D0847867

DATE DUE

GAYLORD

PRINTED IN U.S.A.

The Gray-Flannel Pigskin

The Gray-Flannel Pigskin

Movers and Shakers of Pro Football

William Henry Paul

J. B. Lippincott Company
Philadelphia and New York

U.S. Library of Congress Cataloging in Publication Data

Paul, William Henry, birth date
  The gray-flannel pigskin: movers and shakers of
pro football.

  1. Football—Biography. I. Title.
GV939.A1P37   796.33′264′06273   74–10669
ISBN–0–397–01025–7

To my mother and father,
which will surprise them but no one else

Contents

Introduction

ONE DAY LAST AUTUMN I received a call from Don Klosterman, the General Manager of the Los Angeles Rams. Don told me that there was a reporter named Bill Paul of *The Wall Street Journal* in the Rams' offices at the time. Paul was interviewing Carroll Rosenbloom, the owner of the Rams, in connection with a book Paul was writing about professional football. Rosenbloom, according to Klosterman, had suggested that I write the introduction to the book.

I told Klosterman to have Paul get in touch with me when he had finished the manuscript and, if I liked the book, I would be glad to do it.

I liked the book. In fact, I liked it very much. It is as highly readable as its title is catchy. And it is a major contribution to sports journalism because it fills a vacuum. No other book like it has been written before.

No question about it, this is the age of professional football in the world of sports. The game has swiftness and contact, or violence if you will, and these are quite possibly the principal characteristics of the contemporary society.

9

It is no longer a game just for men. On Monday nights alone, a large percentage of television viewers are women, and it is now fact, not legend, that the social habits of America have been substantially changed on Monday nights in the autumn.

So this book comes at exactly the right time, for it tells where it's really at in professional football. It is not one of those quick, mass-production jobs about a jock or a coach who is enjoying instant glory. It is not one of those laborious technical manuals so dear to a tiny coterie of sportswriters who write for themselves rather than for the public. You will not find charts of plays here, with all the X's and O's. There is no explanation of the zone defense. Instead, you will discover where success and failure truly originate in this enormously visible, overwhelmingly glamorous, but very difficult business. And you will discover it in terms you will identify with—in terms of people. The people who own the teams, the people who general-manage the teams, the people who are business managers, the people who scout for new players and the people who publicize the teams.

There is no bigger name in pro football today than O. J. Simpson of the Buffalo Bills. But he almost quit before he achieved his current eminence. A man you probably never heard of, a publicity man, induced "the Juice" to stick it out. That's the kind of thing you will learn in this book. You will find out why Carroll Rosenbloom is the favorite owner for most of the players. You will meet Jim Finks, former General Manager of the Minnesota Vikings, and then you will know why the Vikings are in contention every year.

Have you ever heard of Jack Steadman, General Manager of the Kansas City Chiefs? If not, you will. He is the hard-core reason for the continuing success of the Kansas

10

City organization. Two women, the Morabito girls, own the San Francisco franchise. They will never sell it. It has become their life. A black former director of player personnel is now working hard at becoming an owner. How did he get to dream of this opportunity? What impels him?

These are just some of the people you will be reading about in this book. And you will be interested because they are interesting people. Some of them are exceptional people. But above all, they, and the business of which they are a part, have been the subject of careful, diligent study by a fine reporter who can draw pictures with his words and bring life to the surge chamber of professional football—the front offices.

The Gray-Flannel Pigskin tells it like it is for the first time where it counts the most.

HOWARD COSELL

Preface

AT THE RISK OF SOUNDING MELODRAMATIC, these are the best of times and these are the worst of times for professional football. Certainly pro football's popularity is at an all-time high. Season tickets show up in wills and divorce decrees, while countless wives argue that their husbands are as good as dead, or at least wedded to the TV screen, on an autumn Sunday afternoon.

But the problems are many. Mostly, they're about money, about players who want more, and about clubs that once had more than they do today. Those who are profiled in this book are part of the best of times. But there are others—several of whom show up on these pages —who help make these the worst of times. Both kinds are found inside the front offices of pro football.

W. H. P.

April 1, 1974
Malvern, Pa.

Acknowledgments

FIRST AND FOREMOST, I would like to thank Ray Paul, an author in his own right who spent untold hours helping his little brother in every phase of this project.

Also, I would like to thank Ray Lincoln, the editor who first went to bat for me, and John Kinney, the man who believed in this book as much as I did.

And I would like to thank Carl Wooten and Frank Topper of *The Wall Street Journal* for both their undying enthusiasm and incisive comments.

Finally, I would like to acknowledge my debt to the late Arthur Daley, an exceptional sportswriter for *The New York Times*, for some of the stories of the NFL back in the 1930s as told in his book, *Pro Football's Hall of Fame* (Copyright © 1963 by Quadrangle/The New York Times Book Co. Quotations from this work are reprinted by permission of Quadrangle/The New York Times Book Co.).

The
Gray-Flannel
Pigskin

1
Pro Football: Quo Vadis?

Both Valerie Lane, a hairdresser from California, and Pete Rozelle, Commissioner of the National Football League, were featured in the October, 1973, issue of *Playboy*. As *Playboy*'s Playmate of the Month, Miss Lane was most revealing. As the subject of *Playboy*'s Interview of the Month, Mr. Rozelle was not.

The difference was that while Miss Lane made her figure public, Commissioner Rozelle kept what figures he has to himself. The commissioner told his interviewer he has only a "general impression" of the finances of the twenty-six teams that comprise today's NFL, and that while he might know how this or that particular club fared financially the year before, in general "I'm not aware of clubs' specific financial conditions."

At first glance Commissioner Rozelle's financial unenlightenment is difficult to believe. After all, he has been professional football's chief executive since 1960. And as such he has had to negotiate television contracts and other multimillion-dollar odds and ends requiring more than a cursory knowledge of NFL finances. More than that, the commissioner can be quick with a specific figure when it

19

tends to portray NFL owners as something other than modern-day robber barons in opposition to the image projected successfully by, among others, former NFL player Bernie Parrish in his book *They Call It a Game* (Dial Press; Copyright © 1971 by Bernard P. Parrish).

Parrish starts his ninth chapter, entitled "Owners and Their Earnings," with the statement: "Most owners of pro football teams are not comfortable unless they are wearing $400 business suits, $100 alligator shoes, and $25 monogrammed shirts with solid-gold cufflinks."

Rozelle tells his *Playboy* interviewer that "the 26 clubs pay out in excess of $5,000,000 a year in medical payments and in salary to injured players who don't perform for all or part of the season."

And Rozelle tells an interviewer from *U.S. News & World Report* that as an industry, professional football grosses only slightly more than $150 million a year, a revenue figure that might easily be topped "by a big department store."

But while the commissioner obviously knows more than what he picks up while munching the olive in his martini, he may in fact not know as much as you would expect. For one thing, the league office in New York is itself the size of a modest corporation (each of the twenty-six clubs is assessed by the league in the neighborhood of $135,000 a year, or a total of about $3.5 million), which means Rozelle spends at least some time keeping his own house in order.

But more importantly, so many factors work today at significantly altering a pro football team's profitability from year to year that even some club executives have difficulty projecting accurately another team's financial picture.

Unlike, say, the steel or automobile industries, the football industry has no group of Wall Street analysts whose job it is to forecast financial results. Nor, with only two exceptions, are the corporations that make up the football industry required by law to make public their profits and losses. (Quite frankly, no Wall Street analyst would waste his time closely following an NFL club. The figures are just too small.)

The last time a survey of individual club finances was taken was back in 1969. The survey showed that the average annual pretax profit of a club was $452,000, a figure which by itself is of limited value because of the different ways in which club profits are taxed.

For example, a few owners like Carroll Rosenbloom of the Los Angeles Rams and Lamar Hunt of the Kansas City Chiefs include their particular club's earnings as part of personal income, which means the taxes paid, if any, on those earnings may vary widely from year to year depending on the success or failure of the man's other business investments.

A number of other clubs are ordinary corporations, which means their earnings are taxed at the going corporate rate of 48 percent. A few clubs are partnerships, which means their owners are taxed in the same way as Rosenbloom and Hunt. One ordinary corporation, the New England Patriots, is publicly held and directors choose to distribute a portion of the club's after-tax profits to its more than 2,000 stockholders in the form of dividends. Another ordinary corporation, the Green Bay Packers, is also publicly held, but Packers' profits are retained by the club and earmarked for use in club operations, not for any one owner's personal income.

Even if that 1969 survey had given specific, club-by-club figures, those figures would by now be woefully out of date. Several clubs—including Buffalo, New England, Dallas and Kansas City—have since moved into new and larger stadiums. The effect is league-wide because a visiting team is guaranteed 40 percent of gross ticket sales after taxes, if taxes are applicable to the home team's city or state.

Moreover, most clubs have either been receiving or paying out money these last few years in connection with the 1969 merger of the American Football League into the National Football League. Terms of that merger call for the ten AFL teams to pay a total of $18 million over a period of twenty years to two NFL teams, the New York Giants and the San Francisco 49ers, as compensation for infringement upon the two clubs' territorial rights by two AFL teams, the New York Jets and the Oakland Raiders, respectively. (Of that amount, $10 million is earmarked for the Giants and $8 million for the 49ers.)

In addition, terms of that merger call for three clubs, the Pittsburgh Steelers, the Cleveland Browns and the Baltimore Colts, to receive $3 million each over a period of years for agreeing to switch from the National to the American conference in the realignment that followed the merger.

No matter how current, probably no set of industrywide figures could reflect adequately all the local variables in any club's annual profit picture. For example, the Oakland Raiders could have grossed an additional $250,000 in 1973 if four of their scheduled home games had been played on the road and vice versa, according to Raiders' Executive Assistant Al LoCasale. The reason is stadium size. One week Oakland played Cleveland, whose stadium holds around 80,000, in Oakland before a crowd of about 50,000.

The schedule setback, however, was partially offset by a break in player injuries. In 1972 Oakland had seven players with injuries that forced them to the sidelines quite early in the season. They subsequently were paid to stand around with their hands in their pockets. But in 1973 the Raiders suffered only two such early-season casualties, which meant a saving in the neighborhood of $150,000 compared with the prior year.

In 1973 the New York Jets also suffered from a very personal problem. Both the Jets and the baseball Mets play in Shea Stadium on Long Island. The park is municipally owned and the Mets, by virtue of playing many more games there than the Jets, are the primary tenant. The clubs' rental agreement prohibits the Jets from playing at Shea until the Mets have finished their season, and in 1973 the Mets kept going well into October because they were in the World Series.

This forced the Jets to reschedule a number of games, and in the one instance where it was not a home-and-home series, the New Yorkers estimate they lost $75,000 in game income. The game was with the Pittsburgh Steelers, and although the Jets technically were the home team, Pittsburgh's stadium seats 10,000 or so less than Shea. (It could have been worse: at least the league picked up the traveling expenses.)

The NFL's inability to show Congress the current financial condition of its member clubs was a significant factor in the 1973 passage of a bill lifting local television blackouts of pro football games sold out three days in advance—a move owners immediately predicted would spell economic disaster for pro football.

A report by the Special Subcommittee on Investigations of the House Committee on Interstate and Foreign Commerce said that Congress originally allowed television blackouts because it "was believed to be necessary in order to protect gate receipts." Thus "in order to determine whether the continuation of these policies is warranted it is essential to know the current financial condition of the clubs. This information, however, was not made available to the Subcommittee for this review. The NFL advised the Subcommittee that it did not have such information."

The subcommittee report added: "The burden of proof . . . for the necessity of continued financial protection should be on the league."

Of course one might take issue with the wisdom of Congress's decision to lift the blackout rule when the subcommittee report states that a thorough investigation of this matter requires knowledge of individual club finances, figures not available to the congressmen. The speed with which the bill was passed (Congressman Jack F. Kemp, a former pro quarterback, said, "The last measure that passed this body as quickly was the bill on the Gulf of Tonkin") implies that the elected officials really weren't concerned with making a thorough investigation.

Be that as it may, if pro football wants continued "financial protection" from Congress, then it should be prepared to make its figures public. When Congress gave pro football a blackout rule in 1961, that action constituted an important exemption from antitrust laws. Congress did the NFL a favor—and over the years it's done others. Now that Congress, in a less friendly mood, wants to know why this favor should be continued, it's in the league's own best interests to make its financial picture visible. How else can the NFL show need if, as Rozelle says, need exists?

Instead, in that same *Playboy* interview the commissioner bemoaned the fact that more specific figures are not available and called for a joint House-Senate study of pro football finances. Such a study, he said, "would eliminate suspicion." Rozelle added: "Everyone keeps saying the NFL won't open its books, but I've told the owners they're going to have to, and they've said they will."

24

Fine. But shouldn't the league take the initiative? It's the league that comes to Congress hat in hand. Any congressional study would be a one-time shot. What's needed is an ongoing analysis able to reflect those local variables which can have such an impact on individual club finances from year to year. To eliminate suspicion, the information gathered by the league might be placed on file for examination at any time by congressmen and others, including members of the general public. The latter are entitled because taxpayers own the airwaves and, until the blackout was lifted in 1973, they permitted the NFL to control those airwaves which, in turn, helped club owners make money.

The obvious drawback to this idea from the league's point of view is that the NFL Players Association—the union—will be in a much stronger bargaining position. But it's difficult from an owner's point of view to see how the union, even with the additional information, could do that much better than it has these last few years. In 1968 one NFL club paid its players a total of $1,491,000. In 1973 this same club paid a total of $2,402,000, roughly a 60 percent increase. (And that was for a period after the merger of the American Football League into the NFL, which eliminated the costly salary wars of the early 1960s.)

Perhaps by the time this book is published the adverse financial impact of the end of local blackouts will have convinced clubs to make their figures public. Even before the effects of the 1973 legislation were known, many executives this writer met in connection with this book's research strongly urged that clubs open up their records. Several others, however, remained to be convinced, and in more than one case it promised to be like pulling teeth.

But what really is the alternative? For pro football to be treated just like any other business?

Now that would mean economic disaster. Already some

clubs with smallish stadiums are worried—and with good reason—about their ability to stay competitive in coming years with clubs whose stadiums seat tens of thousands more. Daniel M. Rooney, Vice President of the Pittsburgh Steelers, a team playing in a stadium with a capacity of only about 50,000, says that the dollar difference between his club and, say, Kansas City (78,000) or Los Angeles (76,000) or Miami (80,010) is the Steelers' most serious problem. "We all know what happens when one player discovers that a guy in his position on another club is making a lot more than he is," Rooney says and shrugs.

Probably the most important underpinning of the entire sport is the exemption Congress granted in 1961 allowing the NFL to negotiate television contracts on a league basis rather than team by team. Quite obviously if the three networks were able to make separate bids on each and every team, a bid on the New York Giants or Los Angeles Rams would be much higher than one on the Green Bay Packers or San Diego Chargers, with a chance that one or more really rotten clubs might be left out altogether. The league has always maintained that perhaps the most important reason why its teams are fairly well balanced is that all clubs receive equal slices of the TV pie, baked in 1973 at a temperature of more than $45 million. But that policy might easily break down if the difference between the haves and the have-nots became so pronounced. Moreover, the size of the pie would undoubtedly be smaller, which just wouldn't go over big with dollar-conscious players and their union leaders.

Also, it doesn't take a mathematician to figure out that the financial effect of lifting the blackout is negative rather than positive. Though actual figures are the subject of much debate, the fact is that after this bill was passed in 1973, most clubs had several thousand more "no shows" (fans who buy tickets but who for reason of weather, etc., decide not to attend) than in previous seasons. Although those clubs did get their fans' ticket money, they didn't get their beer money, their hot-dog money, their program money, their parking money or their pennant money. At the same time, many clubs paid for the vendors who sell hot dogs and beer and for the ticket takers and ushers who chauffeur fans to their seats. They also paid for several thousand unused programs.

As many have pointed out, the total effect of the no-blackout legislation will not be felt until 1974, when fans have to choose between the color, but also the cold and the inconvenience, of attending a game in person versus the lack of color, but also the warmth and convenience, of staying home and turning on the television. While Representative Torbert H. Macdonald (D., Mass.), a strong proponent of the no-blackout bill, denies that this legislation is, to use the congressman's own words, a "mortal wound" for pro football, even Representative Macdonald admitted during hearings on the bill that it might be a "shoulder wound."

Before the era of television, the pro football business was strictly small potatoes. The following is an actual budget of a National Football League team for the year 1948. (It was obtained, as were all specific club figures then and now, with the understanding that the name of the team would be withheld. And even though that arrangement is not completely satisfactory, it provides more specific income and expense data than were available to Congress.)

Administrative salaries and wages	$ 18,400
Players' salaries and bonuses	$201,100
Head coach's salary	$ 25,000
Salaries of two assistant coaches (total)	$ 16,000
Visiting club guarantees	$125,000
League assessments	$ 18,500

Stadium rental	$ 55,600
Game expenses (including ticket printing, medical supplies, ticket sellers, ushers, special police, laundry, etc.)	$ 17,600
Training camp expenses (including food, lodging, training equipment, medical supplies, etc.)	$ 14,000
Team travel	$ 28,500
Away-game lodging and meals	$ 14,700
Equipment (footballs, etc.)	$ 5,700
Advertising and promotion	$ 12,300
Insurance premiums	$ 10,100
Legal and accounting	$ 5,400
Taxes, payroll	$ 5,200

There were several other smaller items, ranging down to $140 a season for special police for home games and $100 a season for use of a practice field before away games. All told, this club's 1948 budget came to only $657,000—about 10 percent to 15 percent of most clubs' operating budgets in 1973. (This club lost money in 1948.)

Television's appearance in the early 1950s could not have been more fortuitous. A four-year salary war between the NFL and the All-American Football Conference—the American Football League of its time—had left many clubs in financial jeopardy. Up to that point, the history of pro football was a history of franchise failures. But with TV on the scene history did not repeat itself.

Not that television looked like a godsend when it first arrived. In 1950 the Los Angeles Rams contracted to televise home games. The result was a 46 percent drop in attendance, despite the fact that the Rams were Western Conference champions that season.

After that, the NFL established its home blackout policy, and in 1954 Federal Judge Allan K. Grim became the latter-day father of professional football when he turned back a Justice Department challenge to that policy. "Grim was the turning point of the whole thing," says Marshall Leahy, former counsel for the NFL and today counsel for the San Francisco 49ers. Congress's exemption seven years later turned one judge's opinion, always subject to reversal, into the law of the land.

Not all owners knew what they had when in 1961 Congress also permitted the league to negotiate TV contracts on a league-wide basis. Arthur J. Rooney, Sr., for some forty years the owner of the Pittsburgh Steelers, says that a number of owners at first felt an emotional attachment to CBS because that network had consistently contracted with most teams during the era of club-by-club negotiations. These owners wanted CBS to have an unimpeded shot at the new league-wide contract. But Rooney and several others finally convinced them that to make the NFL TV contract biddable would put more money in club coffers.

The impact of this congressional action was as immediate as it was big. In 1962, the first year under the TV exemption, the league's television contract netted about $4.5 million, or about $332,000 for each of the fourteen NFL teams. The year before, even the big-city Washington Redskins had received only $250,000 for both radio and TV rights while the small-town Green Bay Packers had gotten less than half that much—$120,000.

As the popularity of professional football grew rapidly during the 1960s, so too did the size of the TV pie. That in turn led players to seek—and rightfully so—a bigger slice of that pie. At the same time, however, inflation reared its ugly head. The result was that for at least some clubs—and it only takes a few to mess up the competitive balance within the league—there wasn't enough to take care of all outstretched hands.

That the costs of running a football team, like the costs of

29

running a household, have skyrocketed these last four or five years can be seen clearly in the following figures of one NFL club. In 1973 this club paid $534,000 in salaries for coaches and front-office executives, up 41 percent over the $380,000 paid in 1968. In 1973 this club had home-game expenses totaling $296,000, up about 45 percent over $204,000 in 1968. Transportation and lodging expenses rose about 38 percent to $195,000 from $141,000. Medical expenses including insurance premiums rose 40 percent to $150,000 from $107,000. And training camp expenses rose about 34 percent to $228,000 from $170,000. (Oh, yes, between 1965 and 1972 league assessments increased eightfold.)

To ensure the continued profitability—and hence the continued competitiveness—of all its clubs, the NFL appears more and more to be relying on initiation and other special payments which have nothing to do with the game on the field. One team which has been a big winner on the field the last couple of years has been as big a loser off, actually winding up in the red from operations in 1972. But thanks to special payments made by other teams, including monies from expansion teams in Miami and Cincinnati for the privilege of joining the NFL, this club managed to show a net profit in 1972 in excess of $400,000.

NFL plans currently call for the number of teams to be expanded to thirty-two from twenty-six over the next few years. Each new team will pay a multimillion-dollar initiation fee that will be divided among other teams in the league. One estimate is that each existing club will receive a total of $2 million in expansion monies from these new teams.

The problem with this course of action is that the league has to keep adding more and more teams to keep the money coming in. There's no telling when or if the value of an NFL franchise will suddenly tumble from its present heights. At the moment, any franchise sold on the open market would reportedly bring in the neighborhood of $18 million. That's because there are a number of wealthy people who consider owning a pro football team like owning a Rembrandt or a Picasso, only with more action and excitement.

But what if there's a scandal? Take your pick: gambling? drugs? Already the sport has been the subject of a special grand-jury investigation in Cleveland. And after that there were much-publicized rumors about drugs and drug pushers within the ranks of the players. So far, nothing serious has surfaced. But even if nothing does, what's to prevent the popularity of football from declining on its own? According to Dan Rooney of the Steelers, the lifting of the blackout may well have started such a decline already.

"Right now," he says, "there is high interest in professional football. But emotions are strange. People want to do what others are doing. Placing the home game on television eliminates the demand. Some are trying to dispute this, but we have already witnessed this in Pittsburgh with our team doing great. I am not only referring to no shows. Businessmen, salesmen particularly, must get tickets for associates and customers. In Pittsburgh they are still interested but, believe me, not to the extent that they were."

Mr. Rooney adds that as interest drops, so does ticket demand. And sooner or later you no longer have sellouts, which only reinforces in the fan's mind that interest in pro football is waning. "It's downhill from there," he says. "You can't play around with people's emotions."

If the people don't get to the sport in that way, they may get to it in another more direct way. In Atlanta last year Jesse Outlar, a sportswriter, was walking to his car in the parking lot after a Falcons football game when a nineteen-year-old youth allegedly robbed and shot him in the stomach. This was in broad daylight, not the twilight or the darkness that greets many fans after late-season games. Jesse survived—barely.

The incident prompted sportswriter Jerry Izenberg of the Newark *Star-Ledger* to write: "We used to make jokes about the old stadium in Buffalo where even the cops feared to tread an hour after a ball game. We laughed in print. But we didn't laugh on a lonely street corner outside the ball park in late autumn darkness after a night game when guys with bicycle chains came around."

Buffalo now has a brand-new stadium. But if you think that solves the problem, you're wrong. A few years back the San Francisco 49ers moved from Kezar Stadium in the heart of town to Candlestick Park on its southern fringe. One compelling reason for the move was the fear that sooner or later a player or his wife or family was going to be seriously hurt or even killed in the crime-infested Haight-Ashbury neighborhood surrounding Kezar. But Jane Morabito, one of the 49ers' owners, says one of the women in her group was robbed in daytime in Candlestick's parking lot after one game. Mrs. Morabito adds that the woman feels lucky that robbery was the only crime committed.

She was.

Another way pro football is vulnerable is through player strikes. Certainly football players have the right to strike. Almost every worker around does. Although Congress in the national interest may order railroad workers back to work for a ninety-day "cooling off" period, no one is about to call professional football vital to the national interest.

Football players, however, bear a special cross. If they decide to strike, they face the distinct possibility of turning off the same fans who provide them a livelihood. That's what started to happen the last time major-league baseball went through the trauma of a walkout. It got so the issues meant nothing. "Play ball!" sportswriters demanded in unison.

This of course did nothing to bring the problems of the sport out in the open where they could be solved. Football too has its fair share of problems, pay scales for pre-season games being perhaps the one that ignites tempers the fastest. Strikes could be a good thing if such problems finally were resolved.

The players, however, are short on bargaining power. Even though a strike certainly is what makes management sit up and take notice, it does likewise with the general public. A lengthy strike can't help but alienate the $10,000-a-year factory worker who sits behind the goal posts every Sunday and who sees this kind of labor dispute only as a bunch of players all making more money than he is and all wanting to make even more.

If sportswriters and others who influence public opinion were to make a concerted effort to outline dispassionately all the issues at hand, and also try to point out that a little delay in the fun right now may make pro football a better, more stable sport in years to come, then a strike, even a long and bitter one, might serve a useful purpose. Unfortunately, as little as a congressman knows about pro football finances, the average sportswriter knows even less.

Yet another way pro football might lose its appeal is if enough people start reacting to the charges of racial discrimination that have been made by more than one NFL observer. That discrimination does exist is undeniable. There isn't a business where it doesn't, nor will there be one until the day that the naming of a black to the board of General Motors isn't some big deal for which the rest of the all-white board is to be commended.

Black-white tension is a constant concern of front-office executives. That's one reason why long ago John Free, Business Manager of the New York Jets, arranged player

seating for the pregame meal on the basis of food prefer-
ence. Steak at one table, pancakes at another, and so on.
That way you avoid all the blacks sitting together and all
the whites sitting together.

In an interview on college scouting in 1973, one front-
office executive said with a note of pride that his team
may be the only one with more black players than white.
"The color of a man's skin doesn't matter here," he said,
a good indication that many teams give consideration to
race when choosing their forty-man squads. In showing a
form for judging collegiate talent used by one of the three
scouting combines that service the NFL, this executive
asked that if the form were to be printed in this book, the
box marked "Race" be deleted. He said knowing a man's
race can sometimes help indicate the kind of formal football training he's had. "People, though," he added,
"wouldn't understand."

In 1973 a sociologist at the University of California at
Fullerton charged that subtle discrimination is widespread
in the NFL. Jonathan I. Brower said that his two-and-one-
half-year study had revealed that racism in various degrees
is practiced by those at every level of the sport, from scouts
to coaches to owners.

Brower's reasons for this are applicable to almost any
business. One point he makes is that white coaches tend to
feel more comfortable with white players and consequently
tend to lean toward whites in fielding their teams. Another
is that since many scouts are white middle class, they
don't always read correctly black players' attitudes fos-
tered by a different environmental experience.

These are not earth-shattering problems. But even these
societal rather than football-only problems must be
watched carefully because of the fishbowl in which the
pro football business operates. All it takes is one story in
one newspaper and, as Rommie Loudd, the black former

Director of Pro Personnel for the New England Patriots, says, you've got outsiders ready to pick up the banner even though they might not know which banner they're picking up.

Frank Dolson, an often biting sports columnist for the *Philadelphia Inquirer*, wrote in early 1974: "Professional sports need loyal fans to survive, but how long will fans remain loyal if the athletes, the coaches, the managers, the owners are so demonstrably disloyal? . . . Already the cynicism is growing, the loyalties are fading. . . . When the dollar signs drive scores out of the headlines; when what a player's agent says becomes more important than what his coach or manager says; when a man's salary creates more excitement than his batting average, sports are in trouble."

People will lose respect for pro football unless owners act with a little more dignity than did Philadelphia Eagles' owner Leonard Tose when Congress lifted the blackout. Tose announced that he would put obstructed-view seats on sale and that unless all such seats were sold seventy-two hours before game time, he would declare the game not to be a sellout and, consequently, not to be televised.

Tose's action prompted two state senators to introduce a bill that would have fined him for such a move. Tom Fox, a reporter for the *Philadelphia Daily News*, disclosed that a local businessman by the name of Jerry Rubin, known in the City of Brotherly Love as the "Carpet King," tried to purchase every one of Tose's rotten-view seats for one game just to foil the scheme. Rubin was motivated, so Fox said and so *Sports Illustrated* later told the world in a less-than-complimentary article, by jealousy: Jerry's wife allegedly had dumped him for Leonard and Jerry saw this as his chance to get "Old Eagle Eyebrows," as Fox called Tose.

Tose isn't the only man in a position of power in the NFL whose actions have embarrassed the league as a whole.

When Miami owner Joe Robbie decided to approach Baltimore Colts' Head Coach Don Shula about the Dolphins' head coaching job without first, as required by league rules, informing the Baltimore management, his actions were certainly something less than forthright. (Robbie was investigated and penalized by the league office.)

Robbie's callous attitude toward his players finally caught up with him in early 1974 when, despite two consecutive Super Bowl victories, Dolphin standouts Larry Csonka, Jim Kiick and Paul Warfield decided to sign with the rival World Football League. Sportswriter Dave Anderson of *The New York Times*, one of the best in the country for cutting through the crap spouted by management and players alike, wrote:

"Joe Robbie has only himself to blame [for losing these players]. He has alienated virtually all the Dolphin players with his aloof manner, his brusque treatment, his domineering attitude. . . . They [the three players] remembered locker-room arguments over Robbie's ticket policies. They remembered being ordered to produce cash for their Super Bowl tickets by a deadline date rather than have the club accountants deduct the cost from their paychecks. They remembered how Robbie discriminated against the single players by inviting only the wives of married players to the recent Super Bowl game as the club's guests. They remembered how Robbie tried, usually without success, to show off players at parties for his friends. . . .

" 'Deep down,' Csonka has said of Robbie, 'he's a big businessman. It's impossible to have a real friendship relationship with him. Sooner or later, a player doesn't mean any more to him than an expensive Xerox machine does. When a player is outdated, that's it.' "

In 1973 more than one team was fined many thousands of dollars for violations of the forty-seven-man player limit. Specifically, these teams (whose names were never disclosed) were fined for allowing players signed to so-called "futures" contracts to practice with the other forty-seven men on the team. A futures player is the property of a specific club, but his contract forbids him to work out with other players signed to regular contracts. The futures player, who is paid a minimum $5,200, is supposed to work out on his own and be ready to join the team if and when he's needed.

But suppose you're a coach with a pair of offensive guards who are both one or two years away from retirement. Next year you may find yourself having to trade for or draft one or two new guards. That can cost $200,000 easily. But if instead you've got a couple of futures stashed away whom you've been training on the sly with the rest of the squad all season long, you're all set for guards next year and can use your money to buy somebody else.

"Each team has an average of three or four illegal futures," says one front-office executive. "And a couple of clubs probably have many more than that. Futures players are the way the rich get richer. We all have to do it in order to compete."

Another whose actions have been far from exemplary is George Allen, General Manager and Head Coach of the Washington Redskins. In 1973 Dave Anderson, of the *Times*, wrote after the alleged widespread use of drugs by one of Allen's players on the Redskins:

"In the narrowness of George Allen's tunnel vision, winning is the Redskins' law. Winning by any means. George Allen created the law. He has traded draft choices he didn't own. He has filed false injury reports with the National Football League office. One of his mottoes is, 'Losing is like dying.' In that atmosphere, the disclosure . . . was not surprising that at least a dozen Redskins were swallowing amphetamines not prescribed by the team physician, in violation of the NFL's new drug code."

Another sportswriter, Leonard Shapiro of the *Washington Post*, added after the 1973 season that "several" Washington players were "dismayed to read the day after a free-for-all against the Cardinals that Allen freely admitted he encourages fights during games to fire up his teams. This was not the sort of image they"—or the league office, it's fair to say—"cared to project."

Still another whose actions have not always been beneficial to the image of pro football is Bud Adams, owner of the Houston Oilers. One time Adams reportedly told Ernie Ladd and Earl Faison of the San Diego Chargers that he would hire them when and if they played out their options with San Diego. Such a conversation constitutes a violation of the league's tampering rules. But even after a sportswriter broke the story, Sid Gillman, who at that time was in charge of San Diego, let the deal go through. Then Gillman filed a complaint with the league and Adams was fined and the deal was voided.

Another time, according to an October, 1973, article in *Dun's Review*, Adams did his best to embarrass his publicity man, Jack Scott. He did so by leaking news stories to a favored reporter, Wells Twombly of the San Francisco *Examiner*, and then the next day blaming it on Scott. "I had twenty-seven front-page bylines and nine-tenths of them came from Bud," *Dun's* quoted Twombly as saying. "Bud just enjoys playing with lives. He reminds me of a guy with puppets. When he's tired of the puppets, he burns them."

But while professional football is a precarious business whose future may not be rosy, that doesn't mean that today any owner is just one step away from the poorhouse. Of course some are given credit for having more money than they do. Art Rooney, who may or may not have as much money as people say he has, gets a kick out of telling how every time his wife reads in a newspaper about all the money he's supposed to have she asks him, "Where is all that money? I know I never see any of it."

On the other hand, it would take a number of owners a number of years before any red ink from their football franchises forced them to change their rather comfortable standards of living. And before that happened, Lamar Hunt of the Chiefs could always auction off the valuable antique Spanish choir stalls he keeps in his posh stadium offices because he has no room for them at home in Dallas, while Carroll Rosenbloom of the Rams could dispose of his wife's luxurious antique French chests which she keeps in a cottage out back because there's no room for them in her magnificent Bel Air home.

No one knows the average net worth of a pro football owner except God and the Internal Revenue Service. But Eugene Klein of the San Diego Chargers has to be considered one of the more wealthy ones after the business deal he pulled off in 1973. Until that year, Klein was Chairman and Chief Executive Officer of National General Corp., a diversified entertainment, publishing and insurance firm. National General was acquired in 1973 by American Financial Corp. of Cincinnati under terms which gave Klein $3 million in cash and $14 million worth of securities, these securities bearing interest of $1.4 million a year until 1980 and perhaps half that much until 1992, according to *Business Week*. In addition, American Financial agreed to pay Klein an annual salary of $130,000 a year for five years even though Klein said he has no plans "except to spend a lot of time with my football club."

But as well-heeled as Klein is, he's not in a category with Bud Adams. Adams controls a financial empire estimated to be worth $100 million. It includes Ada Oil Co., said to be the largest distributor of Phillips Petroleum products in the western hemisphere. It also includes one of the largest

Lincoln-Mercury dealerships in the United States and the largest independent auto-leasing company in Houston, the largest independent travel agency in Houston, four Texas cattle ranches, a herd of registered cattle valued at $1 million, a multicrop farm in California, a Texas hog farm in Houston, etc.

It's also true that, as a business, professional football is probably the healthiest sport around. That may not be saying too much, given the sorry state of some other pro sports, particularly basketball, which claims that less than half of the seventeen franchises in the National Basketball Association make money. But the fact is that no pro football franchise is believed to be operating in the red at the current time. And while that can't be proven until there is a comprehensive study of individual club finances, figures compiled on the following seven NFL teams appear to show that pro football teams generate solid, though in most cases hardly lavish, profits.

The New England Patriots. Because the Patriots are a publicly held corporation, their figures are a matter of public record. Documents on file with the Securities and Exchange Commission in Washington show that in 1972 (final 1973 figures were not yet available when this book went to the printer) the Patriots earned after taxes $545,313 on gross income of $7,725,766. In 1971, the club had earned $481,664 on gross income of $7,419,659.

The Green Bay Packers. Though the Packers are also publicly held, the club is not regulated by the SEC. However, figures obtained and published in May, 1973, by the *Washington Post* show that in 1972 Green Bay earned after taxes $480,203 on gross income of $5,402,902. The year before, the Packers had earned $766,361 on gross income of $5,183,052. (Dominic Olejniczak, President, blamed the sharp drop in 1972 profits in part on those

40

local variables discussed previously. "For instance," he told the *Post*, "we spent $100,000 in improving our stadium.")

Team A. This privately owned club is taxed as an ordinary corporation just like the Patriots and the Packers. In 1972 earnings after taxes were about $450,000 on gross income of about $5,750,000. In 1971 profits came to about $550,000 on gross income of about $5,250,000. One top club official said before the end of 1973 that '73 was expected to show earnings "about the same or a little less" than 1972 on gross income of about $6.2 million to $6.3 million.

Team B. This privately owned club is a partnership, which means that different owners have their share of the earnings taxed at different rates according to their other income in the same year. But had this club been taxed as an ordinary corporation in 1972, earnings after taxes would have totaled slightly more than $600,000 on gross income of about $5,100,000. (1971 figures were not available.)

Team C. Another privately owned corporation, this club's earnings after taxes in 1972 were $300,000 on gross income of about $5,250,000. Both the gross and the net figures are about the same as the year before.

The Denver Broncos. The Broncos, a privately owned corporation, did not make their figures available. However, in testimony before the House subcommittee investigating the no-blackout bill in 1972, Gerald Phipps, Chairman of the Board of the Broncos, said that if home-game attendance decreased by as much as 10,000 per regular season game, his club would no longer be profitable. Based upon that statement, the subcommittee computed that the Broncos' annual profit must be in the neighborhood of $560,000.

The Houston Oilers. Like the Broncos, the Oilers did not open up their books to this writer. But in the *Dun's* profile of Bud Adams, the Oilers' owner said that his club's earnings after taxes in 1970 were about $600,000 and that earnings have declined by about $100,000 a year since then, putting 1973 profits at about $300,000. No gross-income figures were given.

Together, these figures indicate that many NFL teams probably have gross incomes in the range of $5 million to $6 million. The overall average for the entire league is probably in the neighborhood of $7 million because there are a number of teams not included in the above list whose stadiums are significantly larger. The figures also indicate that for teams taxed as ordinary corporations—and they constitute a majority of NFL clubs—net earnings are probably in the $400,000- to $600,000-a-year range. Again the overall average is undoubtedly higher, perhaps in the $750,000-a-year range. This is because there are at least three or four clubs who by virtue of special payments from other clubs or more favorable tax statuses clear more than $1 million a year, and one or two upwards of $2 million. (At least one club executive says, "I can't relate to any of your figures," because they're all much lower than those of his organization.)

To put these figures in perspective, a Wall Street analyst would look at an owner's annual rate of return on his investment. Taking $600,000 as the amount earned by a club in a year's time and $18 million as today's price for an NFL franchise, an owner's annual rate of return comes to only 3⅓ percent. Pretty lousy. Even a savings account would yield in excess of 5 percent a year, while short-term notes would give significantly more than that.

Owners are quick to point out their low rate of return as proof that there isn't the money in pro football that everyone thinks there is. But it's also true that very few owners paid anything close to $18 million for their franchises. Jack Kent Cooke, owner of the Los Angeles Lakers basketball team, Los Angeles Kings hockey team and the Los Angeles Forum, reportedly paid only $300,000 several years back for a 25-percent interest in the Washington Redskins. The capital appreciation of a pro football franchise has been amazing—and perhaps unwarranted given the sport's variety of problems. Nevertheless, it has made several old-line owners millionaires.

To be sure, a sports franchise can also be a wonderful tax shelter for its lucky owner. But if there's a common misconception about the business of pro football, it's that every owner can take advantage of the tax laws every year he owns a club and, consequently, make huge profits year in and year out.

The way it works is that when you buy a franchise, the IRS lets you attribute a major portion of the price to the value of player contracts. Then over the next three to five years, the IRS lets you amortize or depreciate the value of these ballplayers much as if they were pieces of machinery. On a balance sheet, depreciation is a debit. Thus by depreciating, you can either offset (on paper, that is) the amount your team has earned in a year's time or, if your franchise has operated in the red, add to the amount of the loss.

Either way, you've got yourself a tax shelter. And if like Hunt and Rosenbloom your football team is taxed as part of your personal income, it's possible for the paper loss from the football team to be used to reduce the amount of tax you must pay on your other, often quite profitable, operations.

In the light of future uncertainties, some pro football clubs are attempting to stabilize their business operations right now through both diversification and management restructuring. The purpose of diversification is to have something to fall back on in case the fans stop coming to the ball park. The purpose of restructuring is to put money men rather than football men in charge of a club's financial operations.

The Kansas City Chiefs are without doubt the best example of what appears to be the future look of football front offices. The Chiefs are only one of the operations watched over by Jack Steadman, Executive Vice President and General Manager, and owned by Lamar Hunt. Others are an amusement park and a restaurant and banquet center inside the Chiefs' stadium which are open to the public except on game days. Steadman also plans to book conventions and entertainment spectaculars into the stadium and possibly to build hotels and other structures on land adjacent to the park.

Steadman himself is an example of the new look. He's a businessman with a degree in accounting, not an ex-quarterback or a legendary college coach. He watches the checkbook while Hank Stram, the Chiefs' Head Coach, watches the players. Steadman is Stram's equal before Hunt.

Another good example is the Pittsburgh Steelers. For years the Steelers were just a football operation, but now that Dan Rooney has taken over from his father day-to-day responsibility for running the club, the Steelers are thinking diversification. Already the club owns some 200 apartment units, and plans call for double that number by the end of 1974. In addition, Rooney says the company is taking a close look, with an eye toward acquisition, at communication firms.

"If you want to stay in the football business," says the Duquesne University accounting graduate, "you've got to get into other businesses."

Still, NFL executives would be wise to take a long look at their new competitor, the World Football League. Under the direction of Gary L. Davidson, a sun-bleached southern California attorney who organized both the ABA and

44

the WFL, the WFL brings to pro football some significant front-office changes which, on the average, could cut an NFL club budget by 10 percent or more.

For instance, the fledgling WFL has trimmed the size of a team from forty-seven players, including seven non-dressing reservists, to thirty-three players, all of them dressing. This nearly 30-percent reduction in manpower works to cut overall club expenses not only by slicing the player payroll but by chopping travel expenses, insurance expenses, equipment expenses, injury expenses, etc.

Of course this cutback in personnel also cuts down on the quality of the game—or does it? More than one NFL executive claims that on most forty-man NFL squads only about twenty-nine men do nearly all the work. That's because no matter what the situation, you're going to go with your eleven best men, and often one man is the best in several areas.

The idea of trimming the roster has been suggested at more than one NFL league meeting. And at more than one meeting the idea has been thrown out. In large part, that's because no coach is going to vote to diminish the size of his squad, and many head coaches are also general managers attending those meetings.

Another WFL cost-cutting step calls for scouting college talent through a single, league-wide scouting system rather than through each team spending several hundred thousand dollars working on its own and in a consortium of teams. When you consider that come draft time, most blue-chip prospects are known far and wide by every team, it would seem to make sense for NFL clubs to pool their scouting resources.

Probably that would eliminate the chance of one team's discovering an unknown college player who goes on to become a superstar in the pros. But that happens infrequently, and, anyway, many such unknowns could still be unearthed if this league-wide scouting system were sufficiently large enough to research many small, out-of-the-way schools. Even a big-budget, league-wide scouting program could save individual clubs a great deal of money.

When Davidson announced his plans for the World Football League in the fall of 1973, more than one NFL official chuckled a bit loudly. Said one West Coast executive: "It's one thing to throw ten guys on a plane and send them around the country in their underwear like in basketball, and quite another to charter a jet for a party of eighty with thousands of pounds of equipment."

But then when the rival All-American Football Conference opened for business in 1946, George Preston Marshall, owner of the Washington Redskins, referred to it snidely as a WPA project. And when Lamar Hunt challenged with the American Football League in 1960, it was suggested that the first thing the AFL should do is find itself a football. But both challengers were successful (the AAFC's top three teams eventually merged into the NFL while all the AFL teams joined the older league), and Gary Davidson promises to be no less a foe.

Davidson himself is a hustler. His mother was a grocery clerk who split from her husband when Gary was an infant. By the time Davidson was in the eighth grade, he had already organized neighborhood baseball and basketball teams. He worked his way through law school doing such odd jobs as collecting bodies for a mortuary.

On the eve of his graduation from UCLA law school in 1961, Davidson got into a barroom skirmish with a certain unidentified sailor. The sailor threw the first punch, Davidson the second. But the blow that counted—the last one—was delivered by a bartender who picked Davidson up by the seat of his pants and threw him out into an alley.

Since then, Davidson has more than held his own against the establishment in both basketball and hockey. He's a

46

businessman first, a sportsman second. He treats franchises like divisions of a company—if a franchise is losing money, he moves it and brings in better managerial talent. With both basketball and hockey, Davidson saw that the established leagues were expanding, but not at a rate commensurate with Americans' growing interest in the sports. He recognized the value of a proven star and sent his club owners after such headliners as Billy Cunningham and Bobby Hull with seven-figure contracts.

Now with football Davidson is attacking the NFL at one of its weakest points. He realizes that the multimillion-dollar price tag on an NFL franchise is due more to snob appeal than to any tangible assets. He also realizes that by offering a number of rich men the chance to buy a franchise for only a fraction of what it would cost to buy into the NFL—if, indeed, they could buy in at all—this leaves these wealthy men with millions to pass under the noses of established NFL stars. And Davidson realizes that it only takes one Joe Namath to establish a beachhead for his new league, buying it time to improve the quality of the product. (He's already got Csonka, Kiick and Warfield, all from Miami, among others.)

All this has made Davidson none too popular with many sportswriters. Wells Twombly of the San Francisco *Examiner* says: "He [Davidson] has created a need for teams where no need existed. He has made sports a marketable item, to be packaged like so many soggy French fries." Adds William N. Wallace of *The New York Times*: "He [Davidson] has found apparently a bottomless pit of wealthy American males with ego deficiencies who will not be content with their capital gains until they own some jocks and can smell the wintergreen."

Who knows whether the WFL will be around in ten years? Contrary to what many seem to think, the American male just might be ready to absorb even more football than he does right now. Ed Beiler, host of a Los Angeles radio show called "Superfan" where listeners phone in their questions and/or beefs, says: "The WFL is the best thing to happen to pro football. It's time that Rosenbloom stopped considering southern California his own private preserve."

Whatever the outcome, player salaries are likely to go up now, in some cases perhaps by 50 percent or more. Obviously, the NFL should seriously consider Mr. Davidson's financial innovations. Clearly, the future stability of pro football would be helped.

Ironically, Gary Davidson and Pete Rozelle face the same problem: a concentration of power in the league office. In Davidson's case, it's because very few of his nouveau owners know anything about running a football team or league. In Rozelle's case, it's because there are different factions within the NFL, most notably the AFL versus the old-line NFL, which have trouble coexisting. Wellington Mara, owner of the New York Giants, has referred to Rozelle as being like an "iron hand in a velvet glove."

But again for the sake of pro football's future stability, perhaps there should be a reevaluation of the powers Rozelle has.

In 1973, for example, that iron hand came down on Lance Rentzel, a wide receiver for the Los Angeles Rams. Rozelle suspended Rentzel for conduct "detrimental" to pro football. The action followed Rentzel's arrest and conviction for possession of marihuana. (He was placed on probation.) The action also followed Rentzel's two prior convictions for indecent exposure which had led Rozelle to put Rentzel on league probation.

The incident raised an important question that is two-fold: does the commissioner have the power and, if so, is

48

it in the best interests of the sport for him to use that power whenever he and he alone decides that a suspension or similar public action is warranted?

The answer was no on both counts according to Ed Garvey, Executive Director of the Players Association, who called Rentzel's suspension a "callous disregard" of the player's rights. "Doesn't due process apply to football players?" Garvey was quoted in the press as saying. "What's happening to Lance is the most incredible thing I've seen in the three years I've been with the Players Association. Have we got a commissioner or a league chaplain?"

The answer was yes on both counts according to Upton Bell, former General Manager of the New England Patriots. "There must be authority or else players will take more and more on their own," Bell was also quoted in the press as saying. "Even the meekest will start making demands that go beyond the interests of the team. They might even start wearing odds and ends for uniforms."

The Players Association went to court in an effort to overturn Rozelle's action. And in Los Angeles, Superior Court Judge David A. Thomas answered the first half of that question when he ruled in effect that Rozelle does have the power to suspend, etc., whenever he alone decides he should act. In rejecting the association's argument and letting Rentzel's suspension stand, Judge Thomas said that a good public "image" is important to the sport and that Rozelle should act to maintain this image, which the judge said includes "the portrayal of players as high type, admirable young men who are worthy of the respect and emulation of the young."

But while Rozelle legally has the power to act unilaterally, is it always in the sport's best interests for him to do so? It's one thing for Rozelle to have absolute power over the NFL's internal affairs—matters such as tampering and trading draft choices you don't have to trade. In these matters, an iron hand can be quite useful. But when an issue so clearly relates to the sport's appearance in the eyes of the general public, maybe the power would better be vested in a kind of board of directors which might include a representative from management, one from labor and two from the public sector, with Rozelle acting as chairman and voting only to break a tie.

Rozelle complains that football's court battles and name-calling sessions seem to generate as much publicity as the games themselves. "I think squabbling in public will eventually ruin football, and there's no doubt that it's hurting us already," he told his *Playboy* interviewer.

The alternative is to make the NFL more visible in its workings. This is the same idea behind making available to Congress and the public financial information on individual clubs. Legally the NFL doesn't have to do anything. But a Players Association poll showed that more than 90 percent of the active pros believe that Rozelle favors owners' interests over theirs. And as Rozelle himself puts it: "Considering what Americans have been confronted with in the last ten years, domestically and internationally, it's clear that we need emotional outlets; we have to have some peace from our problems. . . . People are interested in pro football because it provides them with an emotional oasis; they don't want football to get involved in the same types of court cases, racial problems and legislative issues they encounter in the rest of American life."

Rozelle adds: "If we end up giving our game the same problematical coloration as the rest of the news, I don't think we'll be the popular escape valve we are now."

2

The Godfather

Carroll Rosenbloom
Owner
The Los Angeles Rams

IT'S STILL DIFFICULT for Carroll Rosenbloom to believe what happened on January 12, 1969. Specifically, what happened that Sunday afternoon before more than 75,000 spectators in the Orange Bowl in Miami and millions more at home watching on TV.

It was on that day that Joe Namath, quarterback of the New York Jets, called his shot. Namath and the Jets were reigning champions of the American Football League, the league whose two previous champions, the Kansas City Chiefs and the Oakland Raiders, had both been thumped by Vince Lombardi and the Green Bay Packers in the first two Super Bowls ever played.

Out in Las Vegas, the "smart" money said it would happen again. But in one of the few pregame newspaper interviews that will ever be remembered, the forever-cocky Namath "guaranteed" a Jets' victory over the Baltimore Colts, champions of the supposedly invincible National Football League.

Ruth, too, had once called his shot. But when the Babe hit one to where he had pointed seconds before, tens of millions of TV-viewing Americans weren't around to immortalize the event even before the instant replay could be run.

The Jets scored first—second, third and fourth. "Broadway Joe" completed 17 of 28 passes for a whopping 206 yards. Three times in the first half the Jet defense intercepted Colt quarterback Earl Morrall. It was over long before it was over.

Especially for the Colts' owner, a guy by the name of Rosenbloom. "I felt like the worst Judas that ever lived," he recalls. "I was the first guy in the NFL ever to get beat by the AFL. I had let all my friends down. There was only one thing for me to do—get a razor and go slit my throat."

To Carroll's way of thinking, he was even worse off than Judas. At least Judas wasn't asked to host a postgame gala for some 350 guests under a tent outside his home in Golden Beach, just up the road from Miami. All the world knew the 16-to-7 final score when Rosenbloom walked through his front door "still wondering how I could cut my throat."

He was met there by his wife, Georgia, who said, "You have a friend waiting for you in the den."

"Friend?" Carroll responded. "Why, wife, I don't even want to see you just right now."

"Go on in," Georgia urged in that understanding tone a wife had better use after her husband has gone and booted the big one. "You'll be glad to see him."

So in Carroll went, and there, drink in hand, soaking his back in the bathtub off the den was a man famous for a lot more than an aching back—Senator Edward M. Kennedy.

Ted, as Carroll calls him, was a good neighbor from nearby Palm Beach. Indeed, he was a close personal friend going back to days long before brother Jack was in the White House. That afternoon he had taken his father to the game, thanks to a platform Carroll had specially built so that Joseph P. Kennedy, Sr., could get around in his wheelchair. Though due back in Washington early the next morning, Ted just wanted to stop by to console an old friend.

And so there they were, Ted Kennedy sipping while lying naked and Carroll Rosenbloom seated on a stool letting out a tear or two and, in his own words, "acting like a fool." Although this scene might seem a bit ludicrous now, it didn't then to these two men.

"Look at it this way," Kennedy told his friend. "Out there this afternoon, at least nobody died."

Rosenbloom says he snapped out of it after that. And even though he could think of a thousand things he would rather have done, he then went for a dip in the Atlantic because "Ted said that's what we're going to do whether you want to or not."

The essential Rosenbloom is that man in the bathroom— all emotion, all out in the open and all for the sake of winning. "It's odd," he says, "how normal, successful people will get into this sport and turn into idiots." Says Carroll's longtime friend and business associate Herb Hutner, "Carroll goes straight at you, either to help you or to get even with you."

A millionaire several times over before the age of forty, Rosenbloom today in his sixties still works hard to be the "charming manipulator," as one sportswriter once put it. The Wall Street world of business is fine, and Carroll is on the phone every morning at seven huddling with his East Coast financial adviser at the opening bell of the New York Stock Exchange. But Wall Street is an exclusive club where success is not broadcast coast to coast. And a man like Carroll Rosenbloom needs a more public forum to demonstrate his talents.

There is no more prestigious an arena at the moment than pro football, the number-one spectator sport to all but diehard baseball fans. A 1972 survey by Louis Harris and Associates, Inc., showed that football was followed by more people eighteen years of age and over than any other sport in this country. The same poll showed football followed by a whopping 65 percent of those who earn $15,000 a year or more, compared to only 55 percent for baseball.

Put another way, you can close a deal worth $50 million for a new ball bearings plant in Saint Joe, Missouri, and you'll be lucky to make page 46 of *The Wall Street Journal*. But win the Super Bowl and every paper in the country, including *The Wall Street Journal*, probably will mention the fact right there on page 1.

Since 1972 Rosenbloom has owned the Los Angeles Rams. For some twenty years before that he owned the Baltimore Colts. For proof that Rosenbloom is a manipulator at heart consider that he, in effect, managed to sell his Baltimore club without paying the consequences—namely, an estimated $4.4 million in capital gains taxes. Consider also that he is the only man in modern NFL history to own two different franchises and that, if given his own way, he would have become one half of the first two-team, father-and-son owner combo in pro football.

That last fact is still today known by only a handful outside the commissioner's office in New York. Rosenbloom says that originally he contemplated buying the Rams for himself and giving the Colts to his oldest son Steve. "Carroll hates to sell anything," says Herb Hutner.

Rozelle, however, quickly put a stop to that idea. The commissioner decided that such a plan has certain obvious drawbacks, not the least of which is to open up the NFL to possible charges of fixing. "We had a little chat," Carroll recalls, adding somewhat forlornly, "and I guess Pete was right."

Yet Rosenbloom had another Rams purchase plan up his

sleeve. This time the twist was that while the L.A. franchise would be acquired *for* Mr. Rosenbloom, it would not actually be acquired *by* Mr. Rosenbloom. Instead, another group of investors headed up by Midwestern businessman Robert Irsay would purchase the Rams from the estate of the late Dan Reeves, the Rams' previous owner, and then swap it for the Colts.

"Compare it," Rosenbloom said, "to your buying a hot dog at the same time I buy one. You like the looks of mine and I decide I want yours. So you hand me your hot dog and I hand you mine, with no money changing hands." And, consequently, no capital gains tax being paid.

The principle at work here—known as cut out the tax man—is rather commonplace in the Wall Street world Rosenbloom also inhabits. For example, when Carroll sold the family work-clothes business back in the 1950s, terms included an exchange of hot dogs, or in this case stock. But the Rams deal is special because not often is such big-board philosophy applied directly to the supposedly fun-and-games realm of professional sports. It's special also in the way Rosenbloom carried off his plan, namely with a certain savoir faire.

For Rosenbloom, savoir faire means luck, or at least it did in the Rams deal. For even before Rosenbloom entered the L.A. picture around June, 1972, an agreement in principle had been reached for the sale of the franchise to a Florida attorney by the name of Culverhouse. William A. Barnes, coexecutor of the Reeves's estate, says the only thing that was needed to consummate the $17 million deal with Hugh Culverhouse was execution of a definitive agreement.

Unfortunately for Culverhouse, the contract he drew up contained certain stipulations Barnes claims were not agreed upon during the negotiations. As a result, the deal faltered long enough for Rosenbloom to show that savoir faire also means knowing when to stick your foot in the door. Recalls Barnes: "Rosenbloom called and asked if the Rams were still for sale. I said yes but that he'd better do something dramatic if he wanted the club. The next thing I knew I had a check in my hand," with the balance expected forthwith.

But, as was previously indicated, the check was not signed by Rosenbloom. If you read the fine print in your Webster's you'll discover that savoir faire also means knowing the right people—such as the commissioner of pro football—who can suggest the name of an investor who might make an instant owner. Needless to say, if the commissioner likes the guy, he's worth his weight in gold—well worth telling that fast action with the checkbook will make him one of the lodge brothers.

Of course, the classic Times Square definition of the phrase in question has something to do with fish and the process of letting one off the hook. To make sure the newcomers didn't take too great a liking to southern California, Rosenbloom himself drew up a special agreement specifying procedures for the franchise swap. As expected, it took just a matter of days for other owners in the league to approve the deal, leaving an irate Culverhouse to ponder his French lessons.

(Culverhouse subsequently sued the Rams for breach of contract. About a year later he received a "small cash settlement," according to Barnes.)

The emotion isn't there when Carroll is conducting business. But he more than makes up for it whenever he sees some bruisers in shoulder pads—especially his own. "Never mind he's the owner," says Joe Scibelli, Rams' cocaptain and veteran offensive guard. "He's part of our club." Adds Merlin Olsen, Ram defensive tackle: "I appreciate knowing that he'll hurt when I hurt."

Hurt? The word doesn't do justice to the self-imposed

agony that sits next to Carroll every game. Agony gets that seat because Carroll's wife, Georgia, says she would go out of her mind if forced to sweat out all her husband's contortions. (She and her friends occupy their own box.) Georgia says he fidgets, he paces, he moans and he groans. And then the band plays the national anthem.

Agony's friend superstition also is there. When he was in Baltimore Carroll always went through a pregame ritual that involved, among other things, patting the head of Johnny Unitas, the Colts' starting quarterback, accepting a strand of tape from defensive back Lenny Lyles, and circling the field with Colts' Head Coach Don Shula, who was later to be embroiled in a much-publicized feud with his boss.

So superstitious is Rosenbloom that for years before he finally gave up smoking in 1973 he always carried two different brands to the game—one for offense and one for defense. He's so nervous that one time on the eve of the 1958 championship game between the Colts and the New York Giants he actually slept in six different beds. (Friends who were supposed to stay with him at his New York hotel never showed, and Carroll just kept bouncing from one mattress to the other.)

But although he may sometimes act like a little kid, no one ever doubts that Rosenbloom is the boss. Be they players or be they coaches, either they do things his way or, like former Rams' Head Coach Tommy Prothro, they find themselves looking for another job. And if they, like Prothro, sue the Rams and Rosenbloom for $1.9 million, no sweat.

After all, the guy does live in a palatial home in Bel Air complete with servants, priceless antiques, a swimming pool and a tennis court. At one time or another, he has been the largest single stockholder in such major corporations as Warner Communications Inc. and Universal Controls Corp.

During his nearly quarter century in pro football, he has lent interest-free money to more than 400 of his players. And when he's asked how much he's worth, he answers not only that he does not know, but that it would take a hell of a long time just to add it all up. ("What difference does it make?" he asks. "After the first million you can fake your way to ten.")

Prothro, who was dismissed by Rosenbloom in January, 1973, charged, among other things, breach of contract and damage to personal reputation. Specifically, the suit alleged that Rosenbloom "conspired" to remove Prothro from his job both by interviewing other candidates for the same position and through "active, knowing and willful interference with the authority and duties of the head coach."

Cocaptain Scibelli says that, in his opinion, the problem really was that both Prothro and Rosenbloom have substantial egos and that "Prothro probably felt that Rosenbloom was trying to come on too strong." Olsen concurs that there probably was a "cross-rubbing" of egos, and adds that it was Prothro's style not to discuss things with the boss, an attitude probably hard to accept for the man whose superstition it had been to know the first play Coach Shula planned to run when the Colts went on offense at the start of a game.

Whatever the merits of the charges, the case eventually was settled out of court with Prothro reportedly receiving an undisclosed amount of cash. What is perhaps more intriguing than the actual settlement is the reaction to the affair by Rams players such as Lance Rentzel, a wide receiver and also author of *When All the Laughter Died in Sorrow*, a book about his personal problems published in 1972 by Saturday Review Press.

It appears that what to Prothro was meddling was to Rentzel a rare demonstration of affection by an owner for his players. "If you want to use the word love, it's applicable," he said one day in an interview. "Both owner to players and players to owner."

Rentzel adds: "People don't realize how important an owner is. I have a friend on the Philadelphia Eagles who said [in 1972] that he felt he was being treated like another one of Tose's truck drivers. [Eagles' owner Leonard Tose owns a trucking firm.] But if I have a problem, I know I can always go to Rosenbloom. I can talk with him and kid with him, but still there's a kind of awe about him. If a guy works too hard to be first class, he fails miserably. Rosenbloom just is."

Such sentiments are echoed by former Rosenbloom players. "I hate to see Carroll go," Mike Curtis, Colt middle linebacker, reportedly said when Rosenbloom announced his move to L.A. "He was a damn good owner." Said tight end Tom Mitchell: "More than anyone else, the players are going to miss Rosenbloom." Added running back Tom Matte, now retired: "You don't find men like Carroll Rosenbloom very often. I don't think the city of Baltimore realizes how much it's losing."

Close friends of Carroll are quick to bring up all the old players he has helped out of his own pocket. One of the most famous is Gino Marchetti, the Colts' stellar defensive end in the 1950s and today a member of the Pro Football Hall of Fame in Canton, Ohio. "Carroll is one of the finest men I have ever met," Gino says. And not without good reason. Shortly before Marchetti was due to retire, Rosenbloom asked him what he planned to do with the rest of his life. When Gino mentioned something about going home and going into business with his brother, Carroll shuddered and instead put him into a deal for a chain of fast-food restaurants that Carroll himself had been considering. The chain has since grown into Gino's Inc., a New York Stock Exchange-listed firm that has made Rosenbloom nothing, but has made Gino Marchetti a millionaire several times over.

The old players don't have to be his own. When Rosenbloom first arrived in L.A., he overheard some veteran Rams players discussing how to help their former teammate Lamar Lundy, who in the 1960s was one of the "Fearsome Foursome" on the Rams' defensive line, but today fights a costly battle against a crippling disease. "I know how you all feel about Lundy," Carroll said at an informal players' meeting. "And I don't want any of you or Lamar worrying about his financial problems. Whatever it takes, I intend to take care of his expenses." A promise, it should be noted, that Rosenbloom has kept.

Nor does it matter how old the old players are. Marty Brill, a gifted halfback on Knute Rockne's undefeated 1929 and 1930 teams at Notre Dame, died in 1973. But several years ago Brill, who played with Carroll for a year at the University of Pennsylvania before transferring to Notre Dame, decided to look up his old friend just for a few laughs.

"You old faker," Rosenbloom joked when Brill walked into Carroll's hotel room relying heavily on a cane. He soon saw, however, that the cane was no joke. Brill had degenerative arthritis which, by that point, had all but made him a wheelchair victim. Rosenbloom remarked how they ought to do something about that, but when nothing more was said for several months, Marty wrote it off as an idle comment.

Not so. A year later when the Colts were playing an exhibition game near Marty's California home, Rosenbloom asked in a letter that Marty let the Colts' team surgeon look him over, which Brill did. When the surgeon recommended surgery, Brill said he couldn't afford it nor could he accept his old friend's generosity. "The doctor said I was crazy," Marty later told a sportswriter. " 'What do you think Rosenbloom is worth?' he said. I said, 'Oh, maybe $30 million or $35 million.' He said, 'Marty, he's worth a hundred million if he's worth a dime.' " So Brill went under the knife and the operation was a success.

Perhaps Rosenbloom himself sums up best the reason for his apparent generosity. Quite frankly, he once said: "I need the adrenaline that comes from winning and being appreciated. We all need a carrot in life and somebody to give us a good word."

But what happens when the good word falls on deaf ears? What happens when the carrot is rejected, when fans, sportswriters, even politicians fail to show their appreciation? Well, as Carroll's friend Herb Hutner put it: "Carroll goes straight at you, either to help you or to get even with you."

Nowhere is that statement more on display than in the events leading up to Rosenbloom's departure from Baltimore in 1972. Carroll was convinced the city didn't love him after he sponsored a luncheon in 1970 for some fifty sportswriters from the Baltimore area. First he wined them and dined them; then he shook them up by asking, point blank, why the Colts' "love affair" with their fans had gone on the rocks.

A long silence followed, broken finally when one writer reportedly stood up and said, "Well, I guess we've gotten kind of used to winning."

"Would you prefer it if we lose?" Rosenbloom shot back in anger and dismay.

Silence.

The problem was that Rosenbloom on the one hand and Baltimore fans, sportswriters and politicians on the other both felt they had given more in this common-law marriage than they had received in return. Rosenbloom felt he had given the city a consistent winner (including championship teams in 1958 and 1959) and the focal point of civic pride. The city felt it had swelled Carroll's bank account through fifty-one consecutive home sellouts for a team that they,

61

not Rosenbloom, had made possible back in the early 1950s by buying the tickets necessary to convince league brass that Baltimore deserved the franchise Dallas fans wouldn't support.

John L. Steadman, Sports Editor of the Baltimore *News-American*, was a key figure among anti-Rosenbloom forces. Steadman today declines to discuss what happened, but his columns at the time drove Rosenbloom to charge on television during half time of a game in August, 1971, that Steadman was waging a "vendetta" against the Colts, trying to turn fan opinion against the club just because he had been passed over a few years before for the position of general manager.

Steadman denied the charge, but a careful reading of several of his columns does suggest that he may have felt shortchanged for the drumbeating he and others did trying to secure an NFL franchise for the city that had lost one previously through no fault of its own. For example, when Rosenbloom threatened to move the Colts out into the Maryland suburbs in 1971, Steadman wrote: "Baltimore made the Colts. It wasn't the other way around. It was Baltimore which built the present Memorial Stadium and it was this writer who led the campaign in this newspaper for a professional football franchise to be returned here."

Later that same year when Carroll and his son Steve both blasted Colt fans for not patronizing a preseason game against the Kansas City Chiefs, Steadman wrote: "He [Steve Rosenbloom] wasn't here, nor was his father, when the Colts' fans put up $300,000 in December, 1952, and January, 1953, for season tickets with the promise [of a franchise] from [League Commissioner] Bert Bell. Baltimore is the only city where fans put up the money in advance to permit a football team to go into business."

To be sure, Steadman did have a point. Rosenbloom

wasn't yet around when certain civic leaders went to Bell in 1952 in search of an NFL franchise. Originally, Baltimore was part of the short-lived All-America Football Conference along with San Francisco (owned by Tony Morabito), Cleveland and others. With quarterback Yelberton Abraham Tittle leading them on, Colt fans in the late 1940s were perhaps the most rabid, if not the most gentlemanly, in the land. Indeed, after the Colts were upset in the 1947 division championship by quarterback George Ratterman and his Buffalo Bills, extra police had to be called in to quell an angry mob that set fire to the stands and formed a posse to search out and destroy an official whose questionable fourth-period call they blamed for their team's loss. (The official was smuggled out on the Buffalo team bus.)

But despite strong support at the gate, the Colts, like most clubs at the time in both the AAFC and the NFL, lost a bundle of money trying to outbid the other league for the cream of the collegiate crop. Red ink drowned original Colts' owner Bob Rodenberg, a Washington businessman, in just his first season of action. The fallen banner was picked up by a group of seventeen civic-minded Baltimore businessmen. Unfortunately, they lasted only two years before financial setbacks forced them to sell a majority interest in the club to a cemetery owner by the name of Abraham Watner.

Watner's first—and only—season (1950) was also the first following the signing of a peace treaty between the two leagues. But by that time the Colts were so mired in red ink that the cost-conscious new owner reportedly even tried to ration chewing gum on the basis of one-half stick per man per game. But that only caused dissension in the ranks and particularly shabby play on the field. (1950 record: 1 win, 11 losses.) The final blow came when Watner, rebuffed in his attempt to obtain player help from other teams in the league, decided on his own to sell the franchise back to the league for $50,000.

And for a while it appeared Baltimore was out of the pro football business for good. One reason was Washington Redskins' owner George Preston Marshall, who quickly announced to the rest of the world after Watner threw in the towel that never again would he relinquish his territorial rights by allowing a club to play up the road in Baltimore. "We'll be known in the future as the Washington-Baltimore Redskins," Marshall was quoted in the press as saying.

But up the road that same group of businessmen who still held a minority interest in a now-defunct corporation plotted the return of the Colts. (Rosenbloom is still not in the picture.) Watner's franchise sale was illegal, they concluded, because other Colt directors had not voted their approval. When the league wouldn't listen, they sued. And they appeared in a good position to win when Commissioner Bell offered reinstatement—providing Colt fans would purchase at least 15,000 tickets over the course of six weeks.

A dumb agreement from a Baltimorean's point of view. Not even in their best year at the gate did the old Colts sell anything close to 15,000 season tickets. And that was for eleven breathing, bleeding bodies, not just some promise on paper from the league commissioner.

Dumb? Just four weeks and three days after Bell's announcement, all 15,000 tickets were sold. Spearheading the drive was a local automobile dealer who moved his shop to Memorial Stadium and unleashed his entire sales force on the city. (Melodrama department: even women carrying small children made the wintertime trek to Memorial for their tickets.) To the winner went the breathing, bleeding spoils who had drawn only flies in Dallas the season before.

Now Bell had a problem. For even though he had promised Baltimore fans a team, he had not actually lined up a financial backer to run the franchise in the event the deal went through. Enter Rosenbloom, grudgingly.

"He twisted my arm," Carroll recalls. "He told me it was my civic responsibility, that I was Baltimore's last hope. He made it so that if I didn't take the club, I was one son of a bitch."

And so, it turns out, the old Penn bench warmer at first didn't even want to be an owner. But from here on Steadman's point begins to wane. For almost immediately Rosenbloom plunged into the task of building a winner. The change from grudging to dedicated came suddenly in the fourth game of Carroll's first season in charge. The Green Bay Packers were beating up on his boys when, late in the game, a Colt halfback-turned-pile-driver ripped into two Green Bay tacklers instead of just stepping out of bounds.

"If they want to play that hard," said Rosenbloom, "I want to go with them all the way. If they've got that kind of spirit, I can't sit back, can I?"

He didn't. After that first futile season, Carroll declared: "Baltimore deserves a winner. I am promising you that winner. I don't care how much money it takes."

He proceeded to hire as his head coach Weeb Ewbank, a talented assistant coach for Paul Brown and his perennial champion Cleveland Browns. (Another irony of the Kennedy bathtub game was that Ewbank was the Jets' coach, having been dismissed years before by Rosenbloom in the aftermath of a row.) The Colts' owner also beefed up his scouting department, and soon such future NFL stars as Marchetti, Alan "The Horse" Ameche, Raymond Berry, Jim Parker, "Big Daddy" Lipscomb and, of course, the kid found throwing footballs in a sandlot, Johnny Unitas, were wearing Colt uniforms.

Rosenbloom put out for his players and they reciprocated. In 1953, for example, Carroll distributed his club's modest profits in the form of $500 Christmas presents to each of the forty players. When the league outlawed the practice, Rosenbloom installed "incentive clauses" in his players' contracts, a standard practice today. The Colts' owner pioneered in placing situation-wanted ads for his players in Colts' programs, and almost as soon as he took over he started lending money and acting as financial adviser to many on the Colts' squad. (A business associate of Rosenbloom says that out of more than 400 such loans Carroll has made to date, only one business venture failed so badly that the player, whom he declined to identify, couldn't pay back the loan.)

In just five years, the Colts changed from a tailender into a conference champion. And when Ewbank brought his Western Conference winners into Yankee Stadium in 1958 to meet the New York Giants, champions of the East, it turned out to be one of the most exciting football games ever played. The Colts won, 23 to 17, but only after more than eight minutes of a sudden-death overtime period when "The Horse" plunged 1 yard for the winning touchdown.

The following year the Colts again upended the Giants, 31 to 16, to repeat as NFL champions. And from then until Rosenbloom left town in 1972, the club compiled an amazing record of 119 victories, only 52 defeats and 5 ties, good enough for one Super Bowl winner, one Super Bowl runner-up and two squads that made it into the play-offs during the pre-Super Bowl era.

But not good enough to preserve the wedded bliss between the city and its football team. The first overt sign of marital discord came in the late 1960s when Rosenbloom sought but did not obtain certain improvements in municipally owned Memorial Stadium, among them installation of artificial turf so that the Colts could practice at home before baseball season was over. Outraged, Rosenbloom charged the stadium's other tenant, the Orioles, with alienating the city's affections for the Colts. He charged Orioles' owner Jerome Hoffberger with working to kill the plans primarily because improvements were likely to lead to higher rent. "Hoffberger is a political animal," Rosenbloom told a sportswriter. "He has the Mayor (former Baltimore Mayor Thomas A. D'Alesandro) in his back pocket. And that's all right with me. I'd rather have the Mayor in Hoffberger's pocket than in the Mafia's."

Hoffberger vehemently denied the accusation. Whatever the case, years passed and nothing was done to improve Memorial Stadium, even though one local sportswriter went so far as to point out how one lady he knew "had to have rather substantial splinters removed from her clothing, and from something even more personal and dear to her," after sitting in the upper deck one night.

Rosenbloom, it's fair to say, definitely felt unappreciated. "I have had [certain] objectives," he summed up rather plaintively at one point. "One, to have a winning team. That has been done. Two, to provide a comfortable, convenient place for ticket buyers. That hasn't been done but it's not my fault."

On more than one occasion the Colts' angry owner threatened to move his club into his own stadium to be built somewhere out in the suburbs. And when it appeared he really would in 1971, Maryland Governor Marvin Mandel came riding to the rescue—almost. Mandel did manage to bring the city and its football team together. And he did push through the state legislature a $7 million appropriation for stadium improvements. But in the process he irritated a number of legislators, with the Colts getting caught in the political crossfire.

Moreover, by the time Mandel appeared on the scene Rosenbloom had already upped his lease demands to include a football training camp he said he would build with his own money, but which the city was to reimburse him for by reducing the Colts' yearly rent on Memorial Stadium. One civic official termed the new lease demand "a rape and a raid on the taxpayer's body." The Orioles also fumed, and because that $7 million could only be spent if both teams were committed to Memorial well into the future, the Birds refused to sign their lease—leaving a lot of coin to gather dust.

Rosenbloom's growing indifference toward Baltimore fans was emphasized by his decision to switch the Colts from the National to the American Football Conference after the merger of the two rival leagues in 1969. Back in the more friendly days of the 1950s and early 1960s, Carroll had on a number of occasions told the Baltimore community that the Colts belong to their fans and that he merely acts as a "trustee." One time he said: "The football club belongs to the city. The Rosenblooms are merely caretakers, and we try to do a good job. If we don't, they're liable to get new caretakers."

But when it came time for three old-line NFL teams to switch conferences in order for the two divisions to have an equal number of teams, Rosenbloom thought of himself and not Colt fans. Baltimore fans were quite against the move, but Carroll saw it as a chance to play every year in places he liked to be, especially New York and Miami. He also saw it as an opportunity to build what he considered to be the greatest rivalry of the day: the Jets versus the Colts. And, as he admitted quite frankly, he liked the idea of other NFL teams paying him $3 million to make the switch.

To make matters worse, both Carroll and his son Steve, who by 1971 was the Colts' president reporting to Chairman Dad, really laid into the Baltimore populace when only 16,771 showed up on a hot August night to watch a preseason game against the Kansas City Chiefs. As one sportswriter from another city aptly pointed out, "It was just a meaningless preseason game, another chance for the coaches to look at dozens of humpty-dumpties before sending them home to Tarkio and Bemidji and Flag Pond."

But the contest, the Colts' first home exhibition in some ten years, was preceded by bickering over whether tickets to such games should be tacked on to a fan's season-ticket package, as they are in a number of NFL cities. Carroll said it was vital to the Colts' economic health. He claimed that the season before, the season in which the Colts won the Super Bowl, his club had shown a pretax profit of only $180,000, "the lowest earnings of any team in professional football," he said.

The plan was scrapped when press pressure mounted. But when the fans stayed away in droves, Steve told a reporter: "This makes you wonder if the image of the Baltimore fan is really a myth. When a world championship team is not supported in its own city, it's time to re-evaluate the situation." Dad chipped in with: "Maybe the guy who said our fans are too used to winning was right. . . . Maybe our fans are not as loyal as people all over the country think they are."

That did it. Steadman wrote a column entitled "Colt Fans 'For Real'—They Ain't Myths," in which he damned with faint praise by such statements as, "Maybe [Steve] Rosenbloom didn't mean to demean the fans who decided not to come to the exhibition." The fans themselves were more blunt. "It was a downright insult and disgraceful for the Colt fans to be criticized," began one letter to the editor of a Baltimore paper. "After all the years the fans have supported the Colts, how can anyone have enough gall to say he wonders if the image of the Colts' fan is a myth?" started another.

The flak got so thick that one Baltimore sportswriter

seemingly sympathetic to Rosenbloom's position wrote: "Want to pick up some support for your political future? Knock the Colts. Want to make points at the office, earn prestige and popularity at the local bar? Get on your soap box and let Carroll Rosenbloom have both barrels."

Now Rosenbloom wanted a permanent separation, and when the city of Tampa, Florida, came courting, the Colts' owner responded warmly. Biff-bam-pow! In Baltimore the city comptroller vowed in the press to fight any move by the Colts "before the National Football League, in the courts and in Congress." In Washington, Maryland Congressman Clarence D. Long denounced Carroll's actions as "arrogant," and his words as "the words of a businessman, not a sportsman." Back in Baltimore, incoming Mayor Thomas Schaefer said he was "quite irritated"·to learn that Rosenbloom had "made up his mind already without talking with the new mayor," adding, "I hate to threaten anybody with lawsuits," but . . .

As he was later to do with Carroll's father-son owner idea, Commissioner Rozelle nixed the Tampa plan. At the time, more than one observer noted that the Colt commotion came right after Washington Senators' owner Bob Short had moved his team to Texas, in the process moving congressmen to angry words that Rozelle, presumably, did not want to escalate into action designed to strip the NFL of its hard-earned exempt status from antitrust provisions in the law.

The next stop was Los Angeles, where Carroll could woo anew, complete with a new head of blond hair. (He'd been a bald guy as well as a bad guy in Baltimore.)

Wooing? Georgia Rosenbloom says her husband really starts every day huffing and puffing with a half hour of vigorous exercises beginning at six. "He hates to lose at anything," she confides, though that should be obvious to anyone who has ever walked on a tennis court with the long-ago Maryland junior amateur net champion.

It should be equally obvious to such self-professed pool sharks as Howard Cosell, the tell-it-like-it-is, raspy-voiced sports commentator for ABC television and radio. If Carroll is telling it like it was, then one night Howard strutted into a friend's home, slapped a $10 bill on the pool table and announced with all the flair—if not the believability—of a Jimmy Cagney that "pool is a game of skill and brains, and no one can beat Howard Cosell when it comes to brains."

Rosenbloom proceeded to put him away in the corner pocket and then applied salt to the wound by mailing to Emmy Cosell, Howard's wife, a little money tree with ten $1 bills attached and a note expressing sympathy for her having to put up with such a no-good gambling spouse. "I'm Howard's psychiatrist," Carroll jokes with a you-betta-believe-it smile on his face. "Howard's just a poor little Jewish boy whom I'm trying to help through life."

It's hard to believe that Rosenbloom was ever in Baltimore when he strolls into his yellow-carpeted living room in Bel Air wearing white pants and shoes, a pink polo shirt and a powder-blue coat sweater. (The woman who gives Carroll his facials makes a point of saying he is one of her few male customers who isn't afraid to walk in through the front door.)

This is not to say that the Rams' owner no longer rolls up his sleeves and sweats out a working day. Jack Teele, Administrative Assistant with the Rams, says he once found his boss at night in his office dining alone on a can of salmon. Two secretaries say they find it difficult to keep up with their boss, partly because of Carroll's fetish for writing notes in his head and nowhere else.

"Carroll Rosenbloom is successful for one very simple

71

reason," says Bob Oates, sportswriter for the *Los Angeles Times*. "He works harder than anyone else."

But always in a mercurial manner that seems either to leave an opponent smiling or fuming. An example of the former is Edward L. Masry, an attorney in Los Angeles who represents Roman Gabriel, Ram quarterback for twelve seasons before being traded at his own request in 1973 to the Philadelphia Eagles. Masry's unenviable task was to deal with Rosenbloom after his client had publicly demanded to be traded. Gabriel made the demand in the wake of an injury-filled season in 1972 and Carroll's post-season acquisition of another frontline QB, John Hadl of the San Diego Chargers.

Publicly, Masry sued the Rams on behalf of Roman, alleging that the Colts–Rams franchise swap voided any existing contract Gabriel had with the Rams and charging Rosenbloom with acting "maliciously" in preventing his client from negotiating his own contract with another team. But privately the attorney made no bones about the fact that he likes Carroll, that he had been the man's dinner guest once and had enjoyed himself thoroughly. At one point in the Gabriel byplay, Masry asked to use Rosenbloom's office phone, commenting facetiously, "I always use your phone when calling Paris."

To which Carroll responded, "Well, I wish you'd start speaking English with me."

Laughter. (Genuine.)

But more importantly, Masry respects Rosenbloom. "On most clubs," he notes, "the players' attitudes in a situation like this would be 'to hell with the owner.' But on the Rams it's the owner who gets their support." (The suit was withdrawn shortly before the Eagles' deal was announced.)

An example of fuming is Don Shula, Head Coach of the Miami Dolphins, winners of the 1973 and 1974 Super Bowls and the first pro team in many years to go through an entire NFL season undefeated and untied. (1972 record: 17 and zip.) Before residing in Miami, Shula was Rosenbloom's head man at Baltimore. In 1970, while Carroll was off in the Orient on business, Shula and Dolphins' owner Joe Robbie met secretly on the matter of Shula becoming head coach and part owner of the Miami club.

Shula, as per league rules, obtained Steve Rosenbloom's permission before entering any negotiations. But that was only after Robbie, who didn't bother with that formality, made the initial contact. Consequently, Commissioner Rozelle ruled that the Dolphins had violated NFL tampering rules, and the Colts were awarded the Dolphins' number-one draft choice in 1971. But Carroll, in that "get even" way of his, wasn't about to let the matter drop.

Indeed, Shula fumed in the lobby of a Miami hotel when, shortly after he joined the Dolphins, he offered his hand to Carroll only to have Rosenbloom do an abrupt about-face and march off, according to *Miami Herald* sportswriter Bill Braucher in his book, *Promises to Keep: The Miami Dolphin Story* (Dodd, Mead & Company). "I've never had a more humiliating experience," Shula said.

After that the two men kept their distance. But when the Colts bombed the Dolphins the following season, Rosenbloom told a reporter at the game: "I couldn't believe my eyes. I thought [the Dolphins] would be better coached than that."

He kept it up until first the press and then Rozelle fumed publicly. Probably the most vicious comment made by a sportswriter was by Larry Felser in *The Sporting News:* "Rosenbloom has about as much class as the proprietor of a Times Square schlock shop."

Eventually, Rozelle felt duty bound to slap a fine on Carroll for actions detrimental to the sport of pro football. Was it deserved? Carroll was asked many months afterward.

"I guess," he replied without much conviction.

An owner's day is usually not all work the way it often is for a general manager or business manager. Georgia says that when her husband first involves himself in a new project he gives it his undivided attention until, in his opinion, both the men and the ideas he wants are in action. That explains why Rosenbloom spent several weeks and several thousand dollars interviewing a number of candidates to replace Prothro as Rams' head coach, deciding finally on Chuck Knox, an assistant coach with the Detroit Lions, who led the Rams into the play-offs with a 12-and-2 record in 1973, his first year in L.A.

But once such men and ideas are in motion, Georgia adds, Carroll tends more and more to sit back like the general of an army who knows what his lieutenants are going to do before they actually do it. Only twice a season does he ever address the entire squad, once after the final forty men are selected and again before an important game.

The Rosenblooms divide their time among homes in Bel Air and Golden Beach, Florida, and an apartment in Manhattan. (Weekends may find them relaxing in Palm Springs.) Georgia runs the households with the help of a private secretary while Carroll runs his businesses. "That way," comments the man of the house, "there's no chance we'll get into a fight."

Like nearly all club owners, Rosenbloom attends league meetings several times a year. According to more than one front-office executive, Carroll's voice is one of the most powerful among the sport's moguls, ranking up there with Rozelle and George Halas of the Chicago Bears. "Carroll likes to wait until others have had their say," notes one front-office official. "Then he will stand up slowly and give it one hell of a dramatic reading."

On one not-so-unusual workday, Rosenbloom started off—that is, started off after his half hour of exercises and his phone call to Wall Street—with a doctor's appointment followed by an hour or so in the Rams' West Los Angeles offices. After returning a number of phone calls—but not Cosell's—he and Georgia went shopping for about an hour, with Georgia leaving her husband in front of the extremely swank Bel Air Country Club for a luncheon date with politicians with whom Carroll wanted to discuss the prospects of building a new stadium. (Some things never change.)

The meal, however, was cut short by the day's special event—a swimming meet at son Chip's private school. (Georgia picks Carroll up in the air-conditioned Mercedes.)

By 3:30, however, Carroll was back at his desk listening to Rams' General Manager Don Klosterman, whom Carroll brought west with him from Baltimore, describe a trade two other clubs announced earlier in the day. "You're kidding," Carroll shouts at his lieutenant. "Somebody ought to have his stupid head examined for pulling that bonehead maneuver."

One of his two secretaries—just your average, run-of-the-mill gorgeous-blonde-type secretary—brings in the day's waiver list: a list of players other clubs in the league have cut or "waived" off their squads who now, for the standard $100 waiver fee, can be claimed by any other club.

Not much there, Carroll notes before starting a note-scribbling session on the back of an envelope. One scribbled thought concerns a new negotiating posture he wants Klosterman to take in contract talks with a veteran player. Another confirms the boss's approval of a suggested public-relations campaign designed to familiarize Rams' season-ticket holders with the new owner.

Notes written, Carroll remembers Cosell. "Poor Howard." He sighs unconvincingly. "I hope the boy can wait until tomorrow."

With that, he gets up to leave, pausing long enough to ask Sam, the janitor: "How come you're still wearing that

hat? I thought your wife was going to take that silly thing away from you."

Both men laugh.

After a five-minute drive home, Carroll changes into a sweat suit for his nightly tennis match. Usually a winner, this time Rosenbloom and his partner, actress and neighbor JoAnn Pflug, are up against it. Their opponents are Georgia, who claims to be a beginner but is not to be believed, and her rather slow-moving partner—yours truly—whom the Rams' owner seems intent on puncturing with a tennis ball.

He doesn't, and after Georgia puts her husband away, he points out the antique French chests his wife picked up in France the last time they were in Europe. It seems a French ambassador who came to dinner at Bel Air one night informed Mrs. Rosenbloom that her chests were priceless antiques which could not now be brought out of France. Though quite pleased, she has decided to keep them in her tennis clubhouse.

The Rosenblooms' Chinese cook prepares dinner and their Colombian houseboy does the serving. Wine, of course, though Carroll never drinks anything stronger. Conversation among the seven diners includes tidbits about singer Dionne Warwick, whom Georgia saw with her new baby while shopping, and the baby shower everyone seemed to go to last week for Mrs. Mel Torme.

At one point the discussion turns to author Jacqueline Susann and her new novel. "I remember her back when she was still taking dancing lessons hoping to become a star," Carroll mentions, adding with a good-natured laugh, "Now look at all the dirty words she's learned."

After dinner, conversation centers for a while on a practical joke Carroll played a long time ago. It was a snowy day in January, 1960—the day before the inauguration

76

of President John Fitzgerald Kennedy. Carroll and Georgia were with the Kennedy clan at Bobby's McLean, Virginia, home. Despite the white stuff, a touch-football game had been scheduled with future Senator Ted and future Attorney General Bobby acting as the two captains.

The night before, Ted had complained to Carroll that his team didn't have a chance of winning. "Bobby's grabbed all the good players, Carroll. What am I going to do?"

Carroll thought he'd reassure his friend by saying, "Well, you can have me."

"Oh, great," was the reply. "What good are you?"

"I'm real good," Carroll smiled, a plot hatching. "I'll get you some Colt players. That ought to do it."

"Carroll, I love you." Ted grinned.

"That's great." Papa Joe grinned when informed of the scheme. "But don't tell Bobby. He'll be boiling."

The next day Bob and Carroll and Ted and some ringers played a little football, with Rosenbloom in retrospect laying claim to not one but three charley horses. On his first big play—a pass—Carroll developed a bad case of butterfingers. "Bobby hasn't gotten to you, has he?" Ted scolded when the middle-aged receiver made his way back to the huddle.

The game continued, with Bobby's wife, Ethel, sitting on the sidelines, snow on the tip of her nose, refusing to come into her own warm house. As might be expected, the Colts proved too much for Bobby's boys. And when it was over, a slightly disgusted losing captain asked around concerning where brother Ted had found all those good players.

"You know"—Georgia smiles today—"I don't think Bobby ever forgave them for doing that to him."

(Another Kennedy tale Carroll enjoys telling concerns Jacqueline Kennedy, now Jacqueline Onassis, and the time she broke her ankle during a touch-football game. No time out was called. No one rushed to her assistance. Instead, she simply was left to drag herself off the field as best she could while others shouted such encouraging thoughts as, "Hurry up, you're holding up the game.")

Solomon Rosenbloom, Carroll's father, was an immigrant from Russian Poland who went to work at fifteen and built himself a successful work-clothing business in Baltimore. Carroll was the eighth of nine children, the last of six sons. For a while, so the story goes, the Rosenbloom family lived down the street from writer H. L. Mencken who, Carroll says, "gave me my first hard-shell crab."

Never an outstanding scholar, Carroll was proficient in high school in a number of sports, among them football, track and boxing. He went to the University of Pennsylvania to study business. His father hoped that Carroll—like all his sons—would someday join him in the family business.

At Penn, Carroll met a flashy halfback by the name of Brill who, like Carroll, was rather well-to-do because his family owned J. G. Brill Co., a manufacturer of streetcars and buses. Sophomore-year Carroll kicked off a three-year feud with Penn line coach Lud Wray who, Carroll claims, enjoyed having his charges really pile it on one another during practice. So much so, in fact, that after sophomore year Carroll and Brill went to South Bend, spoke to Knute Rockne and decided to transfer to Notre Dame.

Brill did, but Solomon prevailed upon his son to continue his education at the Ivy League school, which only made matters worse the following fall when Wray, according to Carroll, decided to make his player pay for encouraging the star halfback to transfer to another college. As if practice sessions weren't torture enough, that same year Brill came back to Franklin Field in Philadelphia, scored three touchdowns and helped the Irish humiliate Penn, 60 to 20.

Midway through junior year, Carroll was benched and the following summer he wasn't even invited to training camp. The message, however, didn't sink in, and senior year Carroll played with the scrubs who, he recalls still with a great deal of bitterness, "could kick the shit out of the varsity."

"When I got out of college," Carroll says, "I decided I was going to do well, and to do well you have to work. My father once said to an associate, 'You know, it's funny how the more I work the luckier I get.' I did go to work and I worked with Dad. But we couldn't get along because we were too much alike. I wanted very much to break away, and when the opportunity came to go to Virginia to liquidate one of my father's companies I leaped at it. Business was terrible, but some of the fellows still had hope. I began to think and I told my father I had found a man willing to pay 10 percent more for his company than anyone else. I then went to Virginia."

Where, as present circumstances suggest, he did quite well. But not without a big boost from the father he didn't get along with who, behind his back, secretly guaranteed loans the son thought he was making on his own with several New York banks. Success bred challenge, challenge bred success, and before long Carroll was managing a number of work-clothing concerns.

"I was always considered a maverick in business," he says. "In those days people like Penny's, Wards and Sears were buying their goods through a jobber [or middle man], and I just couldn't see such big companies buying through a jobber. So I went straight to the companies and told them they could buy directly from the manufacturer, who was me. They said don't you know the jobbers will blacklist you. Of course I knew, but I couldn't have cared less. Everyone started buying directly from me and I started to make a lot of money."

By 1940, at the ripe age of thirty-two, Rosenbloom retired to the life of a gentleman farmer on Maryland's Eastern Shore. Two years later his father died, leaving Carroll sole trustee of his estate. "I could see my dad sitting on a cloud saying, 'I'll fix that little son of a bitch thinking it's time to quit. I'll make him go back to work.'"

In 1959, Carroll entered the hot-dog-swapping racket when he sold all the family's work-clothing interests to Philadelphia & Reading Corp., which today is part of Northwest Industries Inc., for a reported $7 million in cash and more than $20 million in stock. After that, he became chairman of the board of Universal Controls Corp., an American Stock Exchange outfit which Carroll put together with another investor as a holding company for a number of calculator-oriented firms. After a sharp run-up in price in the mid 1960s, Universal Controls' stock has been a low-priced item ever since, and a few years ago Carroll resigned his position.

There have been a number of successful investments along the way, and today Rosenbloom manages a stock portfolio of some twenty blue-chippers, with several more in the portfolios of his wife and his children. But first and foremost Carroll Rosenbloom wants to be known as a pro football owner. He wants to have his every business decision scrutinized and talked about by millions of people. That sure beats page 46 of *The Wall Street Journal*.

And yet at the same time, as an owner Rosenbloom retains an aura of mystery, an air of inaccessibility normally associated more with politicians and movie stars. An owner doesn't have to explain why he trades Joe Blow or why he fires John Smith as his head coach. If an owner wins—and Rosenbloom gave three of the last five winning Super Bowl coaches their first head coaching job—he assumes a prophetlike demeanor. And if he loses, well, there's always a celebrity in the bathtub.

3

The Buck Stops Here

Jim Finks
Former Vice President-General Manager
The Minnesota Vikings

Jim Finks, General Manager of the Minnesota Vikings, lay in a hospital bed on the fourth floor of the Fairview Southdale Hospital in suburban Minneapolis.

The gall bladder, doctors agreed. It must come out.

The college draft, Jim disagreed. He must run it for the Vikings, gall bladder notwithstanding.

The physicians huddled. Reluctantly they agreed to a postponement. They insisted, however, upon standing by with pain killers when Jim ordered his office moved into his hospital room, lock, stock and scouting charts.

The GM installed a special phone to call Jerry Reichow, his director of personnel, at Viking headquarters a few blocks away, who in turn called the club's representative at the New York hotel where the draft was taking place, who in turn informed Commissioner Rozelle of the Vikings' choices from first round to last.

While nurses stared, club assistants hustled in and out of Jim's room with reports on all the blue-chip college prospects. Coaches and owners from other teams jammed the hospital switchboard hoping to arrange an eleventh-hour trade but usually being asked to call back after Mr. Finks's temperature was taken. Although not in serious danger, Jim had a needle in his arm at the first sign of pain. Doped up but still quite functional, he wheeled and dealed from morning till night for two days looking for the best available brawn.

And he found it. Indeed, Finks's so-called bedpan draft of 1967 is regarded by many as the most successful in Viking history and the one that transformed the club from an also-ran into a Super Bowl challenger in just two years' time.

But, as Finks will readily admit, it's a hell of a long way from a college draft to a Super Bowl. All twenty-six teams get to draft; only nine played in the Super Bowl the first eight years of its existence. Minnesota did. Twice. And twice they blew it. The Vikings were heavily favored to defeat the Kansas City Chiefs in January, 1970, but instead lost convincingly, 23 to 7. As the underdog in 1974, Minnesota lost to Miami by the same score.

So General Manager Finks continued to look for the right combination of hard work and luck which, he says, is what gets a team into the Super Bowl in the first place. If work alone could do the trick, then Commissioner Rozelle's office would by now be flooded with mail from angry fans demanding that somebody ought to break up the Vikings.

Unfortunately, there's a lot to be said for football's luck factor. As Finks himself puts it, "It only takes one or two guys to screw up a season." And when your job is to deal with forty different players with forty different and, for the most part, rather sensitive personalities, somebody, somewhere, sometime is going to screw things up.

Given his position, probably the man most likely to screw up is the general manager. Among those who care little or not at all for Jim Finks are certain players and player agents who have negotiated contracts with him. Among those who feel otherwise are front-office executives of other teams who are trying to hold the line against rising expenses.

"Football is business and I'm a businessman," Finks says simply.

Says Grady Alderman, a veteran Viking offensive lineman: "Jim's got a lot of class, but he's not in a position where he's going to be loved. It's a fine line keeping the owners happy and the players happy, and sometimes you can't always find it."

Finks was unlike other GMs in pro football in terms of the power and responsibilities of his job. The Vikings are one of a handful of clubs in the National Football League without an owner who holds at least a 51-percent majority interest. (The Vikings have five minority owners in all.) Under present league rules, a 51-percent owner is a prerequisite for league membership. But the Vikings, who joined the NFL in 1960, are free to operate their own way, which means that as general manager, Finks had much of the responsibility but not the power of a club owner.

That also means that it's pretty much all the GM's problem when: (1) players won't sign contracts, including the quarterback who led your club to the Super Bowl the year before; (2) the head coach and the star quarterback refuse to speak to one another; (3) the city fathers demand back stadium rent and you don't think they deserve it; (4) CBS won't drop an affiliate from the Vikings' broadcast network even though its signal reaches home, cutting into home attendance (this is in the days of the blackout); and (5) your own four sons turn on a hockey game the moment Dad leaves the room.

Except for number 5, each one of these things turned Finks into a tough negotiator. Perhaps more than other general managers, Jim doesn't back down from a fight, especially when it comes to negotiating players' contracts. That's because he was a hard-nosed quarterback in the early 1950s for Art Rooney's Pittsburgh Steelers. Salaries were more modest then; a six-figure income was reserved for the man on the moon. Even though Jim tends to disagree, others say he got irritated easily by players who came in demanding this, that and the other thing—all of which were unheard of in his day.

What Finks does say on the subject is revealing: "When I was playing ball, there was a more realistic approach to the game. I don't mean that to be as callous as it sounds. But players then realized that football is only a means to an end and not an end in itself.

"Players today look at football as the end and all of everything. A young guy coming out of college really believes this. I try to discourage it. I try to tell every rookie that if he's coming into the National Football League expecting to be wealthy when he's finished, then he's coming into the wrong industry."

Finks adds even more bluntly: "All we are looking for is two or three good players each year. Some of our free agents and draft choices don't have a Chinaman's chance of making this football club unless the incumbent breaks his leg. But you have to keep these guys coming in every year. You have to just keep that sense of competition and keep everybody honest. Also you have to have a certain number of people in training camp to get any work done. You can't work your veterans against each other, twice a day for six weeks, and have them ready to play a preseason and a regular season."

This doesn't mean that as general manager Jim didn't get close to at least some of his players. For example, he can tell you off the top of his head that Bill Brown, a running back and a veteran with the Vikings, is the father of three, including a Korean child that he and his wife Kay just adopted. And that Bill and Kay were high school sweethearts. And that in high school Bill was an all-state performer in both football and basketball. And that, despite such natural ability, Bill is an awful golfer who tends to wrap the club around his neck on the follow-through.

But for Jim such lighter moments were too few and too far apart. Jim Finks is a man who, at least in 1973, didn't appear particularly to enjoy his job. That may be because he tried to do too much. On some NFL clubs, like the Kansas City Chiefs, the head coach handles the brunt of player contract negotiations, leaving the general manager free to devote all his time to the financial operations. On other clubs, like the Philadelphia Eagles or the Oakland Raiders, the owner takes an active, day-to-day role in the running of the team. But in Minnesota, the buck always stopped in Jim's office—which, incidentally, came complete with two extra-long couches for those forty-five minute catnaps he sometimes takes when the headaches pile up.

When everything is going right—when the team is winning and the stadium is filled and the fans love your club—that's when Jim would get restless and a little depressed. "I like action," he says. "When your club is pretty well established, you are forced into becoming a storekeeper. And that isn't very much fun."

Football in particular and sports in general do not necessarily figure into Finks's long-range plans for himself. "Don't get me wrong. I like my job. But I don't want to be a general manager all my life," he said quite strongly. "Yes, I'd like to be an owner, but even as an owner I'd be doing very much the same thing I do now. I just feel that there are a lot of other things in life that I might want to try someday."

In May of 1974, Jim Finks resigned from the Minnesota Vikings, saying publicly only that it was "time for a change." Privately, he added that the move was not based on his inability to become part owner of the club; indeed, he was offered a 2½-percent share just forty-five days before his resignation.

With the Vikings, Finks earned in the neighborhood of $75,000 a year, in the upper range for a general manager. He owns some real estate, interest in an apartment house, but is, he says, more concerned with socking it away for his sons' college education. (Two are in college; two are still to enter.)

A quiet, intense individual, Finks still lives in the same two-story home he moved into in 1964 when, at just age thirty-seven, he was named the Vikings' general manager at a salary only about one-third his future income. Though the world of pro football can include movie stars and politicians if your name is Carroll Rosenbloom, if you're Jim Finks, you can't remember the last time you stayed at a party past midnight.

And chances are, the next morning on your desk there will be another player's contract that has been returned unsigned with a note from an attorney saying, in effect, that the Vikings' offer stinks. One recent letter read in part:

Dear Mr. Finks:
This office has been involved in negotiating pro basketball contracts, but it has not to date negotiated a standard player contract for the National Football League. However, in my joint capacity as an attorney and a member of the state legislature, I have taken it upon myself to contact some fellow attorneys and others who have negotiated said contracts. . . . Based upon my

several days of discussions, it is my professional advice to my client to not accept this offer.

Sincerely,

"I get absolutely no pleasure out of negotiating contracts," Jim said, as he reached for the big bottle of wheat-germ tablets on his desk. There isn't enough time, however, to worry just about contracts. With annual revenue in excess of $5 million, the Vikings are much bigger than their management structure would indicate. The GM is one man, but there are always a thousand things to do. The best way to examine the total job is to look at it by months.

In January, for example, he spends much time attending league meetings, including those of the competition committee. Also in January he chairs several meetings with the scouting, public relations and other departments going over the budget for each in the next fiscal year. (The Vikings, like most NFL clubs, end the fiscal year on January 31 in order to include prior-season proceeds from play-off games—including, hopefully, the Super Bowl.) Though more and more in recent years he has relinquished responsibility for scouting college players, the GM oversees several meetings in January at which plans are finalized for the college-player draft held at the end of the month.

In addition, in both January and February the GM meets with bank officials to arrange for a short-term loan that will cover the costs of doing business until next season's ticket money starts coming in over the summer. In February, he must contact by phone each of the club's seventeen draft choices, arranging for them to come to Minneapolis either alone or with their attorney or agent. At the same time, he reviews the salary scale of each of the club's seventy-five or so employees, paying particular attention to the coaching staff.

In March, negotiations commence with each of some thirty-five veteran players. That requires elaborate study of prior-year performances, plus a good deal of informal checking around with other clubs to determine what other players in the same position and with similar credentials are earning. With that in mind, the GM will also sit down at this time with his head coach, Bud Grant, to determine what trades the Vikings ought to shoot for during the spring and summer.

Contract negotiations continue throughout spring and summer. Along about April 1, the Vikings firm up their airline and hotel bookings for the coming season. (Finks would examine the bids and pass final judgment on winners and losers.) There are more league meetings to attend, followed by the job of making sure that season-ticket applications are in the mail in time to allow for any cancellations that might come in. (Fat chance of that. The Vikings may have twenty-five cancellations in a year's time out of better than 45,000 season seats.)

In June, the coaches go fishing but Jim Finks would stay for the club's annual meeting and, at the end of the month, more league meetings. When training camp opened in July, chances are Jim would still be at his desk hammering out players' contracts. As Grady Alderman indicated, sometimes that hammer swings harder than a player likes and he refuses to sign. When that happens, league rules require the player to play one additional season with his club at a salary not less than 90 percent of his prior year's pay. Then if by May 1 of the following year no contract has been signed, the player is a free agent able to negotiate his own contract with another club, providing the new club is willing to give up whatever players or draft choices Commissioner Rozelle has decided is fair compensation to the old club. (This rule, referred to mockingly by players

88

as the "Rozelle Rule," has been challenged in the courts by the Players Association, which claims a violation of anti-trust laws.)

In 1972, Finks went into July with not one but three players—all stars—who refused to sign contracts. How that happened and what Finks did about it illustrates why Jim has a tendency to whack hell out of the ball when indulging in a lunchtime game of paddle ball.

The three players—running back Clint Jones, wide receiver Gene Washington and defensive back Charles West —sought to bargain with management (meaning Finks) as a single unit, something tried but never successfully in pro football. (In 1966, baseball's Sandy Koufax and Don Drysdale did negotiate as a duo with the Los Angeles Dodgers.) All three players were represented by the same agent, Los Angeles attorney Al Ross, a tough negotiator sometimes described by his detractors as a "Hollywood hustler." All were big names, which meant that when they announced their collective holdout it made headlines on the sports pages of every newspaper in the country.

According to Finks, Ross sought to increase the salary of each player from somewhere in the $20,000 to $40,000 range to somewhere in the $60,000 to $80,000 range. According to Ross, each was making significantly more than Finks says, if you include bonus money.

Explains Finks: "Clinton Jones had not been as productive up to that point as we had hoped. Charles West had had one good year and Gene Washington was coming off two bad seasons in 1970 and 1971."

Counters Ross: "Clint Jones had rushed for some 600 yards the previous season and was destined to make an important contribution to the club in the future. West was an outstanding athlete who should have been compensated a lot more when he entered the league [as a number-two

89

draft choice in 1968]. And Gene Washington was one of the most talented athletes in all pro football. He might not have caught too many passes in 1970 and 1971, but you can't catch them if nobody throws to you."

Adds Finks: "I tried to reason with Al and found I couldn't. He threatened lawsuits. He kept insisting the players were so mad they didn't want to play for us, that I had betrayed them, lied to them, misrepresented them all along."

Counters Ross: "If I were to tell you in detail how Mr. Finks treated the players and twisted them around, your book would be on fire. He said this is what I'm offering, take it or leave it. I thought that kind of negotiation went out with Adolf Hitler."

Adds Finks: "When they told me they were bargaining collectively, I said we might as well forget about it right now. If I were to agree to that concept, it would be the beginning of the end for the Minnesota Vikings. It would destroy any policies we have about awarding contracts on merit."

Counters Ross: "I'm not saying all players should be paid $1 million. But I don't think that Finks bargained in good faith. I know for a fact that a couple of the guys could have gotten $25,000 to $30,000 more each from another team except that Finks wouldn't even talk to that club about it." (Ross declines to identify the other club.)

Whatever the case, in this corner was the immovable object (Finks) and in that corner the irresistible force (Ross). The three players did eventually sign, as individuals according to Finks, together according to Ross. They signed for considerably less than what they were demanding, according to Finks; for not much less, according to Ross.

Whatever the case, bitter memories remain.

90

Says Finks: "Basically, Al gets these fellows' confidence by painting very optimistic pictures of where they can be financially in five or six years. All they need is the money and he'll do the rest. And, by God, he'll get the money from the Vikings!"

Says Ross: "Jim told me I was trying to put a wedge between him and his players. I told him that he was doing a pretty good job of that all by himself."

And more than bitter memories, a lengthy lawsuit grew directly out of these particular negotiations. Brought by the NFL Players Association, it charged the Vikings and others with failing to bargain in good faith with free agents. (The suit is still in litigation.)

Whether or not a player accepted Finks's salary offer, the general manager almost always went through an elaborate ritual before coming up with a suggested figure. The first step of this ritual is determining the player's contribution to the club the year before. How much playing time did he have? How many mental and physical breakdowns in action? The answers are found in the coaches' grades of every player in every game during the year.

This is cut and dried, but beyond this the job becomes more intuition and less analysis of facts. The second step is checking around with other clubs to find out what players in comparable situations are making. One year Finks had a second-string quarterback who thought the offer the general manager was making was far too low. Jim checked around and found that the Vikings' offer was, according to Finks, about 40 percent higher than what other clubs were paying their second-stringers and, in fact, higher than what four clubs were paying their starting quarterbacks.

"I held my ground," Jim says, "and tried to convince the player it was a fair offer." Unfortunately for the Vikings, Finks guessed wrong. The player continued his hold-out and eventually was traded to another club where, after languishing on the bench for a time, he proved himself one of the better quarterbacks in the NFL.

The third step is even more tricky. Suppose a player who entered the league as a late-round draft choice un-expectedly blossoms into a star. Chances are, he's probably making far less than most everyone else on the club—including a couple of early-round draft picks that same year who were able to command high salaries but who didn't live up to their advance billing. When it comes time to negotiate this player's new contract, what do you do? Double his salary? Triple it?

Dave Osborn, former running back of the Vikings, was one such player. Drafted thirteenth out of North Dakota University in 1965, Osborn got, according to Finks, "a very small bonus and a small contract." For two years Osborn wasn't much, but then in 1967 he ran for 972 yards, or a 4.5-yards-per-carry average. "Dave was only making about $28,000 in 1967," Finks says. "It was very difficult to take him from twenty-eight to where he belonged. I just didn't know."

Osborn compounded Finks's problems by telling Finks that whatever he was offered would be good enough for him. "I wrestled with figures for many days," Jim says. "I called a lot of other clubs before deciding to almost double Dave's salary."

Adds Finks: "There have always been inequities in the system. If you start at $30,000 and I only start at $14,000 but I am a better producer than you are, I'll be up to your $30,000 before long. But in the meantime, you've also got the big bonus and you've been earning $30,000 for three years before I even catch up."

The fill-in-the-blank approach to negotiating is quite rare. Indeed, the fourth and final step is usually listening to the player's story on why he deserves more money than he's being offered. This is where diplomacy must prevail. "You have to know how to soothe egos," says Viking lineman Alderman. "You can offer someone a whole lot of money, but make a comment about his race or playing ability and he won't sign. Jim is good at avoiding these pitfalls."

Says Finks: "I have an obligation to listen to everyone's story. One guy may say he's better at his position than the other fellow and he can't understand why the coaches don't play him more. Or he will tell me that he did his job but he doesn't want to say anything about his teammates. Or he'll say we had an awful lot of bad breaks this year but we're going to be better next season. Or that he was hampered by an injury and couldn't get going this year. Or that he was playing a new position. Or that nobody threw him the ball or handed off to him for a run. Or that he can't perform well as a part-time player. Or that punting in this climate hinders him more than if he was in San Diego.

"These may all be good reasons," Finks adds. "But when you get right down to it, what counts most is Bud Grant's opinion of the player. In most cases, if Bud isn't playing a guy, it's because that guy isn't good enough to play."

Even so, sometimes Jim found himself paying a player on the basis of what he thought the player would do in the future rather than on what he'd done in the past. "One time a guy came into my office and promised me that he would be a first-string performer next year. I took that determination into consideration and jumped him $7,000. But he didn't make any more of a contribution than the year before. Still, the next time around he wanted more money, and it got sticky when I reminded him of our conversation the year before."

What does a sticky conversation sound like? The following is one between Finks and this writer who, although not a football player, was nevertheless able to generate a spirited discussion. If nothing else, it shows two things: management holds most of the trump cards, and any player who tries to negotiate without special legal and tax representation may be asking for trouble.

Finks: "All right, Bill, let's review last year [in this case, 1972]. I think we both agree that we had a disappointing season. There are a lot of reasons for it, and I think we in management are in part to blame for it. But the fact remains that a 7-and-7 record was not what we had hoped for.

"Now let's talk about your situation. You've been a regular for us and have done a fine job. But you're going into your fourteenth year. How much longer do you think you can do the job?"

Bill: "Well, I don't think that should be the question. As long as I can do the job day in and day out that's all that counts. I'm an offensive guard, and you know, Jim, that last season you never saw the man I was blocking get to the quarterback. It was always on the other side."

Finks: "Well, there is no point in discussing that. I've got the grades, Bill. I know you've done a good job and that there is every reason to think you may be able to play for us another couple of years. Now here's what I am proposing: I'll give you a $2,500 raise over what you earned last year. As you remember, last year I jumped you from $31,000 to $38,000. At that time I told you that you were getting up into an area where you must personally achieve something like all-pro or even all-conference, but you didn't last year, did you, Bill?"

Bill: "Well, I don't like to put it this way, but I want at least a $5,000 raise. Sure we were 7 and 7, but you just said that I did a good job last season. I've got a mortgage

94

and my wife is expecting our fourth child. I just can't play for less than a $5,000 raise. I just won't sign."

Finks: "Well, that's fine. Why don't you think it over and we'll meet sometime next week. But I do want to say this: I just didn't pick this $2,500 figure out of thin air. I've given it an awful lot of thought. Unless you can come up with some strong arguments, I think that's what we are going to wind up offering you, Bill."

(Next week, or in this case after lunch.)

Bill: "Now you know, Jim, that you can't just pull individual achievements out of a little drawer. Especially when you play offensive guard. You yourself said I did a damn good job and all the sportswriters said it too."

Finks: "I think you did a fine job. I wouldn't be offering you $2,500 if I didn't."

Bill: "If it wasn't for that damn Rozelle rule, I could get a job on any other club in the league."

Finks: "But the point is, Bill, you weren't selected for all-pro or anything else like that. Now here's what I will do for you. I'll put an additional clause in your contract to be tied to individual achievement. I'll give you a $1,500 raise [less than originally offered], a $1,000 bonus if you're selected to play in the Pro Bowl at the end of the season, and $1,000 if you grade as the top lineman on our team." ($3,500 in all.)

Bill: "Well, all right, but how can I be sure that the coach who grades me won't try to screw me for some reason?"

Finks: "I promise you he'll never know that your contract contains this type of clause. That would be as unfair to him as it would to you."

And that's the way we ended. Ed Sharockman, on the other hand, can remember ending on a lot less friendly note. Sharockman was a defensive back for the Vikings who, until his release by the club and subsequent retirement from football in 1972, negotiated his own contracts without the aid of an attorney or agent.

Sharockman, who today is a stockbroker in the Minneapolis area, remembers that "everytime I would open negotiations, Finks would tell me what a horseshit player I was. He told me how bad I was and what a bad season I had. And I would get upset. He really used to upset me. One time he said, 'I didn't realize how sensitive you were.'" Sometimes, Sharockman adds, "I just wanted to kick his head in."

Instead, however, "I might storm out of his office. I figure the best thing to do is walk the hell out and try to forget about it. Hell, we are all human beings and we have feelings. I knew he was doing it for effect because I know what kind of guy he is."

Sharockman adds: "Finks has a job to do and he doesn't care whether he's done it on the basis of real human feeling for people. He feels this is a business. He is just trying to get people to sign as cheaply as he can. As a player, you are always told that this is a team and you are all working together. You sacrifice yourself because this is a team effort. But, on the other hand, when you get into negotiations it's not like that at all. It's done on the basis of a business.

"Finks talked about being honest all the time and being fair. Those were his big words. But I felt that I was always honest with them but that he was never fair. His job is negotiations and to keep the price down and that is what he did."

Sharockman's problems with Finks went beyond contract negotiations. When the Vikings let Ed go in 1972, the season was already two-thirds over. Ed was placed on waivers and picked up by the Eagles, whereupon he decided to retire rather than report to a club suffering through a really rotten season.

Later Ed asked Minnesota for severance pay, in his case about $5,000. But the Vikings refused, arguing that since Philadelphia had claimed him, Ed was no longer the Vikings' responsibility. Ed then went to the Players Association, and in September, 1973, Sharockman lost his case before the National Labor Relations Board.

To be sure, Sharockman is just one player. Bill Brown and others say, in effect, that Jim's a great guy. But more important than any final disposition are the attitudes expressed by the two men involved. Both men feel betrayed by what they see—though in different ways—as the changing nature of the sport itself. Neither can understand how the family atmosphere they knew a decade ago has today become a loose configuration of lawyers, agents, union officials and more lawyers.

Says Sharockman: "It was a Tuesday, Halloween. Bud called me on the phone and asked me to come to the office. I asked him if it was something that could be said over the phone. And I knew then what had happened. He said no, that he would like me to come in, which was nice of him.

"When I got there I expected that at least Finks would be there. Bud started to explain everything to me and that Philadelphia had expressed interest in me at training camp. But I just cut him short. I just wanted to know why Finks wasn't there.

"I called Jim at home and asked why he wasn't there, and he told me that he had to get home and said he had waited about twenty minutes. I asked what happens if I retire? He said, 'Well, you are the property of the Philadelphia Eagles.'

"And that was the extent of it. I never even got a thank

97

you. It was like all those years never existed, like I wasn't even there. I think I was one of the first guys to sign a contract. I started even before our first coach, Norm Van Brocklin. I mentioned to Finks that I had been with the Vikings my whole career and asked him if this was the way he wanted to end it. Afterward, I called Garvey.

"Money," Ed adds, "was never the issue then."

Says Finks: "We thought about doing something special for Ed—until we found out that he had filed a grievance against us. It all happened so quickly that nothing was ever done. Nowadays the players force me to go by the book. Five years ago there was a completely different attitude toward it. I was going to talk to Ed, but he called me on the telephone first. He made it impossible for me to do anything else. The Players Association has taken the attitude of no more paternalism. So now we're negotiating on all economic matters and we're putting things into collective bargaining. Whatever is decided, we'll live by it and so will they. That's all there is to it."

Even though football has been Jim Finks's life, as a boy his ambition was to play professional baseball, hopefully with the St. Louis Cardinals. Finks was born in St. Louis in 1927, but his family moved when he was four years old to Salem, Illinois. He was one of seven children and his father headed up a shoe-manufacturing plant that employed about 700. "A very responsible position," Jim says proudly.

Salem was a small town, and every kid played every sport in its season. "I was a committed jock," he says, "football, basketball and baseball." By the time he was graduated from high school, Notre Dame was willing to give him a football scholarship and the New York Giants were ready to sign him to a baseball contract.

Jim turned the Giants down because, he says, "I felt that getting a college education was more important." He turned the Irish down because by the time his acceptance letter came in the mail, he had already committed himself to the University of Tulsa. (Tulsa's recruiters had previously gotten him to change his mind about attending the University of Illinois, but Jim decided his Tulsa commitment was too definite to consider another change.)

At Tulsa, Finks continued to play all three sports. Even so, "there was no doubt in my mind that after graduation I was going to be a professional baseball player," especially after the Tulsa football team failed to win a game Jim's senior year. (They tied 1 and lost 9.) "That left a very bad taste in my mouth," he says.

Jim never heard from the Cardinals but he did hear from the Cincinnati Reds, who signed him to a contract in 1949. The New York Yankees of the All-America Football Conference also asked Jim to sign a contract, and in a move exemplifying sound bargaining instincts, Jim got the Reds to agree that if for some reason they didn't elevate him after playing six weeks of action in the Class-C East Texas League, he could try out with the Yankees, even though he thought then that he would have very little chance of making a pro football team.

Much to his surprise, Cincinnati gave the fledgling football player its blessing. Much as he expected, the Yankees dropped him after just two weeks. Cincinnati took him back, but then the Pittsburgh Steelers, who with the Yankees had been interested in Finks, asked him to give it a whirl as soon as baseball season was over.

But Jim, who was a catcher, broke his finger less than two weeks after returning to baseball in August. He called Pittsburgh to tell them that he couldn't throw a forward pass (he was a quarterback), but the Steelers told him to try out anyway when the baseball season ended in a couple of weeks. "They really needed bodies then," Jim muses.

Jim reported to the Steelers just ten days before the start of the 1949 season and won a position as both a defensive back and a tailback in Pittsburgh's single-wing alignment. He rode the bench most of that season, but the very fact that he hung in there convinced him that his future lay in football rather than in baseball.

After the season, he went back to Tulsa for two reasons. The first was that, like many football players today, Jim did not graduate with other members of his class. (Unlike many today, he went back to get his degree.) The second was a coed he had met the year before when he was a senior and she was a freshman. Her name was Maxine, and a couple of years later she became his wife.

In 1950, Jim's second year with the Steelers, he became a starting defensive back. After that season, he again went back to Tulsa, this time to work in the oil fields. "I had to do something during the off season because back then you didn't make enough money playing football to live twelve months of the year."

In 1951, with Maxine now a student at the University of Pittsburgh, Jim suddenly found himself the starting tailback late in the season when injuries wiped out the two men in front of him. (The Steelers switched from single-wing to "T" the following season.)

Jim stayed number one QB for the next four seasons, though today the memories of those years are not vivid in his mind as they are for many other former players. "There were just too many frustrations," he says. "It isn't much fun playing when you aren't winning. I had a lot of injuries, and when the chance to coach at Notre Dame came along after the '55 season, I decided that was where my future lay."

(Jim says he doesn't have any scrapbooks around the house. "My mother has them all," he says, though Maxine adds that she's got a couple she kept herself.)

100

Jim spent just one year as an assistant coach at Notre Dame before receiving a call from a friend and former coach in the NFL, Otis Douglas, who was then head coach of the Calgary Stampeders of the Canadian Football League. Douglas wanted Finks to coach and scout for Calgary, but when Jim arrived he also was pressed into service as the team's quarterback. (Hank Stram, Head Coach of the Kansas City Chiefs, replaced Finks at Notre Dame.)

This was 1957, and for the first six games Jim was again an active player, though "my heart wasn't in it," he remembers. "We won three and lost three and then, thank God, we found a quarterback to take my place." But before Jim could settle into his combination scouting-coaching position, something happened to change his entire career.

The something was a fistfight. The participants were Calgary General Manager Bob Masterson and defensive back Harvey Wylie. The Stampeders had just lost a late-season game and were boarding the train for the second game of their weekend doubleheader when Masterson connected on a right cross to Wylie's jaw, presumably because Wylie had fumbled a punt that cost Calgary the game. Stampeder President Red Dutton wasted little time in firing Masterson and elevating Finks to interim general manager.

Finks says Calgary was a great learning ground because "the front office was so small I was involved in everything from signing players to laying out and selling the program to handling the tickets to arranging for all the transportation. I was only twenty-nine or thirty at the time and I was making somewhere between $15,000 and $20,000, more than I had ever made as a player."

The record shows that Jim did a good job as GM. "From a club that hadn't been in the play-offs since 1951, we went to a club that actually made it to the play-offs six straight years. We got a new stadium, attendance nearly doubled, and for the first time in eight years we made some money." Moreover, Jim managed to sign away from the NFL a few college draft choices, most notably quarterback Joe Kapp, who was to cross Finks's path more than once during his turbulent career.

But Jim wanted to get back into the NFL because "being an American, I am more comfortable here." Before the Viking offer in 1964, Finks had feelers from the 49ers and the Rams and from the league office, which considered him for the post of director of officiating.

But no job was offered until '64, and then, as in '57, a fight precipitated Finks's appointment. It was alleged in the press that Finks's predecessor in Minnesota, Bert Rose, was forced to quit by the Vikings' five-man board of directors because of "personality conflicts" with "other members of the Viking organization and various sports figures in the community," as a Minneapolis *Tribune* sportswriter put it. The whole story never came out, but Rose's firing certainly looked suspicious in view of the tremendous job he had done the Vikings' first year, 1960, in making the team a box-office success. (Twenty-five thousand season tickets sold before the first league game.)

There was a lot of unrest among management, owners and coaches before Jim got here. "I don't know why Bert left," he says. "Maybe it was a plot to get him or maybe it was just growing pains. I heard all the stories but, frankly, I don't want to know the reason."

And with good reason. The Viking board disagreed on whether Finks was the man to replace Rose. Again Jim isn't saying as much as he may know, but he does say that a couple of the directors were in favor of another man. "I didn't know how strong their feelings had been. Sure, they agreed. They said Finks is okay and the vote is unanimous. But once I actually got here I realized how strong those feelings had been."

102

But that's all he'll say on the subject.

Even when the Vikings' general manager is able to sign all forty players without a fuss, that doesn't necessarily mean that his personnel problems are over and that he can now attend without interruption to such administrative problems as refusing to pay back stadium rent demanded by city officials.

For example, in 1966 the starting quarterback and the head coach virtually stopped talking to one another right in the middle of the season. The quarterback, Francis Tarkenton, played his position quite contrary to the wishes of his coach, Norm Van Brocklin, himself an ex-quarterback in the NFL. Tarkenton is well known for liking to scramble around the backfield, a tactic that can baffle a defense but also, on occasion, his own teammates. Van Brocklin has always believed that a quarterback should drop straight back and throw the ball from inside a pocket of protection established by his linemen.

"It was all a problem of personalities," says Finks. "Norm and Fran just weren't compatible. Something had to be done."

So together with Van Brocklin, Finks went to New York to see New York Giants' owner Wellington Mara about the possibility of a trade. "I had heard through the grapevine that a deal was possible," Finks says cryptically. A deal was virtually completed when Fran surprised everyone by making public a letter advising Viking management that he wouldn't play another season in Minnesota.

As was mentioned previously, luck plays a big role in a GM's success or failure. In this instance, Finks was very lucky he had already virtually dealt Tarkenton to New York. Otherwise, the Viking executive would have been faced with the unenviable task of trying to trade a player to a club that knew the player wasn't about to play for his team ever again. It's doubtful Finks would have gotten three high-round draft choices from the Giants—the same three the general manager turned into three starters in the bedpan draft the following January. Says Finks: "Not every executive would have shown the class Mara did."

(Finks's hospital luck wasn't all good. After the surgery he returned home to recuperate only to be rushed back to the hospital in an ambulance a few days later. Doctors determined he had developed a blood clot that had traveled to the heart and then, by the grace of God, had kicked over into his right lung. First came emergency surgery, then the last rites of the Catholic Church. "They had just about counted me out," Jim says, with the smile of a Vegas gambler who has beaten the house.)

Whereas the Tarkenton–Van Brocklin feud received a great deal of press attention, most of a GM's personnel problems are attended to behind closed doors. One such problem involved a player who, in the early 1960s, went through money "like salts through a widow woman," as Finks puts it.

"When I first got here," Jim says, "this player [whom Finks declines to identify publicly] had just gone through bankruptcy. But he still felt a strong obligation to repay certain people, so we set up a program to try to retire as many debts as we possibly could. We gave him some money—a lot of money, and on more than one occasion. I would imagine we loaned this player $60,000 to $70,000 over a three-to-four-year period. We also furnished legal advice at no charge. But the guy was a compulsive spender. A credit-card guy.

"Remember, this was back before agents and attorneys represented most players. The player had meant a lot to this organization and we knew that when this guy retired from football, he couldn't go out a bum. He had to have something. But try as we did, we never could do it. He just kept spending."

The player, Finks adds, subsequently got himself a financial adviser who helped straighten out his monetary problems. And although Jim doesn't like agents, he says that this player shows how special advisers can help get a player's head together, which in turn makes him a better performer in uniform.

Another behind-the-scenes Viking personnel problem involved a player who got a girl in trouble one year. Finks knew it. He also knew that the player would be late reporting to training camp because he had to first straighten out his personal life. But when the press asked the Viking general manager why this player wasn't in camp, Finks let on that it was just a salary dispute. He deliberately and successfully misled the sportswriters.

Such girl problems are not that uncommon. One executive of another NFL team says he always has at least one player and sometimes more than one who come to him during a season looking for a good doctor or similar assistance. This official adds that relaxed abortion laws have cut down on the number of players who have come to him the past couple of seasons.

Indeed, some front-office executives are happy when a pregnant girl is the most serious personnel problem they face in a year's time. For example, in 1973, defensive tackle Ernie Holmes of the Pittsburgh Steelers was put on five years' probation after pleading guilty in Ohio to charges of assault with a deadly weapon. When Holmes was arrested, Steelers' Vice President Dan Rooney went to Ohio to bail him out. The club then arranged for legal counsel and, it is understood, helped their employee financially during that time.

When things were relatively normal, Finks's work week during the season began Monday with answering the mail. A lot of Finks's letter writing was either to the league office concerning a variety of things such as reporting attendance figures or official statistics of the game the day before, or to fans who had complained about something like the parking or the location of their seats.

Monday afternoon Jim would try to sneak away for a game of paddle ball with Bud Grant. He usually made it, but sometimes the telephone company did him in. "I'm always on the defensive as far as the phone is concerned. It seems to be impossible ever to get caught up because you're always getting calls from other clubs wanting to discuss anything from player personnel to preseason games next year to how much do you pay for your half-time entertainment.

"And often it's the league office calling. Maybe they want to know why so-and-so got thrown out of the game the previous Sunday. Or maybe the visiting team complained about how they were treated by our people. It really could be almost anything."

Monday night, and for that matter every night of the week, Jim got home around 6 P.M. often only to find more calls, primarily from newspaper reporters or owners of other clubs, who might have been attending to other business during the day.

Tuesday began with a check of the trainer's report on the game the previous Sunday. After consulting with Coach Grant, Finks attended the weekly press luncheon where he says he did his best to stay as unnewsworthy as possible. (The Vikings stopped fan-club luncheons a few years back because although they were great if the club was winning, they were just too hostile when times were bad.)

On Wednesday and Thursday, Finks's work often depended on what specifically came up. Maybe a player wants an advance on his contract or he wants to know whether it's okay to endorse a certain product. At least once a week the Vikings' business manager, Harley Peterson, gave his

106

report on the club's financial position. Several times a week Finks would call in his ticket manager, George Arneson, to make sure that all thirty or so VIP's were taken care of for the following Sunday.

Also at least once a week—and recently many more times than that—Finks talked to the club's attorneys. He might be obliged to give a deposition in a case brought against the club by an ex-player like Joe Kapp, or in connection with a suit filed by a season-ticket holder trying to void many clubs' policy of making preseason tickets a mandatory part of a fan's season-ticket package.

"I've spent the last three days giving depositions," Finks said disgustedly during an interview for this book. "And I spent a week before that preparing my statements. That sure as hell can take the fun out of your job."

Finks, however, learned the hard way that all this detail work, with the notable exception of legal affairs, can, if not attended to properly, have a negative effect on the way his club performs on the field. He learned it after the Vikings won the league championship in 1969 and the right to meet Kansas City in the Super Bowl.

"Back then," Finks says, "you had only one week between the league championship game and the Super Bowl. Even so, we should have been better prepared. We should have made contingency plans. Like we had to allocate some 6,000 tickets and arrange for transportation and hotel space for players' wives, VIP's and others.

"Because we didn't have rooms ready for parents, I know that some of our players gave up their rooms to their parents the night before the game. We had some guys sleeping three and four to a room. Now how much sleep do you think they actually got?

"Also, while the league assigns you a hotel, we didn't bother to install our own telephone system. Consequently, we spent hours trying to reach each other through the switchboard, and often we just had to track each other down by foot.

"And then we mistakenly held back a lot of tickets thinking that many of our more affluent season holders would make the trip to New Orleans to see the game in person. But they didn't, and so our ticket manager was out hawking tickets in front of the stadium the morning of the game.

"The absolute payoff," Finks adds, shaking his head in a never-again fashion, "was when the hotel where we held our postgame reception—it was supposed to have been a victory party—ran out of beer. Damn! Can you imagine that?"

When the Vikings made it to the Super Bowl again in 1974, Finks and his staff did things much differently. This time the Vikings had a suite of offices in their hotel staffed by veteran workers who flew to Houston, site of the contest, more than a week before the actual game. They lined up more hotel rooms and tickets than the first time around. They drew up a master chart showing where everyone, including even players' wives, were scheduled to be every day. And they made sure that there were always enough security police around to protect the players themselves.

"I'm enjoying myself," Jim said at breakfast the Friday before the game. "It's easy when you're working with Merlin the Magician," otherwise known as George Arneson, the ticket manager, who had just scrounged up fifty tickets for Xerox executives after a local ticket agency had fouled up.

In fact, looking at the Vikings' GM, you would have thought that this time for sure Minnesota was going to win. After breakfast, Bill Brown stopped by Jim's table and asked, "Do you like my pants?" Then he turned to an observer and, with a knowledgeable wink, laughed. "The

108

boss gave me these pants. He always gives the trash like me the things he doesn't want."

Finks, a smile on his face, shot back: "When I saw your father last night, I knew who he was right away. I also knew why you're so bowlegged."

There have been other decisions made by the Vikings' general manager that he could not correct. Like the time the Vikings signed a working agreement with a minor-league football team, the Des Moines Warriors. The agreement gave the Vikings an opportunity to sign ten to fifteen players a year off the Des Moines roster, while giving the Warriors first call on any player let go by Minnesota. The deal cost Minnesota more than $50,000 over a two-year period and Finks didn't sign one player.

Other decisions that Finks has made he's stuck by, even though they didn't make him too popular a figure around town. In 1971, for example, Finks challenged the Minneapolis City Council's decision that the Vikings owed $73,784 in back rent for use of the city-owned stadium for play-off games in 1969 and 1970. The council said its contract with the club called for stadium rent per game to equal 10 percent of all ticket sales, after certain deductions. Finks said that was only for regular season games and that the Vikings, like their baseball cotenants the Twins, should only have to pay $2,000 a game for any play-off action.

While the Vikings wound up paying the full amount, all but $6,000 of that amount, or $2,000 for each of the three play-off games in question, was designated for stadium improvements specifically for the football team.

Also in 1971, Finks tried to get CBS to drop a Mason City, Iowa, station from the Vikings' local TV network because the signal from that station was penetrating the club's home territory, in Finks's opinion cutting down on home-game attendance. This of course was before Congress lifted the blackout, and the flood of angry letters from outraged fans and congressmen should have been a tip-off of what was to come.

"Because there was an existing contract where this station was indeed part of our network, we weren't allowed to stop them from telecasting our games," Finks says. "However, there was an agreement made whereby two games a year would not be telecast, those two being the last two home games of the year. Those were the two that concerned us most because that's when our weather is particularly bad."

Finks adds: "You can't let the newspapers and the fans dictate how you're going to run your club. I respect Joe Thomas a great deal because when he became general manager at Baltimore, he made changes like trading Johnny Unitas, who was a living legend there, and he didn't let the flak he took influence his decision. There are some people in this league who don't express an opinion until their third cocktail.

"The biggest weakness you'll find in football is the guy who wants all the credit for doing something. There is enough glory to go around for everybody. But when somebody is going to be blamed for something, you can't find these people.

"I get a kick out of people saying I'm a master trader and all that bullshit. Just stop and look at it for a minute. I had nothing to do with a lot of great players being here. Carl Eller, Dave Osborn, Milt Sunde, Paul Dickson, Bill Brown, Fred Cox. All those guys were brought in by other people, and in many instances by more than one front office man.

"That's why I resent seeing a guy willing to take all the bows. There are more of those kinds of guys than the other kind. But they get caught sooner or later. Bud knows I get credit for a lot of things that other coaches would resent.

110

And I think Bud knows he gets credit for some things that other general managers would resent. But we both know it doesn't make a hell of a lot of difference who gets the credit. I don't do anything unless he knows about it and he doesn't do anything unless I know about it."

Adds Finks: "There are a lot of people in our industry who aren't in touch with reality."

Probably the most controversial decision Finks ever made as Vikings' GM was when he traded the quarterback who led his club to the Super Bowl the year before rather than agree to pay what he considered was an exorbitant salary demand.

The quarterback was Joe Kapp, whom Finks had known since their days together at Calgary. The problem, according to Finks, was Kapp's attorney, John Elliot Cooke of San Francisco. Cooke did all the negotiating, Finks says. "I only wish that Joe and I had had the chance to sit down and try to resolve our problems."

But that wasn't what Cooke wanted, according to Finks. (Cooke himself refuses to discuss the matter because of a suit he has pending against the NFL on Kapp's behalf charging, among other things, breach of contract by the New England Patriots.) Instead, Finks says, "Cooke gave me a figure and left me with the impression that it was not negotiable. Either hit it on the head or forget it."

The figure Cooke reportedly wanted for his client was somewhere in the neighborhood of $1 million to $1.25 million over a five-year period. Finks reportedly offered a two-year pact at about $100,000 a year with an option for a third year. Kapp reportedly had been making about $50,000 the season before.

"Cooke told me," says Finks, "that in his opinion Joe Kapp is the greatest quarterback and don't take my word for it because I have talked to many people. He then mentioned a figure that was shocking. I didn't need to consult with anybody because I knew right then that what Joe wanted was financially impossible. I also knew that we would probably have to find ourselves another quarterback."

All of which was shocking to the public. After all, Joe was a flamboyant player, a leader who had brought his team to the Super Bowl. Surprisingly, though, other Viking players looking back on Joe's departure from the Vikings accepted Finks's decision as the right one under the circumstances.

"I can't forgive Joe for not coming back. We all thought he'd settle eventually," said center Mick Tingelhoff.

"I guess I can say now that I felt Joe deserted us," commented guard Grady Alderman.

Added Finks, rising from his couch and popping down a few more wheat-germ tablets: "I just have some strong convictions about signing football players, what's right and what's wrong. And you can be sure I'm going to stick by my principles."

Paddle ball, anyone?

Jim says his ten years with the Vikings were the "ten most gratifying years in my life." But there were problems between Finks and the Viking ownership that made him think it was time for a change. Jim expects to be gainfully employed again by the time this book reaches the stores. He says he is most comfortable in sports, but don't be surprised if Jim Finks's career ultimately leads away from sports to a job where he can keep intact his ways of, as he puts it, "dealing with people and people problems."

4

The Invisible Man

John Free
Business Manager–Traveling Secretary
The New York Jets

WHEN JOHN FREE was an eighteen-year-old college student back in 1936, he took a summer job as a typewriter salesman. Together with a friend, John was assigned a territory around Hagerstown, Maryland, more than commuting distance from his home in Baltimore but the only territory the company had available.

That summer John and his friend lived in a room at the local Y.M.C.A. Their business office was also that room at the Y.M.C.A. Their storage area for an inventory of some twenty portable typewriters was that same rather crowded room. Their business number was the number on the pay phone down in the lobby, the desk clerk their answering service for a fee of $1 a day.

At first business was about what you'd expect it to be during the Depression. But then one night at the local greasy spoon, the two youths overheard two automobile salesmen who were passing through town discuss Hagerstown's notable red-light district. Not one or two, but three, streets of fallen women. And, joked one of the auto men, if you sell a car to the queen bee, you probably can sell a car to every whore in town.

113

And if cars, reasoned the novices, why not typewriters? Surely such women of the town are probably the only women in town (or men) with any money, right? They're also in a line of work that can't go on forever. And when they're washed up as whores they're going to need another skill, preferably one they can teach themselves in between customers' house calls. And naturally these women will pay cold cash, which will make the sales manager very happy, right?

So the following morning John and his friend appeared at the front door of the queen bee's house. John rang the bell and from up on the second floor a voice shouted down, "I just had an examination, Doc, you're not due again until next week."

"I'm not the doctor," John shouted up. "But I do have something in this case that will change the course of your entire life."

"Get the hell out of here," the queen shouted back down, this time sticking her head out a window.

"Okay." John shrugged. "But you're missing the opportunity of a lifetime."

Now that was an old line even in 1936. But it worked. Downstairs came the curious queen dressed in only a nightgown. What a pair of knockers, John thought. Her name was Sunny, maybe because of her bright reddish hair. "We were petrified to go in," John recalls, though the super-salesmen weren't about to pull back now.

Inside, John extolled the virtues of his machine. He worked on the coffee table in the living room, and at one point the queen shook her head and remarked, "You guys must be nuts." But still she listened, and when John had finished his spiel she went into another room and reappeared with a wad of bills as big as a fist.

By the time the salesmen returned to their office an hour

later, the answering service already had calls waiting for them, all from lady friends of Miss Sunny. By the end of the day, the two boys had repeated their pitch maybe fifteen times. By the end of three days, they had sold some twenty-two typewriters at about $65 a machine. The sales manager was ecstatic and the youths' fame spread throughout the company.

Of course John remembers how one or two of his customers had wanted to barter rather than pay cash. But John swears he resisted that temptation, which gives you an idea of the kind of hard-nosed businessman John Free was in his salad days. Today as the business manager and traveling secretary of the New York Jets, Free lets himself go a little more than that—though not in the way Sunny's friends might have suggested. Still, Free retains a cool and at times calculating approach to his job, whether the task be to tear down an illegal wooden windbreak the Oakland Raiders secretly erected during the night before a game at Shea Stadium, the Jets' Long Island, New York, home, or to find a Brink's truck to spirit quarterback Joe Willie Namath through a crowd of admiring but also overly enthusiastic fans.

Probably no front-office executive handles the variety of jobs done by John Free. On some clubs two or three employees do what the Jets' Free does alone. During the week his title is business manager, the chief cook and financial bottle washer of a professional football team. On a number of weekends his title is traveling secretary, the Moses for an airborne herd of players, coaches, owners, sportswriters and others. On several other weekends his title—this time an unofficial one—is stadium superintendent, the man responsible for such pregame preparations as the hiring of ushers, ticket sellers and ticket takers.

Free's most important job is business manager. A business

115

manager is part accountant, part purchasing agent, part investment counselor, part personnel head. If the Jets are going to play a preseason game in, say, Tampa, Florida, John negotiates the contract with the game's promoter. If a player needs a loan or wants to be paid in twenty-eight installments instead of the usual fourteen, John makes the arrangements. If the computer screws up the players' payroll checks, John's job is to straighten things out. If the equipment manager needs more jock straps, John must authorize the purchase.

A majority of National Football League teams have business managers, though as with every position in the front office of pro football the responsibilities and importance of the job vary with the club. In the hierarchy of things, the business manager usually reports directly to the general manager, who, in turn, reports directly to the owner or owners. As a general rule, how much authority a business manager has depends in large part on the forte of that particular club's general manager. If the GM is oriented toward the game on the field—scouting, drafting, signing, etc.—then the business manager will have heavy responsibility for carrying out the financial end of the operation. On the other hand, if the GM chooses to divide his time between the game on the field and the organization off, then the business manager is, more or less, just another employee.

One variation of this rule is when the general manager of a club is also its head coach, a growing trend. For instance, until he stepped down as the team's mentor at the end of the 1973 season, the then sixty-four-year-old Weeb Ewbank was both head coach and general manager of the Jets. Since no man can be in two places at the same time, this meant that the yeoman's share of financial responsibility fell to Ewbank's longtime friend and business associate, John Free. (Now that he is just general manager, Ewbank still concentrates on player operations, leaving Free with the same all-encompassing job he had before.)

Another variation is when the game on the field is treated almost entirely separately from the front-office operation. Such is the case in Kansas City, where Chiefs' Head Coach Hank Stram handles everything pertaining to the game itself while Jack Steadman, Executive Vice President and General Manager, controls the purse strings. The Chiefs have no business manager as such because Steadman does much of that work himself. (The two men collaborate when necessary, such as on player salaries.)

While Free's most important job is business manager, his most nerve-racking has to be traveling secretary. A traveling secretary is responsible for getting the plane to the airport on time, the buses to the airport on time, the players to the right hotel, the food to the traditional pregame team meal, the injured player to a hospital, and so on and so forth.

Furthermore, if the owner suddenly decides he needs two last-minute tickets for some fat cat and his wife, John must dig them up by hook or by crook. And if there are still empty seats in the first-class section of the airplane after all coaches, owners, their families and assorted VIP's have been seated, then Free must decide who among the press corps shall be so honored. (Usually the papers with the biggest circulations like the *Times* and the New York *Daily News* win Free's favor. The players, in case you were wondering, always fly coach.)

What makes Free's job particularly nerve-racking is Namath. John can never be certain whether there is enough security surrounding the Jets' star. All pro football stars have their coteries, but none loom so large or so frenzied as Namath's when the star himself emerges from the Jets' locker room after a game.

"If John Free wasn't around," says Jimmy Walsh, Namath's former classmate at the University of Alabama and now his attorney, "I'd demand that the Jets supply a road manager for Joe. After all, Joe is the star of the team."

Free does his best to protect the star, though he admits that you win some and lose some. One time in San Diego, for instance, John hired a laundry truck and successfully concealed Joe on the short trip from the locker room to the team bus. In Buffalo he used a Brink's truck to achieve the same end. (Free says Namath was grinning from ear to ear and waving out the back window as the Brink's parted the crowd.)

Another time in San Diego John paid some twenty cops to form a wedge to get Joe to the bus. It worked, but some rather ridiculous fans then decided to jump up and down on top of the vehicle, and a few of them actually threw themselves in front of the bus as it started to pull away from the curb—a near disaster. In Miami, John also paid the police to protect Namath, but the cops fouled up by using dogs, which caused many in the crowd to panic and nearly killed one boy who was trampled on.

Even more frightening was the time in St. Louis when one woman who just wouldn't give up stuck her arm through the bus window in hopes of touching her idol. Just then the bus started to move, dragging the woman and horrifying the crowd. Fortunately, the window was so constructed that it immediately broke away from the rest of the vehicle.

Wrote one sportswriter in 1972: "When Namath's playing days are over, it's quite possible prison inmates the world over might contact Free for advice on how to spring loose."

Free himself likes to recall the time outside cavernous Tulane Stadium in New Orleans after a Jets' preseason win over the Saints in 1973. John asked ten uniformed city

118

policemen if they would form a wedge, and each officer proceeded to wrap one hand around another's billy club. The job done, Free tipped the officer in charge $25.

Whereupon the cop shot back, "I thought you said we were going to get paid for this job."

Never mind that scores of people had a clear view of New Orleans' finest illegally accepting a tip while on duty. The law-enforcement officer stood his ground at the steps of the Jets' bus until Free shelled out $75 more.

"I couldn't believe it," says the Jets' business manager. "A cop doing that in front of all those people." (Usually John slips them the dough in private.)

Of course, sometimes John's trouble on the road emanates from within the ranks. At the college all-star game in Chicago in June, 1969, Jet buses started to pull away seconds after Free had finished explaining to the drivers that they were not to move from that spot until after the game. After throwing his body—which resembles more the before than the after picture for a body-building ad—in front of the vehicles, John wanted to know why the hell these drivers couldn't understand plain English.

"Coach Curly said it was okay," one driver explained innocently, referring to Jets' running back Curly Johnson who often was the thorn in John Free's side during his days with the Jets.

When the Jets are home at Shea Stadium, far more serious problems can sometimes arise. One year the New Yorkers were hosting the Oakland Raiders late in the season in a game the weatherman said would be played in freezing cold weather. The night before the game, Oakland management ordered a wooden windbreak built behind the Raiders' bench. Just how the clandestine carpenters got past the Shea security guard is still a mystery to Free. But when John arrived the next morning he ordered the structure torn down, the lean-to being in his opinion an illegal structure under NFL rules and also a viewing problem for the fans.

The carpenters met Free's men head on, and John decided that this was no time for a free-for-all. So instead he went looking for Commissioner Rozelle, who he knew was in attendance, and Rozelle himself ordered the lean-to dismantled. Free gleefully adds that Oakland owner Al Davis was madder than hell. (The Jets and the Raiders have never been big on one another. Remember when Oakland defensive end Ben Davidson broke Namath's jaw in what the Jets called a cheap shot?)

Free says the worst problem he ever had with the stadium came in 1969 after the Mets won the World Series and Met fans tore up pieces of sod 2 and 3 feet long as souvenirs. The Jets were to open their home season less than a week later, which meant thousands of dollars' worth of new sod had to be ordered and workers had to work long into the night performing the surgery. Free says the Mets paid both for the sod and for the labor to put it down—about $6,000 total. But he grumbles that it subsequently cost the Jets a great deal in overtime to put up the extra bleachers for football and that it cost him more than one night's sleep ramroding the sod project.

Another problem that could have been a lot worse than it was began when a young girl darted onto the field at Shea straight in the direction of—who else?—Namath. John likes to position himself at the end of the Jets' bench (around the 30-yard line) during a game just in case he needs to call in security forces. But on this occasion there was no time to do so. For a moment he thought about making an open-field tackle himself. But he balked when he realized how that would look on TV in millions of living rooms. So he just stood there, helpless, while the girl fortunately did nothing more than plant a kiss on her Joe.

120

At least Free saw the girl, which is more than he can say for the young man who before one game several years ago took it upon himself to buy a number of little white toy footballs, paint the Jets' emblem on each one and then at half time throw them up into the stands as a sort of gesture of friendship. Unfortunately, one football hit an unsuspecting fan in the eye. The fan subsequently sued the Jets, and the case is still in litigation.

Next to the kissing bandit, probably the most visible problem Free has had at Shea is an old car, long parked in one corner of the stadium parking lot and by now literally covered with the numbers of Jet players.

Originally the car belonged to Vern Studdard, a wide receiver on the Jets in 1971. When Studdard was cut, Free says Vern sold the car to another player who, when he was subsequently cut, sold it to another and so on and so forth. Each new owner painted his number on the car, and at this point Free isn't sure anymore who owns the vehicle. "I can't get rid of it," he said disgustedly, "because I don't have the registration card and the police won't let me junk the thing without that registration."

For what he does, John Free earns around $30,000 a year, certainly not a salary to sneer at, but not one deserving of any oohs and ahhs when you consider all the time put in. Free's family was rather well-to-do, however, and since coming to New York in 1963, John has lived with his wife, Ruth, on Morgan Island, an exclusive residential section in the Long Island community of Glen Cove, about a sixty-five-minute drive from the Jets' Manhattan offices on Madison Avenue. The Frees live only about two blocks away from Ewbank and his wife, Lucy, and on a hot summer day Ruth and Lucy often can be found together at the Ewbanks's swimming pool. (Together the two football widows also watch a lot of the Jets on TV.)

Free has received job offers at up to double the annual salary the Jets pay him. But he says he has absolutely no intention of moving on because, like many in the front office of pro football, he has a strong emotional attachment for his particular team. Not only does John Free like to work seven days a week from July through January, he actually seems to need all that work to fulfill a sense of involvement with the Jets, a sense of giving 100 percent to a team effort.

Call him cheerleader. Call him superfan. Whatever the case, when he's on the road Free always dresses all in green, the Jets' primary color. A typical ensemble might include green striped pants, a dark-green blazer with the Jets' emblem on the pocket, a green-tinted shirt with maybe a pattern of little jet airplanes and a green tie with a jet-shaped tie clasp.

Back home Free's basement recreation room is wall-to-wall Jet mementos. On one wall hangs his prized possession: a sketch of him done by noted artist LeRoy Neiman at the breakfast before the Jets' Super Bowl game in 1969. Also on that wall is a picture of him and Namath, the latter with his arm draped around John, after a particularly grueling game.

This theme of emotional attachment has several variations. In San Francisco, Jane Morabito, widow of former 49ers' owner Vic Morabito and today a major 49er shareholder herself, screams, cries and beats herself to an emotional pulp at every game. In Los Angeles, Carroll Rosenbloom, owner of the Rams, moans, groans and sometimes even cries over the outcome of a game. In Kansas City, Jack Steadman remains more reserved, though when asked he calls his work with the Chiefs more than a lifetime's worth of personal fulfillment.

Like Steadman, Free is the quiet type, though on one occasion he was moved to deliver a win-one-for-the-

Gipper locker-room speech. It was in Baltimore before a game in 1972 against the Colts, the team that had so unceremoniously fired his friend and head coach many years before. The Jets had never won in Baltimore. And John told the assemblage that this time, by God, he wanted to win, both for Ewbank and, quite frankly, for himself.

The Jets did win. After the game, as is his custom, John was the last one off the field and into the locker room. When he entered, everyone started to clap. "It's been a long time coming," began Larry Grantham, the Jets' cocaptain until his retirement prior to the 1973 season. "But there's no one we want more to have this. Here's your game ball, John," and the place erupted again.

Silly?

Not in this business.

Not in a corporation where overall success can be as much a result of mental well-being as physical conditioning. Emotion can be important in any business. For example, in October, 1970, staff reporter Greg Conderacci wrote in *The Wall Street Journal* how on Monday mornings vacuum-cleaner salesmen for Scott & Fetzer Company in Cleveland get together to sing their product's praises to the tune of "That Old-Time Religion." Some fifty salesmen sing out lustily, and, argues one salesman: "People say it's corny, but it gets the adrenalin going. Maybe the salesman has had a bad week and feels lousy Monday. The singing keeps him from thinking negatively."

And then there's the Speidel division of Textron Inc., which in connection with the introduction to company salesmen of a new line of toiletries one time really raised the roof by first mysteriously dousing the lights in the room and running movies of auto racing. Then a high-school band marched into the room followed by a dozen models who helped the salesmen into racing jackets.

Next the salesmen were ushered into an adjoining room

where there were 10-foot-high mock-ups of the toiletries plus real sports cars and bales of hay covered by huge checkered flags. More shapely young things poured champagne for the salesmen who, to show they were now in the spirit of things, hurled the empty glasses into a fake fireplace.

(Thanks in part to all the ballyhoo, the sales compaign was a complete success, said one company executive.)

Of course, a business manager isn't a salesman. And certainly no business manager for a football team is going to make as much of a corporate contribution as a quarterback or a head coach. But in this age of bad blood between management and labor, an age of player strikes and umpteen lawsuits against league owners, a team with a winning tradition has to find somewhere that rather elusive element known as cohesion. A head coach most often supplies cohesion, though sometimes a player, owner, or even a business manager can be the source. Whoever is the source, cohesion is that element that somehow subjugates a number of inflated egos (both in management and in labor) for the sake of a winning performance.

There is no finer example of a team without cohesion than the Philadelphia Eagles of 1972. The Eagles' record that season was a dismal 3 wins and 11 losses. At the end of the season both the general manager and the head coach were canned, an obvious indication of the kind of leadership in that club that year.

There were other obvious indications as early as training camp when Head Coach Ed Khayat ordered short hair for all players. Then management "solved" the problem of a collective holdout by the team's two best defensive players, safety Bill Bradley and middle linebacker Tim Rossovich, by trading the fiery and very popular Rossovich to San Diego, foolishly leaving the club without a frontline performer in

124

that position. Eagles' owner Leonard Tose added insult to injury by flying to and from many games and practices in his private helicopter with the Eagles' insignia painted on. (A number of his players called that ego tripping.)

Such seeds of discontent definitely are in the Jets' organization. In 1973, for example, a number of players refused to sign contracts, charging Head Coach Ewbank with being a miser with a buck. Dave Anderson, sportswriter for *The New York Times,* wrote after the Jets' sorry 23-to-7 opening-game loss to Green Bay that year:

"Before the Jets won Super Bowl III, money wasn't the factor on the Jets that it is now. . . . But with their Super Bowl success, they realized they were worth big money. Since then, Weeb has insulted their intelligence, to say nothing of their exchequer, with his minimal offers. By now, many Jets are disillusioned with their contracts, even the better-salaried players. . . .

"Not that other NFL teams don't have contract troubles. But they try to solve them as quickly as possible. Weeb's idea of negotiating is to ignore the player seeking big money, a philosophy that went out with sweatshops."

Winston Hill, an all-pro offensive tackle on the Jets, was one of a handful suspended by Ewbank last year until Hill signed his contract. Hill, who as the Jets' representative to the Players Association—the union—can be outspoken in his low regard for the Jets' front office, credits Free with providing what cohesion the New York club has.

Says Hill: "John's still part of management. He's still one of the bad guys. But he does his best to break down the barriers. He's the man who gets all the ugly problems, and he takes it all. He just seems to float through a problem."

Free does several little things, Hill says. Like he goes out of his way to arrange for a player's parents to have a room near their son when the Jets are playing a game near his hometown. And until the kidding finally got to him, he'd always come up with an original—if not memorable—poem to put at the bottom of the mimeographed sheet of instructions he hands out at the start of every road trip. (The sheet is printed in green, of course.)

"I tried to forget them as soon as I read them," Hill jokes, though not without good reason:

> The ball on the 40, it sits on the tee,
> Twenty-two men wait impatiently.
> The signal is sounded, the ball hangs in the sky,
> Now the season has started and spirits are high.
> Cleveland in Brown, the Jets in their Green,
> Violent colors and noise fill the scene.
> New York gets the ball and moves to a score,
> The game is a preview of 16 more.

Adds ex-player Grantham, a close friend of Free's: "Weeb is a guy who tends to remain aloof from his players. John's the guy who sits down and has a beer with you." (Unlike most teams, the Jets permit players to drink on the road, though most do anyway once they're out of sight of the coaching staff.)

Though he is little known even by Jet fans, Business Manager Free is the man to know if, say, you want your hotel to have the prestige of accommodating a professional football team, a fact duly noted by clubs in their widely circulated media guides. In 1973 a Stouffer's hotel in Cincinnati went so far as to send a group photo of the secretaries in the sales department feigning tears in the hope of getting John to reconsider his decision to stay elsewhere in that city. When that didn't work, one secretary wrote him an impassioned letter telling how heartbroken she was and wouldn't he pretty please reconsider for her sake?

He didn't.

Free, however, isn't sitting in the catbird seat when it

comes to airline bookings. One airline, United, strives to sign up as many NFL teams as possible. (In 1973 it had about half.) But at least one other, Eastern, reportedly put out word in 1973 that in view of operating losses it was already incurring, it no longer felt compelled to solicit football charters, which can be unprofitable for an entire season if on just one trip the plane and its crew are delayed for any length of time by bad weather, an injured player or a postgame traffic snarl outside the stadium.

Like any good businessman, Free in 1973 asked airlines to submit bids for the Jets' eleven-trip schedule—that's six preseason games and seven league games minus two bus games, one in Philadelphia and the other in New Haven, Connecticut, against the New York Giants. He received two bids, one for $98,000 from United, the other $104,000 from Eastern. But United wouldn't guarantee for every trip the type of plane Free wanted, whereas Eastern would. So the business manager hemmed and hawed until finally Eastern told him to sign or it was withdrawing its bid. John signed, figuring it was worth the extra $6,000 to be certain that the right plane, the one he was certain could handle any amount of equipment and any number of passengers, was always there.

But John quickly reassumes his behind-the-scenes power when some big shot comes begging at the last minute for tickets to a game at Shea Stadium. For instance, a few years back a New York publicity man became frantic when his client, actress Ann-Margaret, and her husband, Roger Smith, decided at the last minute that they wanted to see one of the biggest Jet home games of the year. The agent called a friend—Namath's attorney, Walsh—who in turn called John who in turn not only got two of the Jets' owners to give up their own seats and instead sit in the press box, but also arranged for Mr. and Mrs. Smith to attend the owners' pregame stadium reception. (Free sent flowers to Mrs. Smith's hospital room when she fell during her Las Vegas nightclub act two years later.)

The Jets' business manager also calls the shots when for some reason a hotel where the club is staying screws up. This happened in 1973 in Tampa, where the Jets were playing a preseason game. It wasn't that this establishment messed up the all-important pregame meal. Free has it so arranged that players who want steak sit at a certain table and players who want pancakes sit at another and so on. That way there's no black-white seating problem.

Rather, the hotel failed to break down adequately the room charges and personal charges incurred by the players. And the hotel somehow added another couple's bill to the Jets' bill—an extra $75 or so on a bill already totaling close to $3,200. "This happens all the time," said the hotel's rather blasé accountant.

"You're the first hotel in years we've been a month late in paying, but I wanted to get this straightened out," countered Free.

And while another hotel official higher up than the accountant sat and fumed, Free did the accountant's job for him, showing him how the various charges should be broken down. The higher-up, a woman, apologized for the mess-up, hoping the club would come back next year. But Free went through the roof when later he was asked by the accountant's assistant to explain it all again to him.

Of course John has nothing to say about whether or not a player makes the team. In fact, he makes a point of not getting too close to any one player because he says it's tough enough just standing there watching a veteran lose his talents as nearly all do sooner or later. But Free is the man a player or a player's agent or attorney must deal with when negotiating how—but not how much—that player is going to be paid. (Seven checks, fourteen, some money deferred until next year?)

In addition, though the trend in management is away from lending money to players, the Jets still do, and Free has a lot to say on whether a loan request is approved. That may sound like a simple job, but it isn't always. For example, one year one player wanted $500 to replace a furnace that had blown up in the basement of his home. Before making up his mind, Free had to ask the coaching staff whether this kid was going to make next year's team. The coaches didn't know, but they did say he was likely to be around at least until the final preseason cutdown. With that to go on, Free determined what this player's preseason income from the Jets would be next year. (The figure is based on number-of-years experience.) In this case the figure came to about $1,000, which meant that the business manager felt comfortable lending $500. (No interest required.)

Another thing Free does for players is arrange, when asked to, for off-season jobs. Such corporations as Chrysler and Lever Brothers as well as many brokerage houses on Wall Street are always looking for football players for their management-training programs. Free acts as an employment agency.

Also, during the course of a season all players will need to purchase extra tickets for certain games—once in a while for a lady friend unknown to the little woman at home. For one player no longer with the Jets, Free went so far as to write down "Shoes" each of several times this player put in his ticket request. That was so this player's wife, who saw all her husband's expense vouchers, wouldn't catch on, though surely she must have wondered why all the shoes.

The shoe act is just one of several unusual tasks John Free has performed over the years. One time some youths were caught by police breaking into the Jets' locker room at

Shea Stadium. The judge sentenced them to perform odd jobs for the club for a number of weeks, making Free in effect their parole officer.

Another time the Jets' business manager became a modern reincarnation of that Greek soldier who in 49 B.C. ran from Marathon to Athens in full armor to tell the people of the victory over the Persians, and then dropped dead. Well, not that bad, but John's tongue was dragging the time union electricians struck CBS before a game at Shea that was scheduled to be telecast over that network. The night before the game Free's orders were to stand by for the judge to sign a restraining order limiting where pickets could march the following day and then rush it to Jets' President Philip H. Iselin. The next day his job was to gather intelligence on, among other things, the pickets' activities. At one point he was ordered to round up all CBS personnel so that Iselin could inform them of his decision not to televise the game, a decision that, as it turned out, was academic since the TV cables had already been sabotaged beyond repair.

In doing his job Free has had more than one brush with disaster. Jim Hudson, a safety for the club from 1965 to 1970, slipped once in his hotel room and crashed face first into a glass door. When John arrived minutes after the accident, Hudson was still conscious but his face was a bloody pulp. Free rode with Hudson to the hospital, filling out all the necessary admissions forms and, as usual, paying the bills. (Luckily the player recovered.)

In San Diego, Free literally almost lost Namath to a frenzied crowd that managed to reach Joe. They started to grab and claw him, in the process twisting an iron chain tighter and tighter around his neck. "Joe was very lucky that day," John says in a reverent tone. "He just did make it to the bus."

And then there was the plane ride home from Miami, when one of the engines caught fire just minutes before the team was scheduled to land at LaGuardia Airport in New York. As a young man fresh out of the University of Maryland, John had dreamed about a life in aviation. That dream, however, didn't include sitting 30,000 feet above ground trying to keep things light by singing "Onward, Christian Soldiers" with everyone else on board. Although the trip did end safely, it made even those jalopy calamities Free had as a teen-ager seem dull by comparison.

Not that they were dull then. In fact, the way John talks about himself, you get the impression he spent much of his early life first getting into, then getting out of, one jam after another which, when you think about it, probably was pretty good training for his current occupation.

He was sixteen years old when he paid a grand total of $7 for his first car, a broken-down Chevy with no running board, a 2-gallon oilcan for a gas tank and a screwdriver for a clutch. He paid for it out of the 30 cents an hour he earned one summer as a clerk in a grocery store near his home in suburban Baltimore. That Chevy was in such bad shape that one day when John couldn't start it for the drive to high school, his father, who was publicity director for the Commissioner of Motor Vehicles in the state of Maryland, had it towed away as the first car seized in a campaign to rid the streets of unsafe cars.

But John got it back, and he remembers how another time he drove to a swimming hole, got out after thinking he had braked the car by putting it in reverse, and then watched the vehicle roll down a hill he knew ended in a 40-foot drop into 200 feet of water. A rodeo rider he's not, but John did manage to hogtie his Chevy just a few feet before the precipice.

John's wife, Ruth, remembers when before their marriage

John, who was using the Chevy to haul logs, started to crank it up, thinking it was in neutral, only to watch the Chevy take off in reverse, this time with Ruth in it. Not even a lasso would have made any difference this time. Fortunately, Ruth wasn't seriously hurt when the car rammed tail-first into a nearby tree. ("Oh, Lord," she says whimsically, when thinking back on it.)

John's father, Elmer D. Free, was originally a newspaper reporter for the old Baltimore *News*. He later switched to the paper's advertising department and then started his own successful advertising firm in Baltimore.

Dad wanted his son to follow him into the advertising business, but John didn't go for the idea because, as he puts it: "You're not a family man with that business. You're constantly having to entertain clients." An ironic statement when you consider the job Free has now.

In pursuit of his airplane dream, John took a job as a riveter in an aircraft assembly plant after graduation from college in 1939. He didn't know the first thing about riveting but that didn't bother him. He decided he would learn on the job just as he had done that summer in Hagerstown.

In 1939 John took a wife, a girl he'd first met three years before after one of his friends pointed Ruth out as the new kid in town whose family owned a full-size pool table. After the introductions John said, "Why don't you invite us out to your house to play pool?" Perhaps that wasn't the most tactful of suggestions, but things worked out all right anyway.

The riveter was drafted during World War II, and after his discharge in 1946 the aviation dream faded as John decided that the end of the war would mean a slowdown in the aircraft industry. Instead, he took a job near home as a wholesale building-materials salesman.

"I'll never forget that company's aptitude test," he says. "The owner, a man by the name of Dave Gouline, held up his hand and asked me how many fingers was he holding up. Well, he was holding up five, but when I gave my answer I said he was holding up four fingers and a thumb, and he agreed. Now that aptitude test may sound silly, but it taught me that you always have to stay one step ahead of the other guy.

"Before long," he adds, "that company taught me there are twenty-five hours in a working day, eight days in a week and 390 days in a year. And that when you think you've done your job, look around for something additional to do."

John did, taking a volunteer position in 1947 in an organization called Colts Associates, a booster club for the Baltimore Colts football team. John got the job through his father, who was one of seventeen well-heeled Baltimore businessmen named directors of the Colts that same year by Mayor Thomas A. D'Alesandro. At the time, the Colts were members of the All-America Football Conference, a league starring Otto Graham and the Cleveland Browns that rose up to challenge the NFL right after World War II. Though not bad on the field, the Colts rolled up enough red ink in their initial campaign in 1947 to drive out the original owner, who left Baltimore's city fathers with the problem of trying to keep a football team in business.

John's work included making speeches before all sorts of civic organizations. Often he would bring along films of Colt games and a player or two who would sign autographs. He also would bring along gobs of tickets that he would try and peddle all night long. (A far cry from today when Free has to ration Jet tickets with an eyedropper.)

For away games John and others would try to line up special trains so that hundreds of fans could make a weekend of it. "It was a good way to get away from the wife," John recalls. Indeed, he remembers one game in Cleveland when some 4,000 Colt fans made the trip, "of which I'd say 150 came to watch a football game and the rest came to do something better."

It was through this volunteer work that Free met Weeb Ewbank, who was an assistant coach at Cleveland before he was hired in 1953 by Colts' owner Carroll Rosenbloom, the man who later fired Ewbank and who today is a name not to be mentioned in Free's presence.

"I liked Weeb right away," Free says. "I remember in 1956, after he had been in Baltimore three years and we were still losing football games, how both the fans and the press started getting on his back. A lot of people wrote letters to the newspapers, and I went out and rang their doorbells and asked for the chance to explain his side of it."

Then in 1958 and again in 1959 the Colts won the championship against the New York Giants. Free, who still earned a living—and by now a very good one—at that four-finger firm, seemed to have the rest of his life laid out for him. By now he was well known in the community and was a member in good standing of one of the most swank country clubs in the area.

But all that changed that day in 1963 when Colts' owner Rosenbloom fired Ewbank after a disappointing season. In New York a group of wealthy businessmen led by entertainment magnate David A. (Sonny) Werblin had just purchased the New York Titans, renamed them the Jets, and were out looking for a new head coach and general manager. They wanted Ewbank and Ewbank wanted to bring Free, both for John's business expertise and because the Ewbanks and the Frees were quite friendly, which made the idea of pulling up roots a little easier.

"I know he gave up a gretty good job to come with me," Ewbank says, "but he never told me his reason. He just came to me and said, 'Let's go.'"

Says Free: "I think that you can't say you've been a success until you've made it in New York, the Big Apple.

I had a nice home in Baltimore and I made a good living. But I just wanted to see whether I could take this team, which as you know went bankrupt before we got there, and help turn things around."

Ewbank says there was some initial resistance to the hiring of Free. "We had a certain individual we had to get rid of," he says. "And once we did there wasn't any problem."

Still, as Ewbank himself admits, when John started out he was woefully underpaid—would you believe a 20 percent cut in pay from Baltimore? That point was accentuated when Free quickly assumed the unofficial position of the Jets' ambassador-at-large. In those early days, he even answered much of the club's fan mail, a practice that lives on in his habit of carrying hundreds of autographed Joe Namath pictures on every road trip.

(Today Free's salary is higher than that of Jet assistant coaches.)

Free remembers how in those early days no one would trust him because of the abysmal credit rating of his predecessors. On one early Jets trip the bus driver who met the team at the airport demanded cash in advance, remembering how the last time a team from New York had been in town he was left holding the bag. "I only had $400 on me," John says, "and this guy wanted $235 of it. But what else could I do?"

Free was hustling again, though this time it was tickets and not typewriters. "We had a deal back then," he says, "where if your group bought forty tickets to a game, we would supply the bus to get you there. The bus usually cost us $200 and the price of a ticket was $6, which meant we made a grand total of only $40. And sometimes we made less than that. Like I remember telling one group that we'd throw in three cases of beer to sweeten the deal. But we did get the people."

John adds: "When I first came here anyone who could

breathe spoke at the first Lions Club that would take you. I never had a desk of my own. I just always was on the move from office to stadium to Lions Club to bed and back to the office again. Come to think of it, I still don't have my own desk."

Free says the man most responsible for the Jets' rise out of Titan ashes was Werblin. For the game on the field, Sonny bought Namath for the then-astronomical sum of $400,000. "In making the Jets successful," says Howard Cosell in his book *Cosell* (Playboy Press),* "Werblin—and Werblin alone—changed the face of professional football. When he bought Joe Willie Namath for $400,000-plus, he established a market level for talent that, in the words of Art Modell, president of the Cleveland Browns, 'made it economic suicide to continue to fight.' Werblin also negotiated a big-money television contract that enabled the American Football League to survive and grow."

For the Jets' organization itself, Werblin installed a no-nonsense, to-the-penny attitude toward accounting not followed by all the new teams, with Free as the man designated to translate much of that attitude into action.

To illustrate the degree of Werblin's business preciseness, Free remembers making the following announcement over the public-address system of the airplane: "Everyone take your seat so the stewardesses can serve the meal in the least amount of time."

After that, "I sat down and the players sat down and the stewardesses started to serve when Mr. Werblin came back to me and said, 'Get up and make that announcement correctly.'"

John thought for a moment and then, with everyone already munching, stood up again and made the following announcement: "Everyone take *his* seat so the stewardesses

* Copyright © 1973 by Howard Cosell. Reprinted with permission of Playboy Press.

can serve the meal in the least amount of time."

Without question, the key to Werblin's carefully orchestrated football promotion was his quarterback from Beaver Falls, Pennsylvania, via the University of Alabama, Namath. Remember the white llama-skin rug Namath had on the floor of his Manhattan apartment? Remember how that rug symbolized to the press a superior sexual prowess? Well, that same rug was carried on the Jets' books as a club asset. Werblin bought it and Werblin had it put in Namath's apartment.

In short, Werblin built Namath brick by sexy brick. "If Joe were sitting across the table from you right now," Free says, "he'd answer your questions with 'Yes, sir' and 'No, sir.' He's really shy and quite introverted despite what you read about him."

Ironically, Werblin was no longer around when the team he built reached its pinnacle against the Colts in the 1969 Super Bowl. He and the other Jet owners had a parting of the ways the year before caused primarily by strong personal differences on how the club should be run. Other owners were Leon Hess, Chairman of the Executive Committee of Amerada Hess Corp., Townsend B. Martin, a partner in the investment banking firm of Bessemer Securities Corp., Philip H. Iselin and the late Donald C. Lillis. They bought out Werblin for $1.6 million in January, 1968.

But Free was there and working as usual. Because the Jets were decided underdogs, the usually all-confident Free decided not to make any elaborate plans for a postgame victory bash. But after the Jets won he raced to a telephone to tell the hotel manager to move his ass because the world champions were on their way. "Get it going," he ordered, "and don't let it stop."

Free's first problem that afternoon was quickly finding some police with dogs to protect the players as they made their way back to the hotel. That problem he solved. The second problem, one which he didn't solve, was trying to keep the number of guests down somewhere around 250, the number of names he had on his list of invitees. "They came out of the walls," Free remembers, adding that before the afternoon was over more than 1,000 people had partied with another 300 or so on hand at the airport to send them off and another 3,000 to 4,000 on hand in New York to hail the conquering heroes.

(A businessman to the end, Free used a portion of his $12,000 Super Bowl share to buy, of all things, a 32-foot-high, portable aluminum scaffolding. His wife really thought he was crazy. But as it turned out Free had an "in" with a certain New York football team which rents the scaffolding every year for work at training camp. The Jets are just one of several customers, and John proudly states that he's made a healthy profit on his investment.

His wife still thinks he was crazy.)

The Jets' exploits have been far more modest since 1969. And although John Free is not in danger of being tied to a desk all the time, relatively speaking he does a lot more check signing and a lot less partying these days. In a typical week, the Jets' business manager may sign some 150 checks, excluding payroll checks which are handled by a computer. One check may be for such an obvious staple as jock straps, whereas another may be for such an obvious frill as flowers for an actress recuperating in a Las Vegas hospital. One check once was for 15 cents and represented an overcharge on a pair of tickets.

Free's year breaks down into three seasons beginning with training camp in July and followed by the actual season from September through December and then the so-called off season which, in Free's case, is a misnomer. It's a misnomer because the Jets' fiscal year ends February 28 and much of both January and February are spent preparing

138

the new year's budget in connection with the accounting firm of S. D. Leidesdorf & Co. Some budget areas Free works up himself, such as travel and administration. Other areas he merely coordinates, such as talent procurement, tickets and public relations, all departments headed by other men. The final budget, which totals between $5 million and $6 million, is submitted for the approval of Jets' President Iselin.

March is probably the sleepiest month of the year, though at the end of every week of every month Free helps prepare for Iselin's perusal a financial statement showing cash on hand. Iselin comes to the Jets' offices almost every day though he seldom puts in a full eight-hour day. Free says his boss's questions are usually general ones, not ones dwelling on specific financial details. For instance, at one meeting the team physician was also present for a discussion on whether to install so-called heart stations at Shea Stadium for use by both players and spectators. The idea was approved.

By April plans are under way for the opening of training camp three months hence. Site selection presents no problem; the Jets have a long-term agreement to train at Hofstra University on Long Island. Still, there are a few odds and ends left for Free to arrange for, such as: Buying food (about $30,000 worth for seven weeks in 1973, and the figure could have been much higher if the meat had been contracted for later in the year); arranging player transportation (the Jets, as per league rules, pay everybody's way in and also out again for those players who fail to make the squad); preparing the field (it costs about $3,000 just to get Hofstra's playing fields in shape); arranging first-day physicals (all players must take them at a total cost to the club of about $1,500); setting up telephone and telegraph lines (another $1,500).

Later on, when camp actually opens, Free will have to make sure the school's laundry charges are not excessive (another $2,500). And before camp is over he will have written checks totaling about $500 to cover the costs of damage done by players to the facilities. (Little things like footballs that go through windows.)

During the lull before the July storm, Free and his wife will probably use up some of the two weeks and five long weekends' worth of vacation he gets every year. Actually he'd better have used up all that time by July because beginning with the first weekend in August, Ruth Free won't see her traveling husband from Friday morning until Sunday night or Monday morning for two solid months. (Under terms of the Jets' Shea Stadium contract, the football team can't play a game at home until after the Mets, Shea's primary tenant, have completed their baseball season—a catastrophe in 1973.)

At the Jets' Manhattan offices Free has at least eight or ten file cabinets filled with everything from players' contracts to invoices on Joe Namath publicity pictures. "We have all the correspondence that we've ever sent," he says, "and all the facts on every game we've played." Mostly John sits at the desk of the talent-procurement head because the latter is usually on the road. Whenever a phone call comes in for the business manager, the switchboard just puts it through on the phone nearest to where John is standing at that particular point in time.

When the actual season gets under way, Free starts his weekdays at Shea conferring with the head of the grounds crew and keeping records in a little black book of who's doing what, when and why. Primarily he's making sure he's not overstaffed. Often the switchboard tracks John down at Shea, but in any event he calls in before he leaves Shea for Manhattan in case, for instance, two players are hurt in

140

an automobile accident and somebody has to rush to the scene to make sure the car is towed away.

The financial details for a home game appear endless. Checks must be prepared for such things as visiting-team guarantee; stadium rent; ticket sellers, takers and ushers; food for the owners' reception; stadium telephones; electricity; field decorations; statisticians; game announcer; chair rentals, etc., etc.

In addition, John has ultimate responsibility for making sure that none of the flags of the NFL teams flying above the stadium have been shredded in the wind. (A few are every year.) He also must make sure that the cleanup crew is ready for action the moment the game is over. And he must be prepared to pay out more than $300 a game in gratuities to numerous people including ball boys, special attendants and the ever-present police.

Of course, John has certain assistants who do much of this game-day detail work for him. But let the least little thing go wrong and he's the man who has to work things out. Even in the locker room before the game John plays a role. Some clubs, including the Jets, take great pains in making sure everyone is lined up correctly for the national anthem and also for the pregame introductions. Free tells the gathering who's going to be introduced that day and in what order and also reminds them of where the flag is in the stadium if it's an away game and how they're to stand at attention holding helmets in a certain hand.

(Says one player, "All John's repetition can really get to be a pain in the neck.")

On the road John's chief assistant is an Eastern Airlines charter representative assigned to the Jets on a seasonal basis. In 1973 his name was Howard Goldberg. Howard never did see the fourth quarter of a Jets' away game that year. That's because by then he had always returned to the

141

airport to make sure that such details were attended to as name tags on the seats in first class and three beers in a plastic bag for every player. (Beer's the best way to fight dehydration, Free says.)

Howard didn't have it nearly as good as Free's other top assistant, Bill Lattimer. When it rained, as it did and then some during the Jets' last preseason game that year, Howard got soaked. But not Bill. As the unofficial man's man for the Jet owners, Bill's job is to guide Iselin *et al.* to their seats, to their pregame and postgame receptions and to the players' locker room.

Lattimer, who is in his sixties and has been the doorman at the Parke-Bernet Galleries in Manhattan for many years, seems to know most every celebrity, according to Free. For example, when the Jets went to New Orleans it was Lattimer, not one of the owners or one of the players, who knew Al Hirt, the trumpeter, and who consequently got Al to give the New York guests the deluxe treatment. (Lattimer's connections have earned him the unofficial title of "Mayor of Madison Avenue.")

As much as Free's repetition gets to some players, so also does it get to Free himself. Perhaps what bugs John the most are people for whom he does favors who fail to show their appreciation with a note, a kind word, or maybe even a good stock tip like National Cash Register at $26 a share. (NCR subsequently went up into the $40-a-share range.)

Namath bugs Free. Day in and day out Free gets letters from people who have been referred to the Jets' business manager by associates of Namath. Often the request is for tickets, though many people are trying to arrange to meet Joe in person after a game. One letter in 1973 asked whether a high-school band from Joe's home area could perform at half time at a game at Shea Stadium.

John says he has been answering these requests promptly since Joe arrived in Manhattan in 1964. But in 1973 Free bristled when he asked his first favor of Joe (a writer had asked Free to set up an interview with Namath) and Joe didn't do it.

"Right now I've got a whole bunch of requests on my desk from people who know Joe," Free said a few weeks after the incident. "But you can bet I'm going to take my own sweet time getting around to them. If he can't do that one thing for me, well, it really makes you wonder if Joe gives a damn what other people do for him."

What John Free does for the Jets, however, is clear. There's always another check to be signed, another ticket to be dug up, another flag to be replaced, another hotel to be booked, another meal to be ordered, another cop to be paid off. . . . They're all John Free's responsibility.

5

Jack's Boys

Jack Horrigan
Late Vice President–Public Relations
The Buffalo Bills

IN THE FALL OF 1973, O. J. Simpson was a happy man. For five years a running back for the Buffalo Bills, Orenthal James Simpson was enjoying his finest season, rushing for more than 100 yards nearly every game and zeroing in on Jim Brown's all-time season rushing record of 1,863 yards set back in 1963. (He made it.)

As he drove home from practice one day late in the season, he talked about how being in Buffalo several months of the year was a good thing for his personal life. "All my friends in California seem to be getting divorced," he said. "I can think of ten couples in just this past year. I like to come back to Buffalo each year to get my head together again. In Los Angeles there are just too many pressures."

In the fall of 1973, O. J. Simpson bore little resemblance to the all-American running back from the University of Southern California who was the Bills' number-one draft choice in 1969. True, by the time he played his first pro game that year, O. J. was already one rich dude. All number-one draft choices are.

But money can't buy happiness, at least not in Buffalo,

144

New York. O. J. Simpson's personal problems included a coach he couldn't stand, a front office he didn't like, and a city whose fans and sportswriters he felt were intent on bad-mouthing him every chance they got. Though he rushed for a most respectable 697 yards his rookie year, Simpson couldn't wait to get out of town and get his head together again back on the West Coast.

The second year was worse; the third year worse than the second. By 1971 Simpson was ready to quit. The hell with it, he thought. The town, the team—everything was a bad trip.

Except for Jack Horrigan, the Bills' Vice President for Public Relations. More than anyone else, Horrigan is the man Simpson says helped him stick out a most difficult period. Simpson says Horrigan was his shrink, his friend and the guy who kicked his ass when he was moping around feeling sorry for himself.

All the time that Horrigan was helping Simpson he was dying of leukemia. That statement isn't meant to turn Jack Horrigan into some kind of martyr. On the contrary, it's a simple statement of fact. Another is that Horrigan died of leukemia in June, 1973, at the age of forty-seven.

To be sure, most PR men in the front office of professional football are merely guys who assign seats in the press box and who make sure a player makes the speech he's agreed to make at some tiny-tyke football banquet out in the sticks. Public relations is pro football's garbage job, and Jack Horrigan was Buffalo's garbage man.

But this garbage man usually didn't collect until after 5 P.M., after he had finished talking to guys like Simpson. He could infuriate a sportswriter by never returning his call. He could frustrate his wife, Liz, who can't remember all the times he was late for dinner. But Buffalo at that time was an organization whose owner, Ralph Wilson, lived in Detroit (he still does), and whose general manager, Robert

Lustig, was strictly a businessman not involved with the players (he still is). That left John Rauch, the head coach, and Simpson was just one of many players who had absolutely no use for John Rauch.

Horrigan filled a void. He was, says Buffalo *Evening News* sportswriter Larry Felser, the man who kept the Buffalo Bills football club from falling apart.

Today the Bills' center of gravity is Head Coach Lou Saban, who came back to Buffalo in 1972 after a six-year hiatus. Simpson says he owes Saban a lot, too, for when Saban took over the club, he rebuilt the offense around the running of O.J. (Under Rauch, Simpson had done almost everything but run, it being Rauch's philosophy not to build an offense around one back, no matter how talented.)

But as the Bills' bread-and-butter man sat in the smallish living room of his suburban Buffalo apartment that day after practice (O.J.'s California address is Bel Air, Carroll Rosenbloom's neighborhood), he remembered Jack Horrigan with an emotion he said he could only describe as love.

"When I was a senior at USC, I was watching the Steelers and the Eagles, hoping one of those teams would finish last and draft me. Ultimately, I felt I would wind up going to the Rams in a trade. George Allen [who was then the Rams' head coach] sort of led me to believe that he would do just about anything to get me.

"That year there was bad blood between the NFC and the AFC, so that when the Bills took me I knew I would be stuck playing in Buffalo. I had the usual big hassle with the owner over my contract. Fortunately, I had a contract with Chevrolet and I also did a guest shot on a TV show. I ended up signing for not nearly as much as I wanted, but a pretty good contract nevertheless. But by that time it was late in the year and my wife was expecting, so I came to Buffalo alone.

146

"Though I had never seen Buffalo, never really said anything about the place, the local press had already started on me by the time I arrived. Every TV show I had gone on—Johnny Carson, Joey Bishop, whatever—there had been a crack made about Buffalo that the Buffalo press attributed to me.

"I first met Jack Horrigan at the airport the night I arrived. There were an awful lot of people there, and I guess I was perturbed at not getting any privacy. I just wanted to play. I had heard about the hassle with another guy who was already wearing my number [32] and who said he didn't want me to wear it. Everything was a big headache. I got into a car and sat with this guy named Horrigan who started to tell me about a press conference the next day. That bugged me. I mean, like I knew what to say. The guy bugged me and when I found out he was in charge of public relations I just didn't care for him.

"Anyway, I finally got to camp, and it didn't take long for me to see that Coach Rauch was not going to be one of my favorite people. Rauch had been the coach at Oakland and though he had had a great record, he never got any of the credit. Al Davis [the owner] got all the credit, and, consequently, in my opinion, when Coach Rauch came to Buffalo, he decided he was going to make sure he got all the credit.

"I thought he hired a few incompetent coaches. Well, maybe they were competent, but he didn't let them do anything. Everything had to be done Coach Rauch's way. I have never been one for curfews, but in college I never minded them either. But here Coach Rauch would make us stay in Canada the night before a game. And so during blizzards we had to make this long drive. Then he would sit in the lobby of the hotel to make sure we were all in.

"I couldn't believe all the meetings we had. Three, four,

147

five hours a day. And instead of discussing what we were going to do or watching films, Coach Rauch would read from a book. You know, he would open a book and read to us like a third-grade class. None of the assistant coaches knew what was going on. I can recall an incident when the defensive guys had finished their meeting and ours was still going on. An assistant coach came to our room to ask whether we were going to wear pads during our workout that day. Without answering him, Coach Rauch slammed the door in his face.

"Coach Rauch was the type of man who if a guy was messing up, he would make no bones about saying it to the press or anyone else. When we lost, and we lost a lot that year, he would get on you.

"That first year I thought it was a personality thing, but my second year, when I started to realize what was really going on, I was amazed at how with all the money that's put into professional football my particular team could be run so poorly. It wasn't just the coach. We didn't have any practice field. We didn't know where we were going to practice from day to day. You know, like we would show up at the stadium and catch a bus to a different place to practice. It was really unbelievable.

"My second year was when I really had problems. I could see that things weren't going to get better. Nobody cared. Coach Rauch was trading a lot of good players. At practice we had a linebacker coach who thought it was a big deal that his linebackers really hit the backs on running plays. I mean, you're not supposed to get hurt in practice, are you? One linebacker was black, and it seemed the only way this coach could communicate with him was by yelling and screaming at him. Coach Rauch would get a kick out of it.

"It was about this time that I really got to know Jack. I

148

was always in his office for PR stuff, and sometimes we would just sit and talk. He'd tell me that things would work out, that people other than myself felt the same way about the situation. He told me that if it hadn't been for Ralph Wilson, I would have been traded by now. He told me that the owner was keeping a close eye on me and that changes would be made.

"Here was a man trying to say something to me. He wasn't trying to feed me a whole bunch of lies. He wasn't somebody trying to make money for his team, which is so often the case in pro football. To me, Jack wasn't a PR guy. He would show you another point of view, sometimes John Rauch's point of view even when he disagreed with John personally. You could say anything you wanted to Jack without being afraid it would come back to haunt you.

"When I came to Buffalo I was dollars and cents to some people, and number of yards gained to others. But Jack always wanted to know what I was thinking about. One time he asked me, 'When was the last time you really got out and worked with a kid?' You see, I had done a lot of work with youth groups, but I really hadn't done much for a long time. Jack caught me off guard and made me think about my commitment to those kids.

"Like, some of the other people in the Bills' front office I still don't know anything about. I don't know if they've got kids, nothing. I knew Jack's whole family [which is knowing a lot considering that Jack had nine children]. When I came to Buffalo, he was the only guy in this whole organization who really wanted to know me as a person, not just some number-one draft choice out of the University of Southern California.

"Anyway, my third year John Rauch was fired, or resigned depending upon whose account you believe, the day I arrived at camp. He made some bad comments on a local TV show and that was that. They made Harvey Johnson the coach [he had been director of player personnel], and it was sheer chaos. There was a constant power play going on among the coaches.

"I guess that year [1971] I reached the lowest point in my career. We lost games doing the most ridiculous things you ever saw. Guys running off the field the wrong way. Too many men on the field. One day after practice, myself and another player went berserk in the locker room. We started saying we wouldn't play for this sorry organization any more. We screamed and yelled and threw stuff around and left the place in a shambles.

"It was Jack who after the outburst called me as soon as I got home. I was looking for Ralph Wilson's number and I was going to call him to say that I wanted nothing more to do with him and his organization. Jack told me that the situation would be changed, that I should just be cool. He told me there'd be new people here next season and, sure enough, Coach Saban arrived that following year.

"Jack had a way about him. He would get on you, and then you'd get on him. Like he was supposed to be an expert on boxing and I would always come in with a question to try and stump him. He'd call me the 'flop from USC.' When I heard Saban was coming back, he said to me, 'Old alibi Ike,' meaning me, 'ain't going to have any more alibis.' I'd always come in doing the Ali shuffle and then I would grab him while someone else tried to land a few shots. We were always kidding around like that. There was a horrible situation here, and Jack and I both knew it.

"While it never became a big news story, it's a fact that if Jack hadn't talked me out of it, I was going to play out my option and demand to be traded. I felt that if I have to go through all this bullshit, I'm going to put them through some bullshit too.

"Jack was shrewd, man. Publicity is getting to the right people, and Jack knew everyone there was to know in football [through his job first as a sportswriter for the Buffalo *Evening News* and later as the PR man for the old American Football League]. Like in 1966 when Bobby Burnett won rookie-of-the-year honors. There was no way Bobby was supposed to win that. Mike Garrett [of Kansas City] was supposed to win it. Publicity is getting to the right people.

"I can recall Jack telling this sportswriter from Boston that I was going to be MVP [in 1972]. I just laughed, but he asked me if I would bet a dinner on it. I said I'd bet a hundred dinners. Good thing he didn't try to collect in full. As I said, he knew the right people and they all liked him. He could sway people to do things the way he wanted them done.

"People don't treat you like human beings in pro football. They treat you like a size and measurement, and you can't help but treat other people the same way. That's why so many guys talk about dehumanization and football players being robots. I think Don Klosterman and Carroll Rosenbloom of the Rams always have winning teams because, no matter what, they get along with their players. Klosterman's a human being. He ain't just some guy wearing a business suit all the time. The first time I met him, he started getting on me about my shoes. You know, jiving me, saying my shoes were cheap. Here's a cat you can play with, someone you'd love to play for.

"Jack was the same way.

"The last time I saw Jack was at the Super Bowl in 1973. I had breakfast with him and Cookie Gilchrist [a former Buffalo player] in Jack's room. Cookie needed some tickets and Jack had gotten him twelve. I said to Jack I thought I was supposed to get some tickets. Of course I'd never said that at all. Anyway I just started to jive him about not getting me any tickets.

"They brought in his breakfast, and as he started to eat he tipped the table and his cereal went all over the floor. He was having trouble controlling himself. I ordered him some more and the same thing happened again. He was leaning too hard on the table, I think. As Cookie and I left I asked him if there was anything I could do. He said he was just going to stay in the room and rest a bit. He said he was going to try and get some more breakfast."

It was in 1965 that Jack Horrigan first discovered he had cancer of the kidney. He underwent surgery for its removal at the Mayo Clinic, and doctors told him that if after five years he still had a clean bill of health, then the operation had probably licked what ailed him.

For four years the bill was clean, but in the fifth year Jack developed leukemia. "Nobody beats that disease," he told his friends, though for the last few years of his life it was business as usual for the Buffalo Bills' vice president of public relations.

The Bills played miserably during those years. One time when Jack, who as the club's advance man usually went to an away game several days ahead of time, spoke in Oakland, he left them in the aisles with his Daryle Lamonica story. Lamonica of course is Oakland's famed quarterback. He would have been Buffalo's famed quarterback except that the Bills made one of the bonehead trades of all time. (Two of the three players Buffalo got for Lamonica lasted one season apiece, while the third, quarterback Tom Flores, lasted only three and today holds just one club passing record: most passes intercepted in a single game—five.)

They were laying for Jack when he got up to speak at a press luncheon shortly after the Lamonica trade. But before they could touch him he grabbed the microphone and broke into song: "All I want for Chanukah is Daryle Lamonica." And him a devout Catholic, too.

Another time at a similar gathering in Kansas City, he apologized right off for not showing up with a highlight film of his team. "Our photographer," he said, "took it out of his Polaroid before it developed."

Often Horrigan's barbs were directed at the players he knew well. When Jack Kemp, quarterback for the Buffalo Bills before running successfully for Congress in 1970, outlined for Jack a piece of legislation he planned to introduce, Jack told him, "If you can't make it any clearer than that, it won't be tabled, it will be intercepted."

George Ratterman had been the quarterback of the original Buffalo Bills when they were a member of the ill-fated All-America Football Conference in the late 1940s, and on more than one occasion Horrigan told the story of what happened to George when he went to Cleveland to play for Paul Brown. In Buffalo, Ratterman had been able to decide for himself when he would be substituted for—a privilege not extended by Mr. Brown. One time, the Cleveland fans started chanting, "We want George. We want George." So, Brown looked at Ratterman, who was sitting on the bench, and yelled, "Get your helmet and"—Jack would pause for emphasis—"go sit in the stands with your friends."

Sometimes the joke was on Jack. Like the time O.J., in speaking by phone to a luncheon gathering in Los Angeles, was asked by someone in the audience how he liked Buffalo. O.J., who was a rookie at the time, said he liked Buffalo fine, but that in Buffalo they don't call him O.J. Rather, he said, they call him J.O., for "jack off."

"The moment he said that," recalls Jim Peters, sportswriter for the Buffalo *Courier-Express*, "Jack had him by the neck; O.J. said, 'Well, you don't think there are any women there, do you?' And Jack replied, 'No, but still . . .' "

To be sure, Jack Horrigan was very straitlaced. Larry Felser, who has been a sportswriter in Buffalo for more than twenty years, says that back in the good old days when PR men from other teams came to town, "We acted like a bunch of clowns. We'd go out on the town and when we stopped talking about football, we started talking about broads. Booze and broads, that's what most PR guys were good for then.

"But Jack," he adds, "never drank and he never talked about women. You could say he wasn't much fun in a nightclub, but he knew a lot about football and when he was with the league office he worked his tail off trying to get coverage from newspapers, a lot of whom didn't believe in his league.

"Before the AFL came along," Larry says, "a lot of sportswriters couldn't write to save their ass. They were good drinkers, but not much else. It was only when the new league started to hustle that there developed some real professionalism on the part of both the PR guys and the writers. PR men like Jack tried to lead you to a good story. I can remember him at one press gathering shouting out, 'I've got a great story on so-and-so here, who wants it?' "

"We appreciated that," adds Jim Peters, "but at the same time it can turn out bad too. In a number of cities the clubs have tried to make the sportswriters an arm of the public relations department. Nearly every coach thinks his PR guy controls the writers a lot more than he does. There are still a few cities like Oakland and Cincinnati and Kansas City where the sportswriters are just rah-rah guys. In fact, in Cincinnati the publisher of the newspaper is on the board of directors of the club."

Jack used to say that football "is a little boys' game

154

being played by men and you [the sportswriters] are trying to make it more serious than it really is."

At the same time, Jack himself treated seriously some things about pro football that others surely would have let pass. For example, there was one girl on the cheerleading squad who, when she got married, was voted out by the other cheerleaders. Jack thought that was horrible and got the girl reinstated.

Coach Saban (during his first tenure) recalls how Jack would, when still a sportswriter, take him aside and just sort of suggest that he have a five-minute private conversation with this or that player. "He opened my eyes on a lot of things," says Saban. "Like one time there was a player who had marital problems and as a consequence his play was falling off badly. From week to week I watched him slip, but I couldn't get from him what the trouble was. You know how players are when their jobs are threatened. The last person they'll turn to is the coach.

"Jack told me to sit down with this player away from the locker room and stuff like that. He told me he thought it would do a lot of good, and it did. Of course I didn't become a marriage counselor or anything like that. But I did tell this boy to sit down and talk with his wife face to face. And it worked.

"You know," Saban adds, "players don't have a lot of people they feel they can go to. They need someone to talk to, and so do coaches. Jack Horrigan was the type of guy you could do that with. There are a lot of Jack Horrigans around, but the press likes to blow up all little problems that could be solved with just a five- or ten-minute conversation."

Adds Congressman Kemp: "If it hadn't been for Jack, I might never have come to Buffalo in the first place. In 1962 I was put on injured waivers by the San Diego Chargers. The Bills said they wanted me, but I said I wanted more money." (He'd been making $11,000 at San Diego.) "Ralph Wilson said he wouldn't renegotiate my contract during the middle of the season, so I just decided to sit home and sulk for a while. Then Jack [who was with the *Evening News* at the time] called me and said, 'You come and play and after the season you'll find Wilson and Saban will play fairly.' I went, and after that season the Bills doubled my contract.

"Let me tell you something Jack Horrigan told me: 'Listen, Jack Kemp, an individual can accomplish anything under the sun as long as he doesn't care who gets the credit.' "

"It sounds like Dad was some sort of godfather, doesn't it?" says Jerry Horrigan, the eldest of the Horrigan nine. "He even tried to help a neurotic secretary he once had. She may be the only person Dad just gave up on. She really drove him up the wall.

"I can think of only one time somebody really burned Dad. It was when this new football magazine was just getting started and Dad was an assistant to the publisher and the managing editor. He worked on it and worked on it, but in the end, just as it was really starting to go, he was forced out because of legal entanglements. That really hurt.

"Come to think of it, there's also a lot of resentment there on my part about the Rauch thing. Here Dad was being a father figure to all these players. You know what I mean? Here's my father being a father figure to forty other grown men. I kind of resented Dad for spending all that time being a father to others, and I resented Rauch for not appreciating what Dad was doing for the team."

In a way, Jerry burned his father, too, not that Dad ever thought of it in those terms. It was in 1971. Jerry was twenty-one years old and a member of a Catholic Radical Left organization akin to the Harrisburg Seven (Father

156

Berrigan *et al.*). They later were dubbed the Buffalo Five, and one night that August, "we decided to do something concrete against the war, the draft system and a lot of other things," says Jerry.

In short, they broke into the draft-board building in downtown Buffalo. "The point of the action," he says, "was to destroy the draft cards and hopefully carry away Army intelligence records, which at that time were under investigation. I didn't let on to Mom and Dad what I was doing because I didn't want them involved in a conspiracy rap. We were going to confiscate the files and return them to the people who were under investigation in Buffalo. Or we were going to publish them in the underground press to let people in Buffalo know.

"It was important that we get away," but they didn't. Indeed, when the police arrived, they found the Buffalo Five dressed in their underwear because they had thought that would reduce their chances of making too much noise. (The police were tipped off in advance of the raid.)

Jack found out about it on a Sunday afternoon, though no one told him until after the Bills' game for fear it might upset him too much. Dad took quite the opposite reaction, from the moment he learned about it to the moment the jury convicted the Buffalo Five and the judge, surprisingly, handed down a suspended sentence.

Wrote Larry Felser: "The NFL is a conservative operation and identification with anti-war groups is not part of its image. But throughout the long trial in Federal court, Jack Horrigan was at Jerry's side. A reporter asked him for his reasons.

"Jack seemed amazed at the question. 'Because he's my son and I love him,' he answered. 'And I believe in him.'"

Liz Horrigan, Jack's widow, says her father warned her about marrying anyone who was a sportswriter or connected with sports in any way. He probably drinks too much, Liz was told, which is ironic because the only addiction Jack Horrigan ever had was for Diet Pepsi, which he consumed at the rate of eight to ten cans per day.

"When we got married," Liz says, "Jack was twenty-one and I was twenty. Jack passed up an opportunity to go to Notre Dame in order to get married. In high school he never studied or anything like that. He was smart enough to laugh his way through. He used to say that basically he was a lazy individual, and in a way, that's true. He never picked up a hammer, never cut the grass. He always had his children doing that."

(Says Congressman Kemp: "Jack never worked at his job. It was just part of him.")

"Jack's family," says Liz, "lived in South Buffalo [otherwise known as the wrong side of the tracks]. Jack's father had money in the early years, but he lost it all in the Depression. He met me when I was sixteen. Jack never had another girl. I was lucky he had no one to compare me with. It started because my brother was in the service with Jack and had my picture in his wallet. We started to write and then we met in Philadelphia on a weekend pass.

"We planned a large family and," says Liz without realizing her double entendre, "he never had any difficulties with that at all. He just announced that we were going to have our own home within five years [they started out living with her parents] and, sure enough, we did. When Jack's mind was made up to do something, he just did it. Boom.

"Jack always seemed to be working at two jobs at the same time. After the service, he worked for United Press International and also did PR for the local hockey club at night. Sometimes I'd hear him come in at 3 A.M. and then hear him get up and go to work a couple hours later."

In 1948 Jack covered Harry S. Truman's Presidential campaign, whistle-stopping all across the country. He later covered the New York gubernatorial campaign of Averill Harriman. "My experience in politics convinced me of one thing," Jack often would say. "It convinced me that I want to spend the rest of my life in the sports world."

The sports world did present certain problems for the straitlaced Catholic kid who'd married the hometown girl. As Felser recalls: "One time Jack went to the hotel room of a well-known light heavyweight to do a prefight interview. He found the fighter completely irrational. Horrigan then went to the promoter and the fighter's manager. He said he would go to the state boxing commission unless the fight was called off. At first he was threatened and then offered a bribe. He never wavered. The fight was called off."

Liz remembers the stories Jack brought home after being on the road with other sportswriters. "One time Jack and this other writer from Buffalo went down to New York. They stayed in the same room because money then wasn't what it's like now. This other guy set up a couple of girls. You know, girls to bring up to the room for the night. This really caused a knock-down-and-drag-out fight.

"Another time, Jack went to bed only to wake up later and find a roommate in the bathroom with a girl. You know what I mean. I can still remember Jack coming home and telling me this is what those guys do away from home. To us, that kind of sex was shocking, really shocking."

(Jack's idea of an off-color joke was to say there must be something wrong with him sexually because he always had sex on his mind—"and if you don't believe me just look at all those children I've got at home.")

When Al Davis offered Jack the AFL PR job in 1963, one of Jack's editors tried to talk him out of going because, as Liz puts it, "those New York writers supposedly were going to eat him alive.

"But Jack never had any trouble at all. He just walked

159

in there and worked day and night, and the writers respected him for it. Those were the days when the Jets were still the Titans and Harry Wismer's checks were taking crazier bounces than a football. Jack really was the Titans' PR man and he had his hands full. It was a thankless job, that's for sure."

Felser characterizes Horrigan as having been Davis's "no man." "The two battled often," Felser says, "but there was deep respect. The day Horrigan underwent surgery for the first time in the Mayo, Davis, a Jew, bought a votive candle and kept it lit in his office. Late that night, when Davis was preparing to leave, a charlady told him she would have to douse the candle since it was against building regulations to leave a flame unattended. Davis took off his coat and stayed the night."

Upon his return to Buffalo in 1966 as the Bills' PR man, one of Jack's chief duties was fending off attacks against his owner, Ralph Wilson, whose position vis-à-vis a new stadium had much of the populace in an uproar. "Wilson was holding a knife to cut throats," says Felser. "He threatened to move the team to another city unless we built him a new stadium."

Horrigan spent hour after hour on the phone and at luncheons and dinners defending his boss. To be sure, the old War Memorial Stadium where the Bills were then playing was a dimly lit structure in a very bad part of town. But more than that, in order to get Jack to come back to Buffalo, one thing Wilson had done was insure Jack (Wilson owns an insurance firm) when no other insurance company would touch him because of his illness, and also guarantee that the money would be there for his children's college education. Horrigan's loyalty to his boss was deep.

Quite obviously, after someone has died, the people who remember him speak only of what was good about that person. But in Jack Horrigan's case, the good things people

160

now say about him are so numerous that it appears that the story would have been much the same had he not died.

Robert Lustig, the Bills' Vice President-General Manager, says Jack liked to take a number of players to a particular school for deaf children. "The players would line up and run through plays, so even though the children were deaf, and some were even blind, they could 'see' how to grip a football and things like that. Maybe because of his illness, Jack got the biggest kick of all out of going to that school."

(A PR man's job can indeed get quite personal. One PR man on a midwestern club says a woman once phoned him asking for an autographed picture of a certain player. That player, it seems, had been her son's favorite star before he died suddenly. Now the mother wanted to put the picture in the boy's coffin.)

Horrigan never saw the Bills' new multimillion-dollar stadium in suburban Orchard Park. He went to groundbreaking ceremonies, but he never returned, even though he had ample opportunity to follow the stadium's construction. This may sound a bit corny, but Jack's fellow workers feel the reason he didn't go back was that he was afraid he wouldn't be around for the opening of what he had plugged for for many years.

Liz may explain best why Jack chose to be so involved with people, why he worked so hard every minute of the day. (So hard, in fact, that Don Phinney, who was Jack's assistant in the office and who also often drove him to and from work because Jack never bothered to get a driver's license, would himself often be a bit late for dinner.)

"He lived with serious illness so many years, I think he was happy just to be able to greet each new day. He had an appreciation for the sky, people, life in general, that I don't think you have until you're faced with the prospect of dying.

"He was really happy those last years with the Bills. And

because he was happy, I was happy. But there are some bittersweet memories. Jack gave time all over the place. O.J. took hours and hours out of our lives. The only time Jack was really happy was when he was working, involved in stories or going through his picture file.

"Everyone talks about here was this brave man dying and all that. But we never treated it as if Jack was dying. It was a deliberate thing. We just never treated it that way. I know that sounds strange. But when they told me he had six years, or maybe four, or even possibly just two, everything was like you read in poetry. You know, about the man who's been told he has just twenty-four hours to live and who looks around and sees the beauty of everything.

"His whole attitude was that it isn't the amount of time I spend with my family, it's the kind of time I give them. He never went hunting or fishing or any of those tricky little things. We could cram a week together into a night.

"I doubt I'd do it all over again. Times change and women do different things now. But this was the way we were. My dad thought Jack had everything fall into his lap. That was the kind of person he was. He never complained, even around the house those last few years."

Recalls Felser: "One time on a long plane trip home from a West Coast game, Jack had a splitting headache. I offered to get him some aspirin. He declined them. 'Some day I'm going to need pain killers badly,' he explained. 'I don't want to build up an immunity to them now.'"

6
The Ladies-in-Waiting
Josephine and Jane Morabito
Owners
The San Francisco 49ers

Remembered joys are never past.
> —James Montgomery
> *The Cloud*

A PROFESSIONAL FOOTBALL GAME. Half time. An attractive, rosy-cheeked young lady in a bright-red coat is standing at midfield. At her side, making her heart pound faster and faster, stands a dark, good-looking and especially broad-shouldered young male who has kindly agreed to be the object of an upcoming raffle management has dreamed up to entice starry-eyed damsels to its demonstration of brawn.

The lady's task, quite simply, is to draw the lucky winner's name out of a drum. But wait. The male turns. He throws his head back proudly. Breathlessly—as if a statue —he gazes at her insatiably, especially at her bright-red coat. He knows he can no longer control himself. He must do what he must do—in short, he must *snort*.

This certainly isn't your classic Manhattan singles'-bar pickup approach. But then what can you expect from an ill-mannered bull whose immediate future on this wet and wintry night in Buffalo, New York, smells ominously of

163

A-1 steak sauce? (Enough to make any housewife's eyes sparkle.)

The lady in red cowers, remembering how as a little girl on a farm an angry heifer once gave her a similar look just before flipping her high into the air. The lady is Josephine Morabito. It is 1946. She is visiting Buffalo with her husband, A. J. (Tony) Morabito, and Mr. Morabito's corporation, also known as the San Francisco 49ers. It is one of a number of games she and her husband attended before his death from a heart attack in 1957.

Many years—too many to Josephine's way of thinking —have passed since that night the bull made a pass at her. Few today in the front office of pro football remember much about either Tony or his younger brother Vic, who succeeded Tony as president of the 49ers until his own death from a heart attack in 1964. Fewer still know how Josephine and Vic's widow, Jane, today run the club their husbands left them.

To be sure, the Morabito women run a football team in a way unique among National Football League owners. For example, while other owners customarily meet several times a year, the Morabito women attend only one such gathering, the annual business-with-pleasure session held in Hawaii or similar locale in January after the Super Bowl. (Other club executives attend other meetings.) Jane, who tends to enjoy the sport's jet-set atmosphere a bit more than Josephine, says she goes in January in part because of the cocktail parties thrown by airline and television people— those for whom professional football means money in the bank. Chances are, she adds, that when the others get down to work, she and her sister-in-law will head for the golf course with wives of other front-office executives.

Back home, you'll never find either lady behind a desk. Neither woman has one at 49er executive offices in downtown San Francisco. Instead, Josephine may opt for a visit with her grandchildren or work as a regent of a local college, while Jane often plays a round of golf or drinks coffee with the girls. Seldom do the ladies actually make business decisions, except, say, when it's a grave matter such as raising ticket prices or moving into a new stadium. And when it's time to meet the press—as it always is after your team loses or when your team's star player refuses to sign his contract—the Morabito women are as successful at staying away from TV cameras as Howard Hughes.

Though Gloria Steinem won't like hearing this, one major reason why the ladies tend not to involve themselves very much in league affairs is that they feel they are women in a world that's marked as clearly as a men's room. Indeed, at present only one other woman is a top pro football executive. And Helen L. Springborn, Vice President and Secretary of the New York Jets, holds those titles only because she is the daughter of the late Donald C. Lillis, former Jets' President. (Mrs. Springborn's activities consist mostly of attending Jet games.)

A few years back, Charlotte Bidwill, widow of St. Louis Cardinals' owner Charles W. Bidwill, did try to carry on her husband's football activities for a time. But several who were there report she tended to say very little at league meetings, her one real contribution being "to keep our language cleaner than usual," according to one club president. (Mrs. Bidwill's son, William V. Bidwill, is now the Cards' top man.)

To make matters even worse for Ms. Steinem, the Morabitos genuinely believe that a man can run a football organization better than a woman. "Men know more about the game," says Josephine. "Personally I don't think my voice would be loud enough to be heard in a room with men from twenty-five other teams."

Not that the Morabito ladies are really as soft as they may sound. On the contrary, both women have been toughened by many years of having to make all their own decisions. In public, however, both widows remain true to the image their husbands wanted them to have, namely, that a woman's place is in the home and not in a picture in some newspaper. As Josephine is quick to point out, Tony always said he didn't give a hoot whether his name was in the newspaper as long as his players' names were. Although the ladies today keep abreast of their club's financial achievements, they have decided to let a man run things for them, just as their husbands would have wanted.

The man who runs the 49ers is Louis G. Spadia, President and General Manager of the club. Spadia is family to the women, and not just because he, like their departed husbands, is of Italian ancestry, though that is an important point. Spadia, who is in his fifties, was with Tony almost from the beginning. He was Tony's office boy after coming out of the Navy at the end of World War II, and, at one time or another, the brothers asked him to carry out every front-office task imaginable—from running the mimeograph machine to selling tickets to signing players to signing checks.

Spadia has no written contract with his bosses. Never has. After his first heart attack in 1952 and before his second and fatal one in 1957, Tony sold pieces of his club to friends and one loyal employee—Spadia. But even if he did not now own 10 percent of the 49ers—together the women own 55 percent: Josephine the largest single stockholder with 30 percent, Jane second with 25 percent—Spadia gives every indication that there's no job he'd rather have. He has an unwritten contract, he says, terms of which are emotional, calling for him to repay the generosity shown over many years by both Tony and Vic.

166

Dick Nolan, the former New York Giants' defensive back and, since 1968, Head Coach of the 49ers, says he never really thinks about the fact that he's the only head coach in the NFL working for two women. "They're not involved with the game on the field," he says, though he adds that each is likely to spend an afternoon or two a week watching the team work out from the balcony of Spadia's office overlooking the 49ers' training fields at Redwood City, California.

This is not to say that the head coach doesn't know his employers. Indeed, during Nolan's first couple of seasons as head coach at San Francisco, his team fared rather poorly in the NFL's Western Division race. After one particularly demoralizing game, he got back on the plane with his head held low only to have Josephine come over and, in Nolan's words, "give me a strong vote of confidence."

Nolan adds: "Those ladies are tough as nails. They really know how to hang in there. They know a heck of a lot about football and after all these years, if anybody deserves to win a Super Bowl, it's them."

Precisely what Josephine thinks. And to a great extent it's that thought that keeps Tony Morabito's widow from ever seriously considering the sale of her team, which at current market prices would probably bring somewhere in the neighborhood of $18 million. Of course, she couldn't sell it without the approval of at least two of the other eight owners, but all know that Josephine is Tony's widow, and that if it hadn't been for Tony none of them would be where he is today in pro football.

A reserved woman who measures both her words and her emotions carefully, Josephine comes very close to dramatic expression when discussing the day she might receive the gold ring traditionally awarded to all members of the winning Super Bowl team. "Isn't that what we're all in it

167

for? Money has never been that important to me," she says firmly, though she laughs at the thought of how during the early years of her marriage in the 1930s she and Tony used to wait for Vic and Jane to come over for a friendly game of poker. Jane, you see, was the only one with a job bringing in good money and she was so bad at playing poker she was always good for a couple of bucks, as even Jane admits.

The laughter is momentary. Josephine shakes her head and wonders where all the years have gone, all the games and all the trips, at first by train and now by plane. "A championship," she muses, "well, it's something I've wanted all these years. It's something Tony always wanted, but never quite got. I feel I keep this team in trust for Tony. He always wanted a championship and so do I."

Jane, on the other hand, seems to be into pro football much more for the kicks and the excitement. A Super Bowl ring is also important to her, but she very much likes to have fun and she'll think nothing of playing co-pilot in the cockpit of the 49ers' chartered jet coming home after an away game. "I'm the worst screamer, panter and yeller you've ever seen." She smiles.

For Jane, unlike Josephine, one very important thing is to have a fall wardrobe bought in time for the first game of the season. ("I've already got five outfits bought," she beamed in the summer of 1973, a good month before the 49ers' first exhibition game.) Jane's private box at Candlestick Park seats eight, and one thing she really worries about is not slighting any of her friends by somehow failing to invite them to at least one game a year.

As you might expect, Jane is more outspoken than Josephine, especially on matters like player salaries and player demands. "I don't think some of these players deserve what they're getting paid," she says flatly, adding that, in her

168

opinion, a lot of what Ed Garvey, Executive Director of the NFL Players Association, has been demanding recently is "garbage."

Particularly annoying to Mrs. Jane Morabito is Garvey's contention made in 1973 just before Jane was interviewed for this book that players should not have to attend those mini training camps that a number of clubs now conduct on long spring weekends. "I think the players are only hurting themselves," she concludes. "Next they'll want to cut back on the training camp and then they'll wonder why they have to play preseason games. Well," she says, pausing a moment for emphasis, "the reason you need pre-season games is to get the revenue to keep a team going."

As Jane's comment indicates, Tony's "family" business has become much more of a modern, profit-oriented corporation in the years since his passing. Of course, so has professional football with the advent of the big-buck television contract and the subsequent arrival of the big-buck player salary. Another factor is that whereas Tony was a happy-go-lucky fan for whom pro football was worth all the red ink it brought his way, the Morabito women look upon this club as their primary source of income. To be sure, neither lady will wind up living off a Social Security check. But then again you won't find the 49ers—unlike a team owned by millionaires such as the Jets—handing out television sets as Christmas gifts to sportswriters. Indeed, Josephine is all business when she asserts, "Like any other enterprise, we're entitled to make a legitimate profit."

Owners often are criticized for making what to them is just a "legitimate" profit. Josephine fights back. "It's the same in this marketplace as in the supermarket," she argues. "Who thought you'd ever be paying 79 cents for a head of lettuce? If I could tell you how to stop inflation, I'd be on Nixon's staff. But I can't, and until somebody can it's going to be necessary to do things like raise ticket prices," which the 49ers did in 1972.

(It should be noted that although the 49ers aren't talking, it appears that the annual income for both Josephine and Jane crosses over into the six-figure range. It should also be pointed out, however, that unlike the rather fixed salary of a corporation executive, the ladies' income figure can vary widely from year to year, in part just on the basis of the schedule their team plays. For example, the guarantee for a team playing in Houston or San Diego is far less than what it is in Kansas City, those teams being extremes within the league.)

Still, as long as Joe Perry is on the 49ers' payroll, at least a chunk of that old family feeling is going to hold on. Perry, nicknamed "The Jet," was a running back for San Francisco throughout the 1950s. Today he is a member of the Pro Football Hall of Fame and is employed by the 49ers as a scout. But more than that, Perry is a bit of a club historian for players who were not yet born when Tony Morabito first acquired his pride and joy.

"We were just like a big Italian family." He laughs. "Even the meals were set out family-style. Wherever we went, Tony and I played gin rummy. He was such a flashy dresser that I don't think I ever saw him twice in the same suit when on the road."

Then, in a far less mirthful mood, Joe adds, "Tony was just like a father to me. I never had a contract, just Tony's hand. I knew he would never screw me, and he never did. I was one of the first blacks in pro football and from my mother I had learned never to take no shit. From Tony I learned not to start any either."

The Morabito women have been tough in their time too. One interesting fact about the merger of the NFL and the AFL is that for a time the two ladies were in a position to kill the whole deal by themselves. And although they never really were close to saying no, it did take a long time before they said yes. In fact, Commissioner Rozelle considered the situation important enough to make a special trip west to discuss the merger personally with the women.

Specifically, Josephine and Jane objected to the so-called infringement upon their territorial rights by the AFL's Oakland Raiders. A similar situation existed in New York, where the Jets were considered to be infringing upon the territory of the Giants. Under Article IV, Section 2, of the NFL Constitution, every team is guaranteed "the exclusive right within its home territory [defined as extending out 75 miles in all directions] to exhibit professional football games played by teams of the league."

That is, all teams save two, those two exceptions now receiving under terms of the merger financial compensation from AFL teams totaling $8 million (49ers) and $10 million (Giants) in equal annual payments stretched out over many years.

"Rozelle came out [from New York] to prove to the girls that they'd be all right," says Marshall Leahy, counsel for the 49ers and an old-guard member of Tony's football family. "The girls didn't buy it right away," he recalls, adding that they were remembering how hard Tony had battled the city's park and recreation commission for Sunday playing dates in Kezar Stadium, which during the 1930s and early '40s was a traditional Sunday site for college football games.

"The girls wanted more than $8 million," Leahy also recalls, adding that Giants' owner Wellington Mara accepted the merger terms before the women. Josephine concurs. "We fought it right down to the wire," she says, though she explains that a lot of the fighting was really done by

Spadia. "We wanted certain playing dates. For example, we wanted to continue the Rams' rivalry and we didn't want to be playing at home on the same Sunday as the Raiders were."

In the end, Leahy says, Josephine and Jane gave their consent, not because they wanted a merger, but because "they didn't want to be the dogs who messed everything up."

One thing this incident shows is that contrary to the general opinion of some forty groups that have tried to buy the 49ers since Vic's death in 1964, these two women are eminently capable of making business decisions when and if they feel the situation requires their involvement. They seldom do, but that's only because they believe Lou can do a far better job than they.

The three agree they have never disagreed on a major decision. But Jane adds that on one very important matter it did take the two sexes some time before they saw eye to eye. The occasion was the search for a new head coach in 1968. According to Jane, Lou was after one particular candidate—not Nolan—who was playing hard to get. "Lou thought this guy was great," she says, declining to identify the gentleman by name. "One minute the guy would say yes and the next minute he'd say no. Well, for heaven's sake, would you want someone leading your team who couldn't make up his own mind? Thank God we didn't get this guy. Nolan has been fantastic."

Jane says she also disagreed with her co-owners on whether the club should move from Kezar Stadium to Candlestick Park, though for one obvious reason the others took her opinion with a grain of salt. The decision to move resulted from a need for the additional revenue found in Candlestick's larger seating capacity. Moreover, the neighborhood around Kezar had become quite unsafe over the years.

172

Even so, "I didn't want to go and I told them so," Jane says in a *nyah-nyah* voice that suggests she is still a bit proud of the stand she took. "I told them I had many happy memories of Kezar [obviously, she was blocking out all those times the fans had booed Tony and Vic unmercifully for the 49ers' sometimes rather sorry play] and they told me I was just being selfish.

"Certainly," she told them.

Keeping the women informed of all important developments is not always an easy thing for Spadia to do, at least as far as Jane is concerned. "When I phone Josie," he says, "I always find her at home. A lot of times she phones me, like today she wanted to make sure that I got tickets for some friends of hers. Jane, on the other hand, is never home. She's always out playing golf or doing something. Sometimes I only catch up to her after we've already made our announcement. But that's all right because I know Josie wants to be more involved than Jane anyway."

Jane agrees—unquestionably. "I hate any sort of regimentation." She squints. "Playing eighteen holes of golf is regimentation enough for me. I'd be terrible in that office. I don't even read that much of what comes in the mail from the league office."

She adds: "The NFL is really a male-chauvinist organization. That's the way it started out and that's the way I think it should remain."

Question: "In other words, you think a woman's place is in the home?"

Answer: "Not me, baby. I'm never home."

One thing that neither brash Jane nor quiet Josephine has yet had the courage to do is troop into the locker room after a particularly important victory. Not that at least one of them hasn't given it some thought.

No, it was Josephine who turned to Spadia after the 49ers' 1970 play-off victory over Minnesota and said, "Gee,

I'd love to be able to go in there." Lou, who like Jim Finks of the Vikings will never be labeled a swinging football executive, still blushes a bit as he recalls thinking, "I just couldn't bring her into a room of naked men." (Josie says it wasn't really a serious suggestion. "They'd have to blindfold me first," she claims.)

Aside from Jane's shouting, the ladies' game behavior is really quite demure compared to someone like Carroll Rosenbloom of the Rams who does everything but stand on his head to appease the gods of victory. The 49ers used to have postgame cocktail parties, but Jane says they were stopped after one rather inebriated guest kicked a chocolate football high enough for it to stick on the ceiling. Thanks to television, which wants West Coast games to start at 1 P.M. local time instead of at 2 P.M. as in days past, and thanks to Candlestick, which is on the edge of town rather than in the middle of it like Kezar, traditional postgame dinners at Trader Vic's and other San Francisco restaurants have also become a thing of the past.

Of course, after a quarter century without a real championship (you can't call the 49ers' 1970 and 1971 divisional crowns real championships since the team subsequently lost in the play-offs), it's easy to understand why the ladies don't get completely carried away. "So many years and too many tears ago, . . ." is the way San Francisco sportswriter Wells Twombly started his 1972 article on the Morabito women for *Pro* magazine, published by NFL Properties, Inc.

"I have been disappointed so many times," Jane says disgustedly. "I really think I wore myself out that time we lost to Detroit," 31 to 27, in the 1957 Western Conference play-off game. (The two teams had finished the season with identical 8-and-4 records; Detroit went on to wallop the Cleveland Browns, 59 to 14, and become the league champion.)

174

"I got home that night and I just cried and cried. I had just gotten undressed and was standing there when suddenly my jaw locked. I couldn't believe it. I couldn't say anything except '*uhhwah-uhhwah.*' It was the middle of the night, so Vic had to call something like six doctors before he found one that would come over. I remember this doctor stood 6 feet 5 inches, and he laid me out on the bed and started putting washcloths in my mouth. But that didn't work so he said I had to go to the hospital. Vic called a girl friend from down the street to stay with my son, and she came running over in a nightgown with curlers and a purse. Then off we went to the hospital where they had to put me to sleep for a couple of minutes before they were finally able to get my jaw back in place. What a mess."

For Tony Morabito, that 1957 season ended prematurely. It ended during the second quarter of the 49ers' fifth game of the season, a home contest against the Chicago Bears. As was his custom, Tony was sitting in his Kezar box with brother Vic, watching the action, when suddenly he slumped down in his chair. A second, massive heart attack. An ambulance ride to the hospital with Tony being kept alive on oxygen and strong stimulants. Frantic work by doctors—all for naught. Tony Morabito was dead at the age of forty-seven.

The players knew by the end of the third quarter, and though the Bears were still vanquished, 21 to 17, the winners' locker room was the scene of utter despair. "Oh, my God," said Frankie Albert, the 49ers' head coach and, before that, its standout quarterback. "I don't know what to say. I wish we had lost by 100 points than have this happen. Poor Tony! Oh, my God, poor Tony! This game was hard enough on a healthy man. But poor Tony was living on borrowed time. Oh, hell, I've got to get out of this dressing room. I can't stand being here."

In many ways, Tony Morabito was like Lamar Hunt.

Both men were young when they bought their way into professional football. Both men were wealthy—Hunt born to it, Tony the beneficiary of his own hard work in a lumber transporting business on the San Francisco waterfront. Both men were thwarted in their attempts to acquire an NFL franchise. Both men subsequently joined forces with other wealthy men to start a rival pro league. (Hunt, of course, was the father of the AFL, while Tony was in from the start on the All-America Football Conference, founded in 1944 by Arch Ward, sports editor of the *Chicago Tribune*.)

The All-America conference was one of a number of rival leagues that attempted to get off the ground at the end of World War II by luring returning servicemen away from the NFL teams they had left when war broke out. The confidence of NFL owners was expressed by George Preston Marshall, owner of the Washington Redskins, who said in an article in *Esquire* that "I did not realize there was another league although I did receive some literature telling me about a WPA project."

The AAFC made it while the others didn't, and one important reason why it did is expressed best by that old sports axiom that a pro league is only as strong as its team in New York. Indeed, if you remember, it wasn't until a group of millionaires led by David A. (Sonny) Werblin bought the bankrupt and ridiculous New York Titans in 1963 and transformed that club into the lavish and glamorous New York Jets—as symbolized, of course, by "Broadway Joe" Namath—did the AFL's future look particularly rosy.

When in 1945 New York Giants' owner Tim Mara got into a fight with Dan Topping, owner of the NFL's Brooklyn Dodgers, the AAFC seized its opportunity. Topping wanted to move the Dodgers into Yankee Stadium, of which he was part owner, but which was situated only a stone's throw away from the Polo Grounds and Mara's Giants. When Mara balked, the AAFC quickly promised Topping $100,000 for a war chest if he would switch to the AAFC and battle it out with Mara. He did.

In 1946, the AAFC's first year of operation, Ward asserted that "all clubs are financed by men of millionaire incomes who are prepared to engage in a battle of dollars with the National Football League if necessary." Tony wasn't really in that class, but for the first year at least he did have two well-to-do partners willing to share the risk. The real money in the new league seemed to be in Los Angeles, where Don Ameche, the actor, was co-owner of the Los Angeles "Dons." For a while, some NFL owners referred to their competition as the "All-Ameche League." But when Morabito and the other nouveau sports owners started throwing top-dollar contracts at returning veterans and graduating college seniors, the NFL chieftains also took to the trenches.

What followed was a war to end all wars—though little more than a decade later the red ink of the 1940s had faded sufficiently to allow history to repeat itself. Tony was particularly adept at signing star players, among them that initial season Frank Albert of Stanford, first of the modern T-formation quarterbacks, and Len Eshmont, slick halfback for the 1940 Fordham Rams football team that made it all the way to the Cotton Bowl before finally bowing to Texas A & M, 13 to 12. Eshmont's college coach, by the way, was "Sleepy Jim" Crowley, one of the halfbacks in the "Four Horsemen" backfield at Notre Dame and the first commissioner of the AAFC.

Tony brought the league much-needed publicity—if nothing else—when in 1947 he tried to sign both Glenn Davis and "Doc" Blanchard, Army's "Mr. Outside" and

177

"Mr. Inside." Tony knew each had a military obligation to fulfill. But he just sort of figured he might get the brass to delay the ninety-day furlough a cadet normally receives upon graduation in June until later in the year, say, during football season. Tony was ready to go as high as $35,000 a man—slim pickings for a number-one draft choice now but roughly 20 percent of Tony's operating budget at that time.

The War Department put a stop to such scheming, but Tony knew that the battle he was really in was for the fan's entertainment dollar. So that same year he pulled off such moves as having the rather durable comedian Bob Hope as the half-time entertainment for a 49ers' home exhibition game. Hope's humor really hasn't changed much in the last quarter century if this excerpt from his show is any indication:

"I used to be a football player. I played for the Santa Monica Ducks, and we were a pretty good team when the wind was behind us. Once in a close game the coach said, 'Stand up, Hope, we want to send the bench in.' "

What wasn't a joke, though, was the red ink on the 49ers' books. A sportswriter estimated before the 49ers' first season of play that the club would probably lose upward of $25,000 the first year out. It lost $150,000, enough to send Tony's two coinvestors running for cover, leaving Tony as the principal owner with a small piece of the action going to brother Vic. Eh, but so what? was Tony's reaction. "I had a barrel of fun and I wouldn't have missed it for the world," he told a sportswriter at season's end.

In describing Tony, Marshall Leahy, Tony's classmate both at St. Ignatius High School in San Francisco and at Santa Clara College, Class of 1931, says: "There are guys in every sport who just like to hang around athletes. Tony was a bench warmer in high school and he failed to make both the freshman and varsity teams at Santa Clara. But he loved football. He used to go to all the high school and college games in the area." (He even took his bride to a game on their honeymoon.)

Leahy adds: "Tony took all the risk. He was in there for all the eggs. He sold his other interests. He borrowed money from everyone. Vic wanted out when things got shaky around 1948 and Tony let him out. Then he brought Vic back about two years later. All the banks in town told him to get the hell out, and to the day he died I don't think Tony ever forgave them for that.

"Tony was a heavy smoker. He also was a worrywart who got terribly involved emotionally in every game. Though his family had a history of heart trouble, he never exercised. He didn't like to fish or hunt either. About the only thing that took his mind off football was a backyard barbecue. For that he'd drive 50 miles just to get the meat he wanted."

And what was Mrs. Tony Morabito doing all this time?

"Raising a family," she answers automatically as if to ask, what else would I be doing?

Yes, but what about the money?

"Well, I think one thing about youth is that you don't realize how precarious a thing can be. Tony was an optimist."

But didn't he ever come home and sort of cry on your shoulder?

"Not particularly. He worried inside."

Pasquale Morabito was Tony and Vic's father, an Italian immigrant who is supposed to have taught his offspring that when there's a principle involved, a Morabito goes to hell and back to defend it. That, perhaps, is the reason why Tony's celebrated feud with the San Francisco *Examiner* lasted all those years. It started when Tony let the paper sponsor an annual charity game, to the dismay of the other newspapers in town. When Tony demanded the following year that all papers share the sponsorship, the *Examiner* blew up—and so did Tony.

"That ended the whole thing," recalls Josephine. "It's a shame, but there's never been another game like that to this day. But when Tony made up his mind, well, forget it, his mind was made up. You don't know too many Italians if you don't know that. It probably wasn't too wise. It probably killed him. But that's the way he was."

Pasquale, Josephine adds, "didn't know the front end of a football from the back end. But Tony's stepmother (and Vic's mother) was a very rabid fan. She would go to the game and Pasquale would stay home with the babies. The first time he went with us to Kezar Stadium he wanted to know if all those people out there had paid to get in. He said it looked pretty good, but he didn't know what Tony had to pay out."

The payout was substantial. Frankly, Tony felt the city was screwing him. In 1949, for example, one San Francisco newspaper reported that rental costs for Kezar Stadium came to 15 percent of gross, while in Cleveland, Municipal Stadium cost the Cleveland Browns, the only AAFC team consistently able to hold its head above water financially, in the neighborhood of only 6 percent to 9 percent. In addition, while the Browns received 50 percent of concessions' revenue, the 49ers got nothing. At the same time, the 49ers were obliged to provide their own ushers, ticket takers and ticket sellers.

Tony the fan could live with these problems. What really got to him was that damn war between the two leagues. More than once the two sides appeared near a truce, a merger. But then this or that owner would get up on his hind legs, make a stink, and the negotiations would break off in a huff. In October, 1948, for example, Philadelphia

180

Eagles' owner Alex Thompson, who had been a peacemaker for the past two years, threw in the towel after Topping commented publicly at a gathering in New York that he figured Mara's Giants would lose about $200,000 that season. "I've made my efforts and now the hell with it," Thompson told the press. "From now on it's really going to be a battle."

To which Tony responded: "Oh no, not again. Every time we make a little progress, somebody blows it all to heck. Well, okay, if it's war the National wants, it's war it will get. But either there will be peace, and soon, or everybody will go broke. Holy smoke! The National guys are screaming about how weak we are, but our Chicago Rockets, admittedly our weakest team, is stronger than their weakest, the Boston Yanks. What's the matter with those National guys? They know darn well that pro football cannot possibly continue for much longer under the present setup. Apparently common sense has been thrown out the window. If this is war, we'll all be ruined eventually."

And Tony physically as well as financially. Leahy, who was with the 49ers' boss at several NFL-AAFC peace powwows, says the latter league's struggle for survival "took an awful lot out of Tony." All those trips back east, he recalls. All the angry exchanges in the press.

At first openly contemptuous, later the NFL tried to divide and conquer by offering membership to the AAFC's two strongest teams both on the field and at the gate, the 49ers and the Browns. The offer was refused, even though in 1949 the AAFC was down to seven teams instead of eight, with many of those drawing only 5,000 to 6,000 a game. (And they were lucky to field seven; the Chicago franchise that year was working on its fifth set of owners in four seasons.)

Said Tony: "We could have taken the National League's

peace overtures at the cost of leaving the other All-American teams holding the sack. But I have to live with myself. The hardheads thought they had us licked. Now the more level-headed members who wanted peace are fighting back, and I got a hunch that peace may not be too far off."

(It's interesting to note that one important mistake the NFL made in fighting the AAFC was letting its Cleveland team, the Rams, go out to Los Angeles to fight the Dons, which the NFL appears to have thought was the AAFC's principal strength. Instead, Cleveland became the AAFC's strength, along with San Francisco, drawing 80,000 and more to every game. In the subsequent war with the AFL, the NFL guessed right. Though Dallas had bombed as an NFL city back in 1951, the league put another team there to battle Lamar Hunt's Dallas Texans. And in the end it was Hunt who had to leave town, though television contracts and Namath's Super Bowl spectacular more than compensated for the withdrawal.)

Eventually, both sides decided that the costs of the ongoing player-signing war, which had doubled and even tripled payrolls in just four years' time, were just too much. In addition, in 1949 AAFC attendance started to drop even in Cleveland. Says Leahy, "Everyone was sick of losing money."

So in December, 1949, at the Racquet Club in Philadelphia, a peace treaty was signed. According to Leahy, NFL Commissioner Bert Bell fashioned the actual treaty document in longhand on a note pad. Both sides claimed victory, though when you consider that no NFL team had folded while only three AAFC teams were brought into the NFL, the greater victory has to go to the established league. (The three were San Francisco, Cleveland and Baltimore.)

But the AAFC argued that there were three more than the NFL had wanted when war broke out. Baltimore was the real coup, the challengers figured. Later when the Colt franchise folded for financial reasons after just one NFL season, Washington Redskins' owner George Preston Marshall vowed never again to relinquish his territorial rights and allow a team in Baltimore (which means, of course, that he was overruled twice).

Just two years after the fighting stopped, Tony suffered his first heart attack. Though this one almost killed him (a priest administered the last rites), Tony refused to get out of football as recommended by his physician. "I'll be worse off if I get out," he protested. "What the heck will I do with myself?"

Though living on borrowed time, Tony wouldn't let up emotionally. In 1956, his long-smoldering feud with the *Examiner* fired up again after a columnist seemed to imply that the fatal heart attack suffered by an ex-49er coach not long after his dismissal was brought on by Tony's action. Outraged, Tony refused to allow *Examiner* sportswriters to travel with the team, as is customary in professional sports, and barred them from all press conferences and training-camp sessions. (Not even George Allen, Head Coach and General Manager of the Washington Redskins, goes that far, though a 1973 article in *Sports Illustrated* mentioned how the temperamental Mr. Allen doesn't let writers covering training camp into the locker room or players' rooms, nor does he let them on the practice field, save for the track ringing the field. And even then, Mr. Allen's rules forbid any writer from indulging himself through the act of sitting down.)

The game on the field did little to improve Tony's condition. Despite a backfield that included Y. A. Tittle at quarterback and Hugh McElhenny and Joe Perry as running backs, the 49ers could never finish higher than second between 1952 and 1957, winding up below .500 in both 1955 and 1956, Tony's last full season.

Though physically only a shadow of his former self (in

choosing pictures for this book, Tony's widow asked that no shot of Tony during his illness be used), the 49er boss continued to perform such tasks as negotiating players' contracts. Leo Nomellini, 49er tackle from 1950 to 1963 and today, along with Perry, a member of the Pro Football Hall of Fame, says Tony remained "a hard-driving guy. If he didn't like something, he'd knock heads together, bang."

Nomellini, who today is Vice President, Public Relations, of Northwestern Title Insurance Co. in Oakland and also host of a sports interview show on an area radio station, says Tony also stayed involved with his players. One time, Leo remembers, Tony promised a player a bonus if he could get down to a certain weight. The player made it, but he was cut from the team that very day. Nevertheless, Tony kept his promise.

Leo says that when he sat down to negotiate his contract, he liked to kid the boss about being hard of hearing. "I would whisper the amount I wanted several times until finally Tony adjusted his hearing aid. Then I'd shout it out, and he'd just about leave his chair."

Leo adds: "I never saw a contract. What Tony and Vic told you they would do they did."

This doesn't mean that Tony was ever loose with a dollar. In 1949, for example, the players demanded an extra game's pay for their play-off game against the Yankees. Tony snapped back that the club had played only twelve games that year instead of the fourteen specified in each man's contract and that, anyway, the contract made provision for a play-off game if necessary. Said Tony: "If you aren't out on the field tomorrow morning at 10 o'clock, we'll forfeit the game to the Yankees. Furthermore, you'll be fined 25 percent of your salaries." (The 49ers won, 17 to 7, then dropped the title game to Cleveland, 21 to 7. The winner's share in that latter game was $266.11 a man, compared to the loser's share of $172.61.)

Spadia was always the guy Tony and Vic played off in their frenetic office. When the Morabito men disagreed on something, they'd call Lou in and ask what he thought. Lou couldn't win because Tony always took Vic's position in front of him and vice versa.

The brothers chose to work in the same office even though Lou remembers it often meant that one couldn't hear himself think when the other was on the telephone. Over the years Tony was always the big brother and Vic the little brother. When Tony was still in college, he used to bring home football players on weekends and Vic sat bug-eyed in the living room hanging on their every word. In the office Tony liked to complain kiddingly about how he had always been the one designated to push around his little brother's baby carriage.

Vic ran a different kind of club after Tony's death. Tony had always delegated to his little brother responsibility for public relations and television, choosing to spend most of his time involved with the actual team. Consequently, Vic was much more the businessman.

In terms of personality, Vic was a brooder, whereas Tony simply blew his top. The little brother took defeat just as poorly as big brother had, which meant that, if anything, the strain on Vic's heart was even greater. But at least Vic had sense enough to come in out of the rain; after Tony's death, he and Jane stopped the Morabito tradition of sitting among the fans—the angry, booing fans whenever anything went wrong—and moved upstairs into a private box. (Josephine stayed on, though as Jane says, "even our fans wouldn't boo a lady.")

Said Vic right after Tony's death, "We are going to carry on and achieve Tony's dream of winning a championship, no matter what the cost." Including, as it turned out, Vic's own death just at age forty-four. Like Tony, Vic survived his first heart attack. As with Tony, doctors pleaded with Vic to get out of the football business. Like Tony, Vic couldn't do it.

Publicly, Vic was always vehement in denying that the 49ers could ever be up for sale. But privately he advised the ladies after his first attack in 1963 that in the event of his death they should sell the franchise.

Like Tony, Vic died only minutes after doctors got him into a hospital bed. But when the ladies discussed what to do, they rejected Vic's idea on the grounds that now it was up to them to fulfill Tony's dream of winning a championship once and for all. Spadia, the guy who used to wear Vic's hand-me-down suits, announced to the world that "the 49ers should have San Francisco ownership and they should have Morabito ownership. There will be no sale to anyone."

And so, Mr. Spadia, what do you say today when other front-office executives kid you about who your bosses are?

"I always say, I know my ladies are ladies. I hope you're as sure that the gentlemen you work for are gentlemen."

They seem to love their club but from afar.

"Sometimes it's best."

They seem to reflect a lot on the past.

"Those two guys are still pretty much around."

After a full decade at the helm, the Morabito ladies today are nearly unknown. "People probably think we're the two pixilated old ladies who live alone." Josephine laughs. Actually, both women are like a lot of women everywhere in that they spend their fair share of time on affairs of the house—Jane's golf games notwithstanding. For example, at the same time as they were being interviewed for this book, Josephine was trying to decide whether to air-condition her home (she decided the price was too high), while Jane was waiting around for her interior decorator, who failed to appear on the designated day. "I'm just the lady next door," Josephine remarks.

186

But with a football team to follow, it's impossible for the women to lead a normal life on weekends from July through December, or hopefully January and the Super Bowl. If the visiting team's owner or owners are old friends, "Lou usually will call us up and tell us when and where we're having dinner," Jane explains. When the 49ers are the visiting team, the ladies and Spadia sometimes have Saturday dinner with Head Coach Nolan and some friends. At dinner, the women never ask how their team is going to fare. "We usually can figure that out by the way Nolan acts," Josephine says.

On the Saturday before an away game, Josephine loves to go shopping, especially for shoes. "After you've been in a city several times," she says, "you get to know the best places to shop."

Jane's home, as you might expect, is a bit more posh than Josephine's. For one thing, Jane has a bar area big enough for a *Wall Street Journal* reporter writing a book on the front office of pro football to drink himself under the table when he is foolish enough to match his hostess drink for drink on an empty stomach.

At dusk, if you stand on Jane's front steps, you can both see and feel the cool fog as it comes in off the bay. Josephine has only to step out back about 60 feet to soak up the rays while lounging beside the large swimming pool that comes with the condominium development she lives in.

It takes Josephine a while to start talking, but once she does she can be right back living nights such as the one with the bull in Buffalo. Or like the night she spent with her husband and his team at some place called the Green Hotel in Pasadena. Okay, so budgets were tight back in the '40s. But booking what Josephine believes was an old ladies' home as a hotel?

And then there was the week she spent in a farm town in Pennsylvania in between games on a three-game eastern road swing during that era of rail travel. The only thing to do at night was watch the cows come back to the barn. The bartender with the bar with sawdust on the floor didn't cotton to a lady in his establishment. (She was the only woman in the entire party.) But he did make this concession, albeit grudgingly: he put water in her Scotch.

(Joe Perry has another memory from that same time that's worth mentioning. In Baltimore one time for a game, Perry strolled into the restaurant portion of the hotel where the 49ers were staying. Before he strolled too far, however, the maître d' came up to him and, as Joe remembers it, said, "I thought you were supposed to stay in your room." It was an obvious reference to Joe's skin color, and the player, who as previously mentioned never took no shit, retaliated by turning over tables and generally wrecking the place. He then straightened things up enough to sit down at one table and casually order his meal.)

Both Josephine and Jane remember certain players, though for Josephine it's usually for their playing ability, whereas for Jane, who was closer in age to players on the early 49er teams, it's sometimes more for their off-field antics.

"He was like a ballet dancer," Josephine says of halfback McElhenny. "Very graceful, and with a little move this way or that way, he was away.

"Such a gentleman," she says of lineman Nomellini. "Just watching him on the sidelines sometimes you could tell he was more than just an exceptional player.

"He left your heart in your throat," she says of halfback R. C. Owens, nicknamed "Alley Oop" for his last-second, up-and-over circus catches of balls thrown his way. "Tittle would loft the ball toward the goal line and you just knew that R.C. was going to catch the ball no matter what."

Jane remembers in particular all the pillow fights on the

188

plane. "Those stewardesses took their lives in their hands just doing their job." She remembers Johnny "Strike" Stryzkalski, another halfback, and the time he gave a player a hotfoot. But Jane, too, remembers McElhenny for his running, and as she does she just sits back in her chair and smiles, saying, "Beautiful."

Even though it's true that remembered joys are never past, it's also true that at some point in time they surely must stop accumulating. As Spadia knows all too well, widows dominate 49er board meetings these days.

If Tony's dream is ever fulfilled, few will be around who remember the man behind it. And that's really kind of sad, because one gets the impression today that money is too much the stuff that dreams are made of on many, though not all, NFL clubs.

You get the impression that Tony was nothing more than Superfan, the guy sitting behind the goal posts just wishing he could pass like Johnny Unitas or run like Joe Perry. Tony sometimes didn't count his pennies, and if when he did he found none were there, well, at least he could always get into the game free.

Rick Morabito, Jane's son, is the next generation of Morabito men. But according to Spadia, Rick currently is content to scout for the club and may not necessarily want to assume the burden of ownership.

But it could never be Rick's dream anyway. For both ladies, "football is a way of life," as Josephine puts it.

And a Super Bowl ring "is what we've wanted all these years."

7

The Dream Deferred

Rommie Loudd
Former Director of Pro Personnel
The New England Patriots

WHEN ROMMIE LOUDD was in his junior year of college football at UCLA, some motion-picture talent scouts dropped by practice one afternoon to watch him work out. After observing him grunt and sweat under a broiling sun, they followed him into the locker room to watch him dress, undress and, the pièce de résistance, walk around the shower room clad in only a towel.

This rather unnerved the 6-foot-2-inch, 220-pound all-American end until one of his coaches informed him that the scouts were there looking for extras to play in the movie, "The Ten Commandments," which was being filmed across town at the time. It seems that the film makers needed several masculine-looking young black men to serve as litter carriers for Moses and the Israelites as they crossed the parted waters of the Red Sea just one chariot step ahead of the pharaoh.

When told that a litter carrier's pay was $50 a day, Loudd readily agreed. (By this time, he already had a wife to support.) But a funny thing happened on the way to the Promised Land: Rommie slipped and fell on his face in the black mud of the Red Sea.

190

In point of fact, this litter carrier received $56.50 a day for his month's toil with Moses. The difference was the extra time Loudd was required to spend in makeup each morning. He was there because, mud and all, the movie makers still felt that he wasn't black enough to play the role without Negro makeup.

Off the screen, Rommie Loudd has never needed makeup for people to know he is black.

Indeed, in 1966 Loudd made headlines when he was named the first full-time black assistant coach in pro football. A year later, the Boston Patriots of the old American Football League promoted Loudd from linebacker coach to director of player personnel—the first black in the front office of pro football. In March of 1971, former Patriots' General Manager Upton Bell named Loudd director of pro personnel, a newly created position and one that he held for just over two years.

As director of pro personnel, Loudd was on the road continuously keeping tabs of the on- and off-field activities of players already in the league. His job was to know what players were like, both in uniform and out, in case they were to become available. "It's a job," Loudd said when appointed, "that I can enjoy for the next twenty years."

Maybe so, but ambition and the sweet smell of black success in a white world subsequently drove this executive to seek to become the first black owner of a National Football League franchise. He succeeded in convincing the town fathers of Orlando, Florida, that he should represent their interests before the NFL. "For me," he said at one point, "being an owner would be the utopia."

But Loudd failed before the league, a franchise being awarded instead to a group in nearby Tampa. Nevertheless, while his dream has been deferred, the very fact that Rommie Loudd was under serious consideration for a franchise proved that he had come a long, long way from such early childhood roles as tap dancer with his uncle in a novelty act that played around San Angelo, Texas, Rommie's hometown. Rommie danced in white nightclubs like The Hangar in San Angelo. He danced to the 1940s swing music of Benny Goodman and others. By his own admission, he wasn't the best dancer in the world. "But," he quickly adds, "I was good enough to get paid."

As director of pro personnel, Loudd was paid to hustle information on other players. Sometimes that information came from a coach or scout. Sometimes it was from an ex-wife or bartender. In either case, Loudd filed important data in one of his numerous player personnel books or in his own computerlike mind.

"My job," he said when still with the Patriots, "is to assist in making good trades and eliminate bad ones." A good trade, he explained quite candidly, is when you get "twice as much as you paid for." A bad trade is when the other team makes a good trade. Sometimes, for example, the other team will try to pawn off a player injured either physically or mentally. "That kind of thing really pisses me off," Loudd said. Indeed, as the Patriots' director of pro personnel, Loudd made it a point of honor to know the real dope on each of the 1,222 players active in the NFL.

When Rommie was a boy in San Angelo, his father, Joe Loudd, wanted him to follow in the footsteps of Dad, who was an all-star catcher on a team called the Black Sheepherders in a Negro league in southwest Texas. For two years, Joe Loudd patiently played catch with his little boy out behind the barn on their small ranch. Then when Rommie was eight years old, Dad blew it by buying his son shoulder pads and a helmet for Christmas. "From then on," says the younger Loudd, "I was hooked on football."

But football wasn't the only thing in life. Even as a player

192

in the American Football League, Loudd wasn't actively pursuing a subsequent career in the front office. For one thing, he recalls there were no black front-office execs in those days.

For another, music—especially jazz—was also his passion. A communications major at UCLA, Loudd seriously considered a career in radio or television for when his playing days were over. (Mud and all, movies also held a special appeal.) Loudd did do some front-office work the year he was a Los Angeles Charger. But it was only after he was out of pro football and into radio for about a year that his thoughts turned once and for all to the front office.

And even then, his front-office career started by chance. It seems that a neighbor who was playing minor-league football for a club called the Chelsea Sweepers needed a ride to the games. Loudd obliged, and because of his unusual size, was quickly enlisted by the Sweepers' coach.

But only as a player. It took half a season before the coach-shy Sweepers named Loudd linebacker coach. The following season he moved up to defensive coordinator and, after two consecutive league championships, he decided that football would always be his number-one passion.

Loudd wanted to coach, however, not join the front office. He went to see Mike Holovak, who at that time was head coach and general manager of the Patriots, to ask for a job recommendation. Holovak was so impressed that he hired Loudd as his own linebacker coach.

A year later Holovak faked Loudd out of position by offering him the job as player-personnel director. The Patriots needed someone to reorganize their disjointed scouting system. It meant a healthy raise and, Loudd decided after two days of deliberation, an opportunity. He took the job because he decided, in effect, that the game on Sunday lasts only sixty minutes whereas the game on Monday, Tuesday and Wednesday lasts all day long.

Loudd was surprised at the offer in part because he didn't think any club would offer such a job to a black. Even today he doubts seriously whether a black will be named a general manager in the near future.

But Holovak, who today is an assistant coach with the New York Jets, says that color meant nothing one way or the other. "Rommie just was there," he says, "and I felt that he would be the best man for the job."

Being in Boston helped. Not long after Loudd was appointed to the Patriots' staff in 1966, the Boston Celtics named a new coach: Bill Russell. In contrast, in 1962 when Loudd was still a player, he and other black members of the Patriots were asked politely—but most assuredly—to sleep in separate quarters when the team played a preseason exhibition game in New Orleans. (Holovak left the decision up to the players, who went along with the request.)

But if being in Boston helped Loudd get into the front office, it also made staying there difficult. Since 1968, the Patriots have had five head coaches and four general managers, a record that not too surprisingly does not appear in any record books. In 1969, things were so bad that the club went into the annual college-player draft in January without either a general manager or a coaching staff.

Loudd credits his ability to keep a low profile as one reason why he endured. Sportswriters, he claims, can be trouble for front-office execs. "I mean, sportswriters either like you or they don't. If they like you, they will project you into some kind of Jesus Christ who can walk on water. If they don't, you can't do anything right."

The one time in Boston that Loudd was squarely in the limelight, he didn't even get his feet wet. Pressed into service to run the Patriots' 1969 draft, Loudd waited nervously for the Patriots' first turn to pick, while sportswriters hovered like so many fourth-grade schoolteachers monitoring a test. A cigarette was in his mouth, but it wasn't lit—which was a good thing since he had the tobacco end in his mouth. The way it turned out, all three of Loudd's first three draft picks made the squad their first year, enough to prompt one journalist to suggest that Loudd might make a good general manager.

Loudd never ducks a scribe. At the same time, he has little use for journalists. "If I'm doing my job," he says, "eventually people in football will find out about me. And that's a lot more important than being known by Joe Q. Public."

Loudd's principal job as director of pro personnel was to maintain a facts-and-figures file on each of the 1,222 players active in the NFL. In attendance at sixty or more games a year, Loudd charted every player's performance in terms of everything from speed and strength to intelligence and leadership. (A quarterback who doesn't talk to his players on the sidelines probably isn't too good a leader.) Using statistics supplied by the league, Loudd also charted every injury and every trade made during the season.

Only a handful of NFL clubs currently assign one man as a full-time scout of players already in the league. Traditionally, that job has been left to college scouts since they're usually free on Sunday anyway.

But league officials say that more and more clubs are beginning to place greater emphasis on the scouting of established players. George Allen, General Manager and Head Coach of the Washington Redskins, has been one catalyst. His "win now" philosophy of football stresses use of established players rather than draftees.

One NFL official predicts that all teams will have a director of pro personnel within the next few years, though he may not be called by that title. In Chicago, for example, the Bears call their man the pro talent coordinator. In Miami, the Dolphins' man is director of pro scouting.

Loudd was not in a policy-making position. He researched and he advised, but the decision on whether to make the trade belonged to the general manager, head coach and, in this case, also the club president. Even so, he felt that "I put my whole reputation on the line every time I recommend a trade."

One trade that the director of pro personnel strongly opposed was the celebrated Duane Thomas deal in 1971. That was the first time the Dallas Cowboys tried to get rid of their sullen star—they succeeded a year later in a trade with the San Diego Chargers. (Thomas is now with Washington.) The deal was Thomas for Carl Garrett, the Patriots' rookie-of-the-year running back in 1969. Thomas reported to the Patriots' training camp, took one look around and bolted. The Patriots tried unsuccessfully to coax him back, but when all efforts failed the league office voided the trade and sent the players back to their former teams.

Loudd wasn't surprised at the turn of events. "This kid had been shoved into a corner emotionally at Dallas. He obviously needed time to get his mind together. He is extremely sensitive and not very trusting of people. I felt that with our situation here [the rapid changeover in men at the top], even if Duane had come in and been a superstar, he still wouldn't have been happy."

There was another reason: "The boy had gone to the newspapers with his problems. He had talked about front-office people. Anything pertaining to race, once it hits the press, brings out all sorts of outside agitation groups who are so willing to come to the front, to fight the cause even if they don't know what the cause is. We are a young ball club trying to build, so why bring those kinds of problems to your team?"

What happened when Loudd's advice was ignored?

Nothing much. To paraphrase Loudd, pride is important, but there are times when it won't put meat on the table.

It's just this sense of proportion that, besides helping Loudd keep his job, made him good at it too. Loudd believed that what a player does off the field is just as important as what he does during a game.

"Rommie was always going deeper into a boy," says his former boss, Mike Holovak. "He checked his background. He looked for other reasons why the boy might or might not be a superstar. Other men in that position do the same thing, but I don't think they did it as thoroughly as Rommie. Take it from me, long hours mean nothing to Rommie."

Agreed, says his wife, Betty. "When Rommie was on the road, sometimes only God knew where he was. And I often wondered how even He could keep up with him."

On one occasion, a Patriots' scout offhandedly asked Loudd to tell him about a player on another team whom Loudd had scouted in college a few years before. After giving that player's height, weight and how fast he runs a 40-yard sprint, Loudd added matter-of-factly: "The boy was a speech major in college and his father owns a car dealership in Michigan."

One example of Loudd's thoroughness was Jim Cheyunski, the Patriots' starting middle linebacker in 1972 who later was traded to Buffalo. When Loudd moved east in 1962, one of the first stops he made in the Boston area was at Ace Cheyunski's gas station in Taunton, Mass. Ace's boy Jim handled the pump, and he was so big that Loudd asked Ace whether his son played football. Ace said yes and that Jim was going to start his freshman year at Syracuse Uni-

197

versity in the fall. From then on, Loudd followed the career of Jim Cheyunski, right up to the day in January, 1967, when the Patriots drafted him on Loudd's recommendation.

People in football agree that when Loudd researched what a player was like off the field, he could indeed get personal. Once when he was still player-personnel director, Loudd recommended that the Patriots draft Julius Adams, a big, 260-pound defensive tackle from Texas Southern University. The Patriots took Adams on the second round of the 1971 draft—right behind Jim Plunkett of Stanford—and the rookie made the all-conference rookie team that season.

Before making his recommendation, Loudd figures that he spoke to some two dozen people who knew what Adams was like when he wasn't rushing the passer. The equipment manager was one source, the locker room attendant another. By far the most persuasive information came from Adams' ex-coach, who spoke about Julius Adams as a husband.

"He told me that Julius is the type of kid who has never had a piece of ass outside his home," Loudd recalls. "He told me that unlike a lot of talented guys, Julius is dedicated. I mean like he wants to be a great football player and he thinks about it every day."

Quite obviously, it's always been important for Loudd to have connections wherever he goes. Relatives help. At Texas Southern, Loudd's cousin has a dormitory named after him. That same cousin has a campus drive named after him at another Texas university. And when there were no relatives to rely on, Loudd turned to dozens of ex-teammates, coaches and, often, bartenders and other street people he met over the years who had comprised what he liked to call his "underground network."

"I know a hell of a lot of people," he says with pride.

Sometimes, the color of Loudd's skin opened doors. There was one time when he was still player-personnel director that Loudd sat down with Darrel Royal, head football coach at the University of Texas. Royal's problem was with black high-school guidance counselors, many of whom were counseling their student athletes against going to the University of Texas because of an alleged racist atmosphere. To help Royal out, Loudd visited with several counselors both by phone and in person. "He told them that this image of Texas was fast disappearing," Royal remembers, "and that they've got the wrong idea about Texas as it is today."

Adds Royal: "Rommie Loudd is a free and easy person. He had our confidence and we had his."

Of course, skin color has produced uneasy moments, too. When racial tension broke out at a midwest university a few years ago, the coach of a professional team in the area told Loudd that the problem was that "the niggers and the whites are just not getting along."

"What did you say?" Loudd responded. "The niggers and the whites? Is that a fact!"

When he was on the road for the Patriots, Loudd said that he could "smell" people who were uneasy about the color of his skin "ten blocks away." Nothing was ever said. It's just that when he walked into the executives' restaurant at another stadium, some people would stare a bit or, if he was at the bar, give him a little extra elbow room. Such gestures have never bothered Loudd, or at least he says they haven't. "After all," he explains, "it's that individual's problem, not mine. If he hasn't adjusted to the twentieth century yet, well, that's just too bad, baby."

But for all that outward composure, a close look at Rommie Loudd—both before and during his front-office career—reveals a strong ethnic awareness. Indeed, to an observer it appears that life for Loudd has always been a series of third-down situations: it's *his* team needing *his* block to spring the runner free. When he discusses having been the first black in the front office of pro football, there's pride in his voice. When he discusses becoming the first black to run a front office, there is determination there.

"I'm not just a man, I'm a black man. This is the truth of the society in which I live."

Much of this sense of awareness can perhaps be traced to a seemingly inconsequential event: the 1947 Rose Bowl game between UCLA and the University of Illinois. In that game, Buddy Young, a black man, ran around and through the UCLA defense all afternoon. He scored four touchdowns, and each time he scored, a boy glued to his radio at home in San Angelo wanted even more to follow in his footsteps.

To this day, Loudd isn't sure why that one game had such an effect on him. "I just know that I suddenly felt like this was my invitation. I saw football as the way to pull myself up in life."

The effect didn't wear off. After his sophomore year in high school in 1948, Loudd decided to leave home to live with an uncle in the Watts section of Los Angeles. There he felt he would have a better chance of getting into UCLA—and a Rose Bowl. (There were no relatives in Illinois.)

The summer before he left home, Loudd didn't tell his friends what he was planning to do. His high-school coach, Allie Thomas, remembers that Rommie waited on tables and did a number of odd jobs around town in order to earn enough for the trip west.

"His family didn't have any money," says Thomas, now the principal of black Shear Elementary School in San Angelo. "The boy felt that he had to do it all by himself."

Thomas also remembers that Rommie was a boy "who

had his mind set on something big. He wanted to be a great athlete. He wanted to do something that would make people proud of him."

In Los Angeles, life for the high-school student (Loudd lost a year's credit in the transfer and had to repeat his sophomore year) revolved around football. He had only one diversion, that is, if you can call the girl he was later to marry a diversion. He met his future wife the second day of classes at Thomas Jefferson High School. Betty Loudd likes to joke that then, as now, it was football first and his girl second.

Both in San Angelo and Los Angeles, Loudd was an outstanding high-school football player. In Texas, he was one of only two freshmen ever to start varsity on teams coached by Allie Thomas, whose career in high-school coaching spanned more than a decade. His sophomore year, Loudd made the Texas all-state team.

Loudd's final game for San Angelo was played against Denton High School in the quarterfinal round of the play-offs for the state championship. Loudd played the entire sixty minutes, as was his custom, holding down an end position on both offense and defense. Denton scored early for a 7-to-0 lead. But then Loudd hauled in a long pass for touchdown that cut the margin to 7 to 6. The extra point was missed, however, and that was the final score.

In California, Loudd had trouble making the squad his sophomore year. He found the caliber of play much better than what he was accustomed to in Texas. But by midseason, he had won a first-string job, which he kept throughout his junior and senior years. Both junior and senior year, Loudd was voted to the Los Angeles all-city team. After his senior year, he was inducted into the city's high-school hall of fame.

Also his senior year, Rommie was named to a high-school

all-American team. That honor entitled him to play in a special East-West all-star game in Tennessee. When the all-star committee requested his picture, Loudd willingly sent one in. But a funny thing happened on the way to the game: the committee never got around to sending Rommie his formal invitation to play. No one ever told him why, but he's convinced it's because he is black. "There were no black faces leaping out of the sports pages after the game," he says. "Two and two make four, right?"

Nevertheless, Rommie received more than two-dozen scholarship offers from colleges all over the country. One was from Tennessee State University, an all-black institution. Loudd figures that if he had stayed in Texas, he probably would have gone to a school like Tennessee State. "But having made my way from Texas all the way to California, I had to ask myself if I wanted to go back and start all over again. I decided I'd better go ahead and attend UCLA."

A full athletic scholarship to UCLA meant the end of working in a gas station on weekends and in a shirt factory after school. Throughout high school, Rommie Loudd never looked as short on money as Betty Loudd knew he was. In part, that may be because of the example set by his father, who always wore the latest-style suit, even if it was the only suit he owned at the time.

At UCLA, Loudd started to follow the example set by his mother, whose exploits as a dancer were legendary, at least around the Loudd household. Jazz was the man's passion. "Jazz is my culture," he says, "and people who play jazz represent my culture." He started by "fooling around with tape recorders," as he likes to put it. That in turn led to a major in communications.

To be sure, throughout college it was Loudd's intention to go on to play pro football. But being a practical man, he felt that when his playing days were over, he stood a

202

better chance in radio or television than in pro football. "A man has to prepare for what's open to him," Loudd says.

In addition, visions of Hollywood danced in his head following the part in "The Ten Commandments." Despite the mud episode, a friend later arranged a screen test for a part in another movie, "Band of Angels," starring Clark Gable. The way Loudd likes to tell it, there was a battle for the job between him and another young and aspiring actor named Sidney Poitier. For more than a month, our man was tutored in how to walk and talk properly. But in the end, Poitier got the part because "he had a bit more experience," according to Loudd.

Be that as it may, Loudd likes to imagine that today he would be "rolling in the chips" if only he had hung around Hollywood waiting for his big break. What done him in, he says with a slight bit of tongue-in-cheek, were those rave reviews he received on the sports pages.

Such reviews were indeed rave. Sophomore year, Loudd was one of only a handful of sophomores to start for UCLA. Senior year, his play at end and linebacker earned him all-American recognition from at least one major publication, *Look* magazine.

At that time, UCLA was primarily a running team, according to Loudd. "If it was third down and 3 yards to go, you knew that we were going to run off tackle with a double-team block by the strong end and tackle." Loudd was that strong end, which meant that he spent most of Saturday afternoon with his head and shoulders buried in some opponent's stomach.

Also at that time UCLA was coached by a man named Red Sanders, who "molded me and everyone else who came into contact with him," says Loudd. The key to Sanders's football philosophy was execution. His teams played fundamental football, but they played it flawlessly, Loudd says.

Execution now is the key to Loudd's football philosophy as well. "When I look at a player today, I don't watch all the fancy moves. I look to see how he blocks and tackles, how he handles the fundamentals."

He adds, "It's always your technique that counts."

The boy from San Angelo wound up playing in not one but two Rose Bowls. The first one in 1953 was a Buddy Young special, with Loudd playing well on both offense and defense in a UCLA win over Ohio State. Thoughts of Buddy Young notwithstanding, UCLA lost the second game, 17 to 14, when the place kicker for Michigan State booted a field goal with less than a minute to play.

"Damn game," Loudd mutters when he thinks back to that game.

Ethnic concerns played a role in choosing which league Loudd would play in after graduation from UCLA. Both the NFL and the Canadian Football League wanted him. Loudd chose the Vancouver Lions over the San Francisco 49ers because, "I felt that most NFL teams had quota systems for black players. I never said so openly, but you could see that blacks never roomed with whites."

There were other concerns, it should be noted, not the least of which was money. In addition, as part of the Lions' deal, Loudd was offered a job as a disk jockey on a local radio station.

Loudd's first year in Vancouver was one to remember. Not only was he named to the all-league team, he was voted one of the city's ten best-dressed men *and* the best new broadcaster in the Vancouver area. (Both mother and father had set a good example for their boy.)

The second year was one to forget. Vancouver listeners still tuned in his hour-long weekend jazz show, "Long Cool." But injuries forced him to the sidelines and, after the 1957 season, Vancouver decided to release their former all-star.

204

Quota system or no quota system, Loudd tried out with the Chicago Bears in 1958. But just as he seemed on the verge of making the team, another injury sidelined him for the entire season.

In 1959, Loudd's playing career reached its nadir when he signed with the Kitchener Dutchmen, a minor-league operation just outside Toronto. It might have ended there, too, except that the following year the American Football League burst onto the scene.

The AFL meant a second chance for Loudd and hundreds of other borderline players, many of whom had been previously cut by NFL teams and were now in a different line of work or toiling on some minor-league team like Kitchener. Some 350 candidates reported to the Boston Patriots' first preseason camp in 1960; the Los Angeles Chargers looked at more than 250, including Loudd.

He signed with the Chargers, who were hungry for experienced ball players, and he helped L.A. to a 10-and-4 season record and the 1960 Western Division championship. As with Kitchener, the pay wasn't so hot. For playing and losing to the Houston Oilers in the first AFL title game, Loudd earned only $1,700—compared to the $8,500 earned by each Washington Redskin for losing to Miami in the 1973 Super Bowl. (The Oilers had a "veteran" quarterback by the name of Blanda who threw an 88-yard touchdown pass to Billy Cannon of Louisiana State University for the score that put the game on ice.)

It was with the Chargers that Loudd got his first taste of the front office. It wasn't a classy job, but he needed the money. For a flat $125 a week, he went around to all the local bars, restaurants and civic associations trying to peddle Charger season tickets. He succeeded, to the tune of about $10,000 in sales.

Also in 1960, Loudd got his first taste of coaching. He helped Charger Head Coach Sid Gillman conduct a tryout camp for some 200 dishwashers and other would-be all-pro performers. (Out of that 200, the Chargers did sign two or three men, one of whom—cornerback Dick Harris —actually made the all-league squad in both 1960 and 1961.)

In addition, the pride of the Vancouver airwaves made his U.S. comeback that year with a jazz program on radio station KCBA in Los Angeles.

But ticket sales notwithstanding, the Chargers gave the now-aging Loudd his unconditional release after the 1960 season. It was at this point that Loudd first seriously considered settling down to the career in radio for which he had prepared. But he couldn't—at least not then—because of the rude send-off he had received from the Chargers. He decided to pull up roots and move east when the Patriots gave him one more chance to play that following year.

The Patriots signed Loudd as a free agent, but before the end of training camp he was established as the starting weakside linebacker. The year before Loudd's arrival, the Patriots suffered through a 5-and-9 season, finishing last in the Eastern Division. With Loudd, and also a quarterback named Vito (Babe) Parilli, the Patriots turned things around in 1961, finishing in second place with a record of 9 wins, 4 losses and a tie.

Loudd wasn't all-pro in Boston, but he was one of the most respected linebackers in the league. "He didn't mind sticking his head into a guy," remembers Houston Antwine, who played defensive tackle for the Patriots from 1961 to 1971. "You knew that if some runner tried to go around Rommie, Rommie would ding him good."

Jim Lee Hunt, who played defensive end in front of Loudd, says that he was one of the best blitzing linebackers in the league, especially when it was time to take revenge on the Chargers. "We always had a ball with the Charg-

206

ers," says Hunt. "I'd curl my man to the outside and Rommie would come storming up the middle blowing everyone out of his way. Once it got so bad that Hadl [Charger quarterback John Hadl] started yelling at his own players, 'Can't you keep that guy off my neck?' " (Against the Chargers, the 1961 Patriots set an all-time team record for fewest yards allowed rushing in one game. The number: 2.)

The Patriots' defense was even better in 1962 when rookie linebacking-sensation Nick Buoniconti joined Loudd & Co. and the Patriots set a team record for fewest first downs allowed in one season—220. For the second year in a row, Boston's record was 9 and 4 and 1, good for a second-place finish behind Houston. ("Every time we went to Texas we got our brains beat out," Hunt recalls.)

But by 1962, the two-time pink-slip veteran was already preparing for retirement, though not for a career in the front office. Indeed, Loudd had a finger in several different pies. He was a sports announcer for radio station WILD in Boston. He ran a private nightclub in the city called the Professional Businessman's Club. (Hunt: "Best damn after-hours club in Boston.") He even had an interest in an outfit called Mother Macree's Goose Grease Co. (Goose grease, in case you're not a soul brother, is a lotion or linament used extensively in the black community to cure a multitude of infirmities.)

And in 1963, the inevitable happened: Loudd was beaten out of his job by a younger player. But before he had time to start feeling sorry for himself, a prominent baking company was knocking on his door asking for help in dealing with certain problems the firm was having with the black community in Boston.

It seems that a militant black group had declared a boycott against Continental Baking Co. because of alleged discrimination in hiring. Allied with a group of both black and white Protestant ministers, the group picketed stores in the Roxbury-Dorchester section of Boston in an effort to cut into Continental's sales.

Loudd was denounced by several black protesters when he agreed to help Continental. But in the end, he was responsible for certain changes in the corporation's hiring procedures.

Loudd rode the circuit with Continental bread salesmen for more than a month, talking to store owners in the same way he later talked to Texas Coach Darrel Royal. Eventually, he helped bring both sides to a meeting where a formal cease-fire agreement was signed. Afterward, Loudd persuaded Continental officials to place want ads in the local black newspaper as well as the *Boston Globe*, and also to work with the ministerial group in placing more blacks on the job with Continental.

After sitting out of football for a year, Loudd's neighbor provided the impetus for his return with the Chelsea Sweepers. Betty Loudd says that her husband could fit football into his hectic business schedule because, come Saturday morning, it's Mrs. Loudd, not Mr. Loudd, who does such household chores as fixing the kitchen sink and putting up the screens. ("He's all thumbs," she confides.)

It didn't take long for the urge to stick it to some running back to return to Loudd. "I guess that once you've played, you never want to quit," he says. It was after the Sweepers beat the Jersey Giants for their second consecutive Atlantic Coast football championship that Loudd, encouraged by some friends, decided to pay a call on Coach Holovak.

"My original goal was to be a head coach," he says, "and I wanted Holovak to recommend me for a job with the Chicago Bears." Loudd says that the offer from the Patriots came as a complete surprise. "I never asked for their job, but it didn't take me long to accept it."

A year later, Loudd was just as surprised when Holovak asked if he wanted to become player-personnel director. "It hit me so quick," he says, "that I needed two days to think it over." During that time, Loudd decided that "pro football is much more than coaching. It's a whole new business that very few people understand."

Mother Macree had to move over when Loudd plunged into the job of revamping the Patriots' college-scouting system. (There was, however, still time for some color broadcasts of football games on TV.) For the first time in the Patriots' six-year existence, scouting operations were run not out of the personnel director's living room, but out of team headquarters in Boston.

Moving operations to Boston did pose one problem. Because there was no parking space around the Patriots' offices in Fenway Park, Loudd estimates that he paid about $500 in parking fines before the team moved to its new headquarters at Schaefer Stadium in Foxboro, Massachusetts, in 1971.

But it was a small price for Loudd to pay to be able to show off his managerial skills. He hit his peak as player-personnel director in 1969 when, without head coach or general manager, the Patriots relied on Loudd and Loudd's system to carry them through the draft. He responded with three top draft choices who all made the team as starters their first year.

When Upton Bell, Jr., became the Patriots' general manager early in 1971, one of his first moves was to promote Loudd to director of pro personnel, a new position in the organization. It was a promotion because of Bell's theory of building a winning football team, which stipulated that it is better to build via the trade than via the draft. Loudd's job was to keep close check on all active players in the NFL.

Loudd had a small, white-walled office on the second

floor of the administrative building at one end of Schaefer Stadium. Some 50 feet away was the club's executive dining room where season-ticket holders can hobnob with one another for just another $2,000 per season. While trotting horses raced the clock on the track of Schaefer Raceway behind the stadium, Loudd raced that same clock trying to cram nine hours of work into an eight-hour workday.

One entire wall was lined with shelves. One shelf housed a dozen or so loose-leaf notebooks containing thousands of pages of information on every player currently active in the NFL, many from the time they were sophomores in college. Other shelves held dozens of reels of videotape of old NFL games. On the floor in front of his desk sat a videotape machine which, when set up, allowed a scout to view the same game over and over that millions of television viewers saw, say, six months ago.

Next to his desk sat a beat-up brown leather briefcase with a sticker affixed that read: "Join the Patriots' revolution." Football magazines were strewn everywhere. The secretary in the outer office was busy answering the telephone. On one day, the calls ranged from an ex-player trying to obtain tickets to an upcoming game, to a scout passing on information that Loudd had requested on a player, to the girl friend of a secretary in the firm who wanted to tell Loudd about this great undiscovered player. (Never missing a trick, Loudd wrote down the player's name, saying, "Women often are your best source of information.")

In order to fully understand the typical work week of a director of pro personnel it's best to start the week on Wednesday morning. Loudd began every Wednesday with a conference with his secretary to set up travel arrangements for the coming weekend. He attended a game on both Sunday afternoon and Monday night, and often there were side trips to renew old—and profitable—friendships. After that, it was time to struggle with the expense account for the prior week. As director of pro personnel, Loudd's annual budget came to about $50,000, more than what most other clubs spend on scouting of established players.

Loudd did many of his own secretarial chores. That's because he found a rapid turnover in secretaries as well as general managers. Most, it seemed, were single girls who came seeking the excitement of being around pro football and either ran off to get married or ran off because they were disappointed.

After making ends meet, Loudd was likely to call Wilbur Harrison, his only full-time scout who worked the West Coast, and discover what Wilbur was doing the coming weekend. Then it was time to stop in at the Mill Falls Restaurant in Newton Upper Falls, Massachusetts, some fifteen miles from the stadium.

Loudd still owns the restaurant even though he's now in Florida. Originally, he was only a silent partner in the venture. But when the establishment plunged into debt a few years ago, Loudd bought out the other partners and, after weeks of burning the midnight oil, managed to straighten things out to the satisfaction of his many creditors.

On Thursday there was a meeting with club president Billy Sullivan or with the general manager or head coach. Thursday was the lightest day for Loudd; he often found time to view films of games from the week before.

Loudd never saw his own team play on Sunday. But before he took off on assignment, he would check out one of his usually reliable "underground" sources: the night clerk at the nearby Marriott Hotel. The clerk was valuable because when visiting teams come to Foxboro, most stay at the Marriott, and a good night clerk can tell you who carouses with whom, when and at what time. "That told me a lot about the harmony in a ball club," says Loudd.

Despite this hectic schedule, it was the moments of supposed relaxation on an airplane that were (and still are) the most trying. "When you're black, weigh 230 pounds and stand 6 feet 2 inches, somebody is going to ask you if you play football," says Loudd with a sigh.

Then, as now, he will try to do some paper work on the flight. But often the passenger asking the question won't get the hint that he just doesn't want to talk football. In that case, he will pull out the headphones, turn on some music and look out the window. (If it isn't a music flight, he may doze off for a few minutes.)

Loudd estimates that with the Patriots he traveled about 150,000 miles in a year's time. While he declines to disclose what his own salary was, he estimates that men in similar scouting jobs earn somewhere between $20,000 and $25,000 a year. If you work that out by the hour, it might fall below the government's minimum wage. "Time was meaningless in a job like that. It was every day of every week of every month of the year."

And Loudd loved every moment of it. Indeed, while he was lucky to steal two weeks of vacation a year, his wife, Betty, says that after three or four days in the same place Rommie would get so restless that he had to go back to work. (He still does.)

After traveling all day Friday, Loudd would check into a motel and immediately turn on his cassette recorder. (The tape is jazz, of course.) To avoid a repetition of the plane incident, Loudd probably skipped going out to dinner and instead had a steak in his room.

After dinner, the workday began. In Detroit, he knew an ex-player who was close to the Lions. In Minnesota, he knew a couple of girls who had dated a number of Viking players. In another city which he declines to identify, Loudd knew some people in the training room who could tell him about the physical condition of that particular team.

212

In Atlanta, there was this sportswriter who always had his ear to the door. "Most pro teams invite newspaper writers to look at films of the game," says Loudd, "So I would call this guy up and ask how did so-and-so look on the film."

In St. Louis, Loudd knew a professional woman who was in business with one of the Cardinal players. He met her through a mutual friend when she was in the Boston area and had dinner at Loudd's restaurant. "This woman wasn't going to be a bed thing for the players," Loudd says. "But by being around them and listening to what they have to say, she learned a lot about their problems, whether it was race relations, lack of product endorsement or too-little playing time."

In another city, Loudd was friends with the ex-wife of a player who liked to keep close tabs on all her old friends. Loudd says she usually called him about once a week after a game. When she hung up, Loudd knew when the next alimony payment was due and things like that. "She could tell you who was working hard and who the players happened to be down on at the time.

"Some women," he cautions, "are just gossipers. But others could tell you if the guy was an excessive drinker or if he was into dope. Some women knew the nightspots the boys enjoy. If I saw one of them, I might ask her what kind of a guy is so-and-so. And she'd tell me that she thinks his ego is too inflated or that he's not the type of guy she'd want her mother to spend much time with."

Loudd adds: "My underground was very important in terms of catching some guy off-color. Say I trade for you and, on the surface, you're a great ball player. But after I've got you, I find out that you're hard to get along with. It was my job to know beforehand what kind of guy you are."

Loudd's behind-the-scenes action got him into trouble only once in Boston. It seems that during the grand jury investigations into professional football held in Cleveland in 1971, Loudd was subpoenaed to testify in connection with a statement he allegedly made to another player. While grand jury investigations are strictly confidential affairs, Loudd says that this player accused him of having told him that he had been blackballed from pro football.

"I remember this kid getting hurt," says Loudd. "Later on, he called me for a tryout and I asked him about the injury. At that point he went to this investigating committee and told them that I said he had been blackballed from pro football."

Was he?

"Well," says Loudd, pausing after the word. "He wasn't blackballed by this ball club. But I certainly wouldn't have recommended him as a player knowing that he hadn't fully recovered from that injury."

Loudd's underground also was important because any face-to-face contact Loudd had with players on other teams was risky. It was risky because of the league rule which makes it illegal intentionally to "tamper, negotiate with, or make an offer to a player on the active, reserve or selection list of another team." In such cases—the league officials say there are several each year—the offending team can lose both money and a top draft choice the way Miami did when it signed Don Shula from the Baltimore Colts.

Still, Loudd asserts that he has never had much use for that or any other rule. "Let me tell you how I feel about rules," he says with uncharacteristic emotion. "Rules don't mean a thing to me because none of the rules that have ever been made have ever favored me, including the Declaration of Independence. You can always get around the rules. I must have a Ph.D. in getting around the rules."

Understandably, Loudd declines to illustrate his point.

But there was one trade he describes which, though not illegal, is not the kind of thing that makes league officials give out gold stars.

This trade brought tight end Bob Windsor from the San Francisco 49ers. It was no secret that Windsor wanted to be traded. Playing behind all-pro tight end Ted Kwalick, Windsor saw most of every game from the bench. He thought he deserved better, and he told the local sportswriters exactly that.

Knowing this, Loudd's assistant approached Windsor after the Pro Bowl game in January, 1972, and engaged him in a little friendly conversation, the exact wording of which went unrecorded. A point was made, however, and three months later Windsor was a Patriot.

Underground investigation kept Loudd busy right up until game time. (Before he was involved in an automobile accident, he used to keep his head clear by starting off the day with some sixty push-ups and fifty sit-ups, exercises he hopes soon to resume.) Loudd viewed each game from the stadium press box. He was armed with his cassette tape recorder because he found that he couldn't write and follow the action at the same time.

There was a lot to follow. Ideally, Loudd was supposed to watch every man on both teams and, by the final gun, be able to grade all of them in each of the thirty different categories on his player performance cards. That's next to impossible, but Loudd and the other scouts have a system where they can view most of them during sixty minutes of action.

For example, he first focused on the center and the middle linebacker because, pass or run, "they will take you to the ball 90 percent of the time." If the play is, say, a run up the middle, "I watched how the linebacker worked with his defensive tackles." If the tackles aren't doing their job, "then the two offensive guards are probably doing theirs."

After the game, Loudd took out his category cards and updated the grade of a player in areas where he felt that player had gotten either better or worse since the last time he was graded. Most categories would refer to basic physical ability. Defensive linemen were watched closely on how fast they get off the snap and how effectively they use their hands to rush past offensive linemen. Linebackers were rated especially on their ability to move laterally and to drop back quickly on pass coverage. (Grades ranged from a high of 1 to a low of 9.)

The card for a quarterback stressed mental ability as much as physical prowess. Besides being graded for setting up quickly to pass and staying in the pocket under pressure, the quarterback was judged closely on such things as courage, leadership and poise.

Loudd defined poise as "grace under pressure." He considers the Redskins' Sonny Jurgensen a study in poise. "It may be third down and one to go," Loudd explains, "and everyone in the stadium will be expecting a run. But Sonny will fake the dive and throw for a touchdown." A poised quarterback like Jurgensen "will beat you in the final sixty seconds by throwing a touchdown from his own end zone."

Joe Namath of the New York Jets is a man who Loudd feels "displays a tremendous amount of courage." Says Loudd: "Joe is always under pressure and playing in pain. One proper hit and his career is finished. Yet, he stands right up there willing to take his chances. I've seen guys really whack him and he never complains."

By the time Loudd would trudge home some time on Tuesday, he looked to his wife, Betty, like something the cat dragged in. "He could sleep for fifteen hours straight," she says in amazement. "Sometimes I wondered if he was ever going to come to."

216

But once he did, Betty says she couldn't wait to get him out of the house and back to work. "He's such a nuisance when he's awake," she says only half in jest. "He's always wanting something—usually food."

Betty Loudd says it has been tough sometimes being married to a front-office executive. Mostly, it's the little things that get to her. For instance, she can't buy meat in town without having the butcher chew her ear off for forty-five minutes about how some team is doing and what he thinks her husband ought to do. Then there was the neighbor who, though only an acquaintance, came to the house in Boston six times in search of 50-yard-line seats to a home game against the Redskins. (Gratis, of course.)

But probably what bugged Betty Loudd most over the years was never being able to park in the parking space with her name on it outside Schaefer Stadium. "I went to every game for two years, and I think that even if I had gotten there at 6 A.M. somebody would already have parked in my space."

What bugged her husband most in Boston was the Patriots' inability to win football games. "I worked my ass off around there for eight years and we didn't win a championship." (In their only title-game appearance in 1963, the year after Loudd's retirement as a player, the Patriots were slugged, 51 to 10, by the Chargers.)

"I'm a poor loser," he says. "I take it very personally. We were just never able to get all the wheels rolling at the same time. When I left, I felt that we had one of the better quarterbacks in the league [Jim Plunkett] and one of the better running backs [Carl Garrett]. We have it, but we still couldn't win."

To be sure, the Patriots tried. In Loudd's first year as director of pro personnel, the club signed five free agents, picked up four more players in trades and claimed eight men off the waiver list. Of those seventeen players, six

217

made the team, including Plunkett's former Stanford team-mate Randy Vataha, a free agent who went on to lead the American Football Conference in receiving during 1971.

"I don't know what more we could have done," he says.

The first thing Loudd did before recommending any player to the Patriots' management was read his "bible" thoroughly. In this instance, that meant the player personnel book containing, among other things, every player's height, weight, age, time in school ("You may not always remember a guy's name, but you always remember his school"), draft number (not too important now) and speed running a 40-yard sprint.

Also in The Book were the grades earned by each player as well as a composite score.

Next, he scanned charts detailing such things as players added and deleted weekly from rosters, players injured (both by week and by team for an entire season) and length of time missed due to an injury. From there, he perused the player's newspaper clippings that had been accumulated from all around the country. Finally, he rolled the tapes of a few of the player's more recent games.

All this, Loudd contends, had only limited usefulness. "Heck, I could see how good a man is just by watching him play. I wanted to know *everything* about him."

Enter those underground sources.

A good example of the underground in action was the 1972 preseason trade that sent defensive end Fred Dryer to the Los Angeles Rams for defensive tackle Rick Cash. Cash, a four-year veteran from Northeast Missouri College, had missed the entire 1971 season with a broken leg. The question Loudd wanted answered was whether that leg was healed completely.

He sent an associate to find out. The associate, in turn, looked up a friend in the heart of the Rams' organization

218

who told him that Cash's leg must be all right because he was last seen playing a strenuous game of basketball. A simple but valuable piece of information for Loudd because the Patriots then traded for Cash, who led all defensive linemen on the club in 1972 in both tackles and assists. (His defensive teammates also elected him their captain.)

Cash says he never knew about Loudd's behind-the-scenes digging. The same thing goes for Bob Reynolds, a ten-year veteran whom the Patriots claimed off the waiver list during the 1972 exhibition season.

Reynolds's career with the Cardinals came to an abrupt end one night when he and an assistant coach exchanged words following a holding penalty against Reynolds which hurt the Cards in an exhibition game. Indeed, Cardinal Head Coach Bob Holloway had to separate the two men, according to Reynolds. "I sort of told the assistant coach what he could do with everything," Reynolds explains.

The next day, the Cardinals put Reynolds on waivers. Immediately, Loudd placed a call to his friend, the professional woman, who just happened to be Reynolds's partner in a publication called *Proud* magazine. "She told me that Bob's attitude was good," Loudd recalls, "and that whatever happened wasn't his fault." The Patriots then claimed Reynolds, who went on to become the team's starting left-offensive tackle.

All this digging, however, didn't impress NFL owners when it came time to choose expansion teams. There were a number of reasons why Loudd failed in his attempt. For one thing, the civic stadium in Orlando seats only about 20,000, far below what's needed for an NFL team. Moreover, according to Bill Clark, a Loudd supporter and sports editor of the Orlando *Sentinel-Star*, civic officials gave only lip service to their support of Loudd and a team in Orlando.

"If they [the civic leaders] had really beat the bush, we could have expanded the size of that stadium. We had the plans. But no one wanted to go out and sell people on the idea."

According to Clark, Loudd did his best to bring a team to the home of Walt Disney World. "He had 27,000 season-ticket pledges and a booster club with a membership of 1,000."

Although the stadium problem certainly could not be overlooked, in a way it's a shame the NFL couldn't find a place for Loudd. Loudd had a dream that really is quite simple:

"We've got to stop patting players on the back. We've got to start helping them with their financial planning. We've got to integrate the players into the community. We've got to get the agents out of sport before they destroy the game. I know one agent who built a home with a player's money and then sold the house to the player. There's too much distrust today between management and players. Changes must be made."

A nice thought. A thought that would go a long way toward securing the future of pro football.

But for now, that dream has been deferred.

In May, 1974, however, another of Rommie Loudd's dreams did come true—although not in the way he thought it would. Loudd and his Orlando group were awarded a franchise in Gary Davidson's rival World Football League. Thus, like Lamar Hunt and Tony Morabito before him, Loudd was forced to circumvent the NFL "lodge" to make it into pro football. It makes you wonder.

8

Everything's Up to Date in Kansas City

Jack Steadman
Executive Vice President-General Manager
The Kansas City Chiefs

JACK STEADMAN was fed up.

After eight years in the accounting department at Hunt Oil Company in Dallas, he was, in his opinion, "nothing more than pencil on an adding machine."

An ambitious man, Jack thought his work spoke for itself. After all, for the past two years he had done extra accounting work for Herbert Hunt, one of five sons of Hunt Oil President H. L. Hunt, the octogenarian whom even J. Paul Getty considers one of the world's richest men.

But for all that work, all Jack felt he had gotten in return was grief, especially from his supervisor, the comptroller, who didn't cotton to Jack's reporting directly to someone in the company other than him—and a Hunt at that.

The first verbal tussle between the comptroller and Jack was only a six-round prelim fought behind closed doors one night after everyone else had gone home. But it set the stage for the main event to come. As was his custom, Jack was working late that night on Herbert's books. According to Jack, the comptroller suddenly called him into

221

his office and started chewing him out for staying late—a ploy, his boss was certain, designed to wring overtime pay out of Hunt Oil.

Jack pleaded innocent, but words were exchanged and a return match guaranteed. Some 150 accountants, secretaries and clerks witnessed the short, but heated, second encounter, fought when Jack was late submitting some vouchers because Herbert wanted something else done right away. First, Jack's boss caught Jack off guard at his desk and, before Jack could get to his feet, dressed him down in a loud voice for messing up the vouchers. Then, as the supervisor turned away the apparent winner, Jack counterpunched, demanding they both go to Herbert's office to find out Jack's side of the story. The comptroller refused, at which point Jack hollered at him, "You're too chicken to go." Immediately, the comptroller headed for his supervisor's office to see about getting this Steadman guy fired for insubordination.

Five minutes later, Jack's phone rang. It was the comptroller's boss, and Jack remembers, "I kind of walked out of the accounting department saying it was nice knowing you all." But under pressure, Jack didn't flinch. "I told him that if the comptroller doesn't understand what I'm doing, he's out of contact with the accounting department. But in any event, he is not going to dress me down in front of 150 of my associates without a confrontation."

Which, if the truth be told, may be what Jack wanted to have happen. Being an accountant, he certainly could put two and two together and realize that what Herbert Hunt thought of him meant a lot more than what the comptroller thought. "I had been there quite a long time and was wondering if I was ever going to get ahead. Working for Herbert, I expected recognition that I had some ability beyond just the day-to-day accounting that was expected of me."

It worked, though for a couple of weeks Jack's wife, Martha, was so uncertain about her husband's future that she bought groceries for their three young children on a day-to-day basis. But before long, Jack was promoted, thanks in large part to a solid recommendation by Herbert Hunt. He was put in charge of restructuring the accounting operations of a Hunt Oil subsidiary, Penrod Drilling Co., and he did so solid a job that he came to the attention of another Hunt offspring, Lamar, who besides being a partner in Penrod, was busily engaged at the time in the problems of a new professional football league—the AFL.

As the comptroller incident illustrates, Jack Steadman's strength is knowing when and where to put the needle to get the job done. With the comptroller it hurt. But today as Executive Vice President and General Manager of the Kansas City Chiefs, Steadman's intention sometimes is only to prick the conscience of local civic leaders who question Jack's elaborate—and expensive—plans to make Kansas City a major-league sports town. Whatever the needle's effect, "Jack doesn't know the meaning of the word 'can't,'" says boss Hunt, the smile on his face an indication of his satisfaction with his lieutenant.

Which is not to say Jack didn't know the meaning of the word "won't." Indeed, for all that positive thinking, Jack wasn't sure back in 1960 whether he really wanted to tackle the general manager's job. True, he was a rabid fan. If you don't believe it, just ask Martha's mother, who arrived in Dallas the Saturday before her daughter's wedding only to find nobody there to greet her. For several hours she waited outside the door of Martha's apartment while the prospective bride and groom watched a Notre Dame-Southern Methodist football game. "You know," Jack now says, "I don't think she's ever forgiven me for that."

But the fact is Jack Steadman was not and is not cut

from the same cloth as other general managers. He's not an ex-player like Jim Finks of the Vikings or Don Klosterman of the Los Angeles Rams. Nor is he the beneficiary of nepotism like Dan Rooney of the Pittsburgh Steelers or George Halas, Jr., of the Chicago Bears.

At the same time, he is not part of the growing trend toward a combination head coach-general manager, like George Allen of the Washington Redskins or Dan Devine of the Green Bay Packers. Of all the general managers in pro football today, probably only Dick Gordon of the New Orleans Saints comes from a background more foreign to the sport than Steadman's. Gordon is a former astronaut.

With the Kansas City Chiefs, as he was with Hunt Oil, Jack Steadman is a businessman. While Chiefs' Head Coach Hank Stram has complete authority over the game on the field, Steadman, a businessman rather than a football man, is in charge of the game off the field. It is a unique setup, and one that has helped the Chiefs to one of the strongest balance sheets in the league, one of the newest and largest stadiums in the league and one of the most corporate-minded front offices in the league, exemplary right down to the thick red carpeting in the posh executive offices.

Such a setup also makes the Chiefs unpopular in certain NFL circles. To be sure, the football fraternity is too closely knit for anyone to go on record against another club. But it is known that the Chiefs' sport-is-business approach to football is frowned upon by many of the more traditionally minded clubs. Says Steadman: "Few clubs operate as a business. What most people in the league fail to understand is that everything we do really relates to financial matters. We've made proposals at league meetings relating to the financial operations of the game." But, he adds, ideas such as cutting back on the number of players a team can carry have gone over with a dull thud. (A rules change in 1973 in effect raised the player limit.)

The Steadman approach to professional football is in the best General Motors and IBM tradition. The name of his game is expansion, expansion through diversification. Ideally, he would some day like to see Hunt's K.C. operations be a consortium of affiliated companies all reporting ultimately to Hunt. At this point, the Chiefs are one of two major Lamar Hunt enterprises in Kansas City, the other being a family recreation park called Worlds of Fun. In addition to the team and the park, Jack also runs for the Chiefs a public restaurant and banquet center known as Arrowhead Inn and located in the stadium.

Says Steadman: "Pro football has become big business, and today the demands of any big business require management leadership that only businessmen with a background of training and experience in accounting, tax, legal and financial matters can give. We feel we are creating a new mold for football organizations of the future. We have developed an organization that can take advantage of pro football's growth potential in today's market."

Unlike many in pro football who steadfastly believe their sport will always capture the public's fancy, Steadman also believes "we must protect ourselves for days when pro football might not be as popular as it is today. Business," he says, "is hills and valleys and the best way to protect yourself against valleys is to be diversified." (Of course, as Leonard Tose can tell you, diversification isn't always the answer. A couple of years ago Tose, owner of the Philadelphia Eagles, brought to market something he called Eagle soda. It laid an Eagle-sized egg.)

Jack's hills-and-valleys analogy is a reflection of the stormy early days he spent with Lamar Hunt and his embryonic American Football League. As most everyone may know, Hunt founded that league after he was thwarted in attempts to obtain an NFL franchise for his hometown, Dallas. This was 1959; Hunt was only twenty-six years old. No sooner had the plans for the new league been announced than the old league declared war against it.

The NFL dropped several bombs, among them threatened expansion teams in Dallas and Houston, both important AFL cities. When that didn't work, the NFL offered these franchises to Hunt and one other AFL owner, providing the new league was disbanded. When that also didn't work, the NFL did award a franchise to a group from Minneapolis that previously was ready to play in the new league.

But Hunt and his league fought back with a not-so-secret weapon: money. There is a story, often told and often denied by Lamar, about the reporter who once told his father:

"Mr. Hunt, your son is going to lose $1 million a year on that new league."

To which Papa replied: "Well, at that rate, he'll be finished in about 150 years."

The figure of a million, however, isn't as farfetched as it sounds. Bud Adams, owner of the Houston Oilers, once told a sportswriter that he expected to lose about $500,000 in his first season but instead lost $750,000. Not that Adams, who owns an oil company, and several of the other owners couldn't afford it.

Still, it is safe to say that in the heat of battle, these nouveau owners sometimes forgot to read the right side of the menu. Hunt remembers a game in Los Angeles between his Texans and the Chargers of Barron Hilton, son of hotel czar Conrad Hilton. Without warning, Conrad showed up in the middle of the second quarter and, while son Barron was screaming about the action on the field, informed his offspring that he had just closed a $42 million deal for the Hawaiian Hilton.

226

"Jeez Christ, Dad," Barron turned to him and said, "it's third and 12!"

Enter Steadman, the accountant, who remembers that "all of a sudden there were new people coming into Lamar's organization who had heard about the Hunt millions and were spending money right and left. It started with thousands, jumped to tens of thousands, then to hundreds of thousands and finally into the millions. It was obvious that the business itself needed to be run on a planned and budgetary basis."

Still, Jack didn't want that challenge. "I was moving into management [at Hunt Oil] and things were looking really good. The thought of going into football, well, I didn't really relish it. Like everyone else, I was reading the newspapers and had the feeling that Lamar was in a death struggle with the Cowboys. Remember I had access to the financial information and, frankly, I was wondering how he could continue to lose money."

The problem, as Steadman knew, wasn't that the well would run dry, but rather that the tax bite just might force Lamar to cut back on his oil operations—the bread-and-butter business. Hunt's football team is a subchapter S corporation for tax purposes. Such a corporation can be owned by one to ten individuals (in this case one), and its operations are included on the individuals' personal income tax returns. For a period of five consecutive years, any losses incurred in running such a corporation can be used to offset gains from the individuals' other business holdings. But after that, the loss can be disallowed. What's more, the IRS can go back and disallow losses from the five previous years.

Bit by bit, however, Jack was drawn into pro football. His first task was to organize basic accounting procedures for the Hunt franchise. Usually, this job would fall to the general manager. But at that point in time, the Dallas

Texans' GM was a businessman who, according to both Jack and Hunt, was long on salesmanship but short on accounting.

The more Jack saw, the more he felt that the concept of cost control was completely foreign to the Texans. Many questions were obvious, such as why was the club buying sporting goods without bids from an outfit in Denton, Texas, when there were four reputable firms right there in Dallas? And why had the club paid more than $100,000 for a direct-mail advertising campaign when logically it semed as though $25,000 worth of newspaper advertising could produce the same results?

Never a man to hide his thoughts, Jack let Lamar know that, in his opinion, the Texans were wasting a heck of a lot of money. Lamar took a closer look, agreed, and offered Jack the GM position. On the surface, it looked like a good deal: more money and a guarantee that if the Texans folded, Jack could have his old job back at Hunt Oil.

But there was another, more personal, problem to cope with. If Jack moved into pro football, he would have to give up his long-standing position as director of the choir in his church. Now, for most people, that probably wouldn't be much of a problem. But for Jack, who says that on several occasions he almost left Hunt Oil to study religious music, it was.

"I talked with my minister and he really was the key to my decision. He said, 'Jack, as I see it, in church you can give the testimony of your life to members of the congregation, while in football you can do the same thing for a great many more people.'"

Today, like many people, Jack is reluctant to talk publicly about his religious beliefs. Still it is important to note the role religion has played in his life. Jack's mother was involved in all church programs and his father was a

228

deacon in the American Baptist Church located across the street from their home in Warrenville, Illinois, a small farm town about 30 miles outside of Chicago. Jack's religious training was strenuous, so strenuous in fact that about the time his family moved to Dallas he began to rebel against both his family and his faith.

"I think everybody goes through a period of life like I did," he says. "I was about fifteen when we moved and I was trying to find myself. I guess sometimes the only way you can find things is to come to a crisis and fight your way out of it."

It was a real struggle, though, and before it was over Jack spent time running with a street gang in Dallas. His gang was made up of members of his high school football team, and one time they passed the word that if any members of the Lakeland Rats (another local gang) wanted to test them, the welcome mat was out.

"See these two teeth," Jack says today, pointing to two up front on the upper level. "A Rat did that. He hit them with his fist and a dentist had to wire them. I still have them but they're sure not straight."

It wasn't until Jack started college at Baylor University that he, in his own words, "placed myself for the first time in proper perspective with God and things." This process started when Jack attended some prayer meetings at night with classmates on the Baylor campus.

But perhaps more than from religion, Jack's change resulted from the girl sitting next to his mother in the church choir that following summer. Her name was Martha and, for Jack at least, "there was a very strong attraction." Unfortunately for him, Martha knew of his reputation. ("I guess it wasn't very good then," he now says sheepishly.) Even so, he was determined to give it a try, so he gritted his teeth and headed for a church youth-group

229

outing the following Friday night. "It so happened," Jack says, "that Martha didn't bring her steady boyfriend that night. So she and I wound up playing miniature golf, swimming and"—somewhat to his amazement—"just having good, wholesome kids' fun."

Overnight Jack became what is commonly known as a square. He tried his hand at choir directing and helped organize youth religious revivals. After he and Martha were married, he even worried—and so did Martha—about what the elderly couple in the apartment below might think about their nighttime behavior. You see, the newlyweds' bed squeaked something terrible and the couple below went to the same church as they and, well, Jack was just certain he and his bride were the topic of conversation at the Women's Missionary on Tuesdays at noon.

This Pat Boone, white-buck-shoes image Jack still has today is sometimes compared to Hunt's own anything-but-a-swinger image. A *Sports Illustrated* writer once commented that "in a crowd Lamar Hunt stands out like wallpaper." Though a wealthy—correction: very wealthy —man, Hunt regularly stands in line at restaurants rather than use his pull to get a seat up front. When his Texans won the first AFL championship in 1961, a jubilant Hunt celebrated in the locker room with a few pull-ups on the nearest water pipe.

Like Hunt, Steadman doesn't smoke and is a demon for physical fitness. (Hunt's specialty is tennis; Steadman, in a sweat suit at 6 A.M., is a mile-a-day jogger around the neighborhood.) But personality match notwithstanding, owner Hunt says the sole reason why he hired this Hunt Oil accountant as general manager of the Kansas City Chiefs, née Dallas Texans, was Jack's business ability.

"I discovered about halfway through our first season [1960] that we had very poor cost controls," says Hunt.

230

"Frankly, I felt a change in leadership was needed. Jack was recommended to me by a longtime family financial advisor for whom Jack had worked on several accounts" —the same man, by the way, that the comptroller had asked to fire Jack.

Hunt adds that, right off the bat, Steadman gave the Chiefs a sense of financial leadership that Hunt feels many clubs still do not have today. "It's very difficult to separate the business end from the football end of the club," he says. "Many areas tend to overlap and many others cannot be accurately forecast, like player-injury expense. For some clubs it's too much trouble to get bids on every expenditure. Frankly, some owners really don't know the sports business all that well so they tend to run their clubs in a sort of fun-and-games atmosphere. Jack, on the other hand, has always done an excellent job at keeping sound business principles in the organization."

And just how important is financial leadership in building a team that can win on the field?

"Very important," Hunt answers quickly. For one thing, he says, if you run a tight ship upstairs, hopefully some of that same precision and attention to detail will carry over to the play on the field.

But more important than that is the front office's direct contribution made primarily in the area of promotion or public relations. "Most teams today are antipromotional," he says. "And it's difficult to get them to change when most are guaranteed a sellout every Sunday." (A preblackout statement.) "But there's a fine line between winning and losing and one key is to make your players and also your fans part of your promotions. If you do that, then suddenly the game is being played not by eleven men but by 80,000 screaming fans."

Hunt says no one is better at business promotion than

231

Steadman, an assertion that seems borne out by the facts. In 1965, the year before Jack started many of his promotional programs, the Chiefs' home attendance stood at only 150,169. In 1966, the year of the big push, the figure soared some 70 percent to 259,071. And in 1967, a year of continued push, the figure rose another 20 percent or so to 315,006.

Of course, the Chiefs' success at the gate was due in part to pro football's growing fan acceptance at that time all over the country. Indeed, average AFL attendance per game rose from only 21,584 in 1963 to 34,291 in 1966, according to league office figures. And while the Chiefs' season record did jump from 7 wins, 2 ties and 5 losses in 1965 to 12 wins, 1 tie and 3 losses (including one to the Green Bay Packers in football's first Super Bowl) in 1966, few would say that Jack Steadman contributed as much to the turnaround as quarterback Len Dawson or wide receiver Otis Taylor.

But if there's any truth to the axiom about home-crowd advantage, then Steadman did make a contribution to the Chiefs' on-field success. He did it using the basic premise that football is part of the entertainment business, pure and simple, and that because it is, "you have to make things happen."

Jack stuck perhaps his most pointed needle squarely into the civic pride of Kansas City, Missouri. It's hardly a secret that for many years people said K.C. was not a major-league city. Remember the jokes about the Athletics being nothing more than a farm club for the Yankees and Casey Stengel? And who can forget—though it isn't worth remembering—that silly Missouri mule mascot of Athletics owner Charlie Finley? (His name, fittingly, was Charlie O.) When entertainment business executive Sonny Werblin took over the New York Jets in 1964, he suggested around the league that the Chiefs should move to another town, one with a major-league television market.

Jack's needle was a pitch to local television and radio people for free time to plug the Chiefs. "We didn't have any money to spend," he says. "We told them what the problem was and asked them for a civic push." Specifically, Jack was pushing the idea of a Chiefs' "Wolfpack," a club to which anyone could belong—anyone, that is, who bought a Chiefs' season ticket. "We couldn't have done it in New York, but Kansas City needed to be a major-league city," he says.

A second Steadman needle was the Chiefs Red Coat Club, again a club to which anyone could belong—anyone, that is, who sold at least 100 season tickets to friends, relatives, Bozo the Clown, anyone. (Unlike the Wolfpack, you got something for being a Red Coater: a red blazer with, yes fans, a patch on the pocket.)

Also, Jack initiated a ticket-by-telephone program that enabled people to buy single-game tickets just by stopping off at their local bank, department store or even friendly loan company. In 1966, the customer-convenience program was expanded to include ticket buying on both the installment plan and the payroll deduction plan. Also in 1966, Jack argued long and hard with a local transit company over special bus service to and from the stadium. Transit officials, remembering the sorry turnouts of a few years back, thought no one would use the buses. But Jack won out when he guaranteed to make good any losses. (The buses were an immediate success.)

Vikings' General Manager Jim Finks says a GM's success usually comes with luck, and Steadman's ticket blitz was no exception. In this case, however, the luck was more bad than good. Near the end of the 1965 season, colorful running back Mack Lee Hill underwent supposedly routine

233

knee surgery. Like Finks, Hill developed a blood clot, only this time the patient died. In probably one of his most difficult acts as GM, Steadman ordered Hill's casket and made funeral arrangements for the family. Hill's death, although a tragedy, did serve to generate a great deal of empathy between the fans and the Chiefs. "People for the first time really began to associate with the club," says Jack.

It's interesting to note that after the Chiefs became a box-office hit, there were some people who thought the team really had taken advantage of the city. One gentleman in particular, a park department commissioner by the name of Holliday, objected to the club's dollar-a-year lease agreement for city-owned office space and practice fields. "It's certainly a gross unfairness for the taxpayers' money to be used to build a building that is then turned over to a profit-making corporation for $1 a year. . . . Maybe the city doesn't need the money but I could use it," Holliday reportedly said when the three-man board considered renewing the lease in 1971.

Steadman's needle pricked right back: "These facilities," he retorted in the press, "were provided to us as part of [our] stadium agreement, and we pay rent for them as a part of that agreement. In the event the Park Department fails to renew its agreement, then under the Municipal Stadium agreement, the city would have to duplicate the facility."

Undaunted, the commissioners filed suit seeking to force the club to pay a higher rent. Unfazed, Steadman reiterated the Chiefs' nonnegotiable position. The suit went to court where the judge threw it out. Subsequently, the board voted two to one to renew the agreement, Mr. Holliday remaining a disbeliever of Mr. Steadman right to the end.

No sooner was that needle sheathed than another drawn to counter a threatened lawsuit by the American Indian

234

Movement, which sought to enjoin the Chiefs from using any Indian reference in its name and logo. The action against the Chiefs was part of a coordinated movement planned against several pro teams including the Cleveland Indians and the Washington Redskins. In effect, Steadman told AIM exactly what it could do with its demand. "Sure we'll change the name," he later said, "when they change the name of the Missouri River." And after a brief war in the press, the whole matter dried up with no lawsuit being filed.

But these needles were only toothpicks compared to the spear Steadman wielded over construction of the Chiefs' new stadium, Arrowhead, one half of the first facility in the United States with separate football and baseball stadiums on a common site. Considering all its prenatal problems, it's a wonder it ever opened.

Not that Jack Steadman deserves to go down in all first-grade history texts as the founding father of Arrowhead Stadium. History of Kansas City's so-called stadium project dates to pre-World War II and winds around several abandoned plans and sites. But it was another Steadman needle, this one of the same species as the Wolfpack needle, that helped push across to local officials the desirability of a separate facility for football.

What Jack did was turn a liability into an asset. The liability was A's owner Charlie Finley (who else?) who about this time (1966–1967) was gesturing to league officials for permission to leave the city for greener, as in greenback, pastures. Seizing upon a situation, Jack convinced local officials that Finley definitely would go and that the civic sting from his action could be soothed by a new super big-league stadium, one just for football that would seat a whopping 78,000—more than can be reasonably built in a modern multipurpose facility. (At the same time, the argument went, a smaller yet equally deluxe stadium could be built on the same site to entice baseball back into town.)

After all these years, officials were intent on finally building some kind of new stadium and the Steadman plan was flattering to their collective civic ego. Indeed, as the Chiefs' 1972 press brochure put it: "Arrowhead is part of the Harry S. Truman Sports Complex that will provide The Greater Kansas City Area with truly the finest sports complex in the World."

That battle won, Hunt left it up to Steadman to get the job done in time to open the 1972 season in Arrowhead. Pressure was great because the Chiefs had virtually sold out and any delay in opening would have meant another season in Municipal Stadium, with its 25,000 or so fewer seats. "I can't even begin to describe the constant crisis surrounding the building of that stadium," says Hunt today.

But Jack can. Before Arrowhead got off the drawing board, it lost its escalators, waterproofing and other features to the high costs of construction. Although one lengthy strike probably is about par for any project, Arrowhead suffered through two such work stoppages. On top of that, work was delayed when a crane accident killed one worker and injured four others. Furthermore, the stadium's all-important public backing was endangered when public officials reacted negatively to the idea of a four-bedroom apartment in the stadium primarily for Hunt's business trips to K.C. and for game-day entertaining.

But as he had done before, Jack turned a seeming liability into an asset—a four-bedroom asset. Specifically, the three-judge court for the county in which Arrowhead was being built questioned the Chiefs' legal right "to construct such an extensive private suite in what was labeled as an administrative area." The judges told Jack that in view of

236

this expenditure, they would find it impossible "to commit any surpluses in the bond construction funds to any further stadium improvements."

Wasting no time, Jack drew his needle at a press conference the following day. He conducted sportswriters on a tour of the stadium, artfully playing down the sunken bath and sauna aspects of the apartment, and playing up the point that others would also be using the dwelling, primarily performers whom the club hoped to book into Arrowhead in future years. In case that wasn't enough, Jack made it clear that the Chiefs' lease agreement made it legal for the club to build whatever it wants to build, just as long as it's pleasing to the eye.

"That story [about the apartment] got us into the stadium on time," says Jack flatly. His point is that after the broadsides were fired, both sides agreed to sit down quietly and discuss the need for better communication. "That's when we set up the weekly meetings with the sports authority, the contractor and others," he says. "And through those meetings our staff was able to virtually take over the contractor's scheduling."

Granted, with Jack running the show there was still asphalt to be laid and ramps to be built when Arrowhead made its debut in August, 1972. "But," he declares, "without those meetings, this place wouldn't be open today."

Depending upon your point of view, Arrowhead Stadium is either very swank or very ostentatious. The apartment in particular is a mind-bender, what with a stained-glass window over the bar depicting Ed Podolak, a Chiefs running back, scoring the Chiefs' first touchdown in Arrowhead. (Said Podolak the first time he saw himself, "I sure must have a big nose.") Lining the wall behind the bar are two sets of sixteenth-century Spanish choir stalls, trophies of a Hunt antique expedition in Europe.

(Actually, the stalls were for the new home the Hunts had planned to build in Dallas before they purchased Jim Ling's manson. That's Ling as in Ling-Temco-Vaught.)

Off the combination office and living room is a conference room shaped in the form of—ugh!—a football. The ceiling there cuts through the second floor, allowing a large chandelier to hang down some 20 feet from the ceiling. A balcony, inspiration by Valentino, rims both rooms and serves as a walkway to the four bedrooms on the second floor. Open the sliding glass doors on the main floor and you find fifty-four seats in three rows of eighteen for the Chiefs' guests to view the game in a patrician setting.

Even though not in the same class as Hunt's "office," Steadman's work area has a certain class of its own. Indeed, Jack has probably two of the classiest-looking secretaries in all pro football. (They're a sister act.)

More than needles and hard work, Jack Steadman is big business in the sense that to him the corporation is first and foremost. "Why write about me?" he asked at one point in an interview for this book. "I'm not exciting. It's the Chiefs themselves that are exciting. It's what Lamar has done to create a first-class business operation here."

Indeed, like many corporate executives suddenly thrust into the spotlight, Steadman went on to ask that special recognition be given his staff, in particular Jim Schaaf, his assistant general manager. "You'd do me a big favor if you would mention Jim," he said. "And please find a place for Martha, my beautiful gal at home who puts up with me and all my crazy hours and work habits."

Though home is only 15 miles from Arrowhead's Tartan Turf, it might as well be a million away when gardener Steadman rolls up his sleeves, turns on his four-speaker outdoor stereo and retreats into what he calls "my own private world free of people asking 'Can you get me a season ticket, Jack?'"

238

If not at Arrowhead or in the swimming pool or garden at home, chances are Jack is at his favorite watering hole, Big Jack's Jungle Juice. Named after the illustrious executive vice president and general manager of the Kansas City Chiefs, it's really a refreshment stand at the Worlds of Fun park owned by Hunt and overseen by Steadman. Unlike most general managers in pro football, Steadman also wears the cap of a straight businessman, much like several club owners. In fact, even though attention here has been focused on Steadman's football job, that job occupied only about two-thirds of his time in 1973, the remainder going toward getting that $20.5-million Disneyland-type park off the ground.

Worlds of Fun, which opened in May, 1973, consists of five major "theme" areas featuring American, European, Scandinavian, Oriental and African motifs. (For the record, Big Jack's Jungle Juice is part of Africa, across the path from a restroom.) The park covers some 140 acres northeast of Kansas City and is only the first stage of a projected 500-acre recreation and commercial center. (Part of Jack's ongoing assignment from Hunt is to develop the other acreage, rather than have it be developed by a large number of outside firms.)

As was mentioned before, Worlds of Fun represents a radical departure from the thinking of football traditionalists—for whom the game is the only thing. Of course, Hunt's grandiose plans to reshape the Kansas City skyline might never have cleared the smog in more developed urban areas like New York, Chicago and Los Angeles. For example, in San Francisco in 1969, entrepreneur Hunt tested the air for another family-oriented recreation and entertainment project on the island site of abandoned Alcatraz prison. Wrote an editorial writer for the San Francisco *Examiner:* "Not even Alcatraz deserves anything quite as ugly and vulgar as the fate planned for it by Lamar Hunt, that go-gettin' son of a billionaire from Little Ole Texas. Nor, while we are on the subject, do the much maltreated and beswindled taxpayers of San Francisco deserve yet another royal rooking, ample though the precedents may be."

For all the coordinated plans Hunt is now deploying in his city on the Missouri, back in 1962 when the Chiefs (then Texans) were thinking seriously about leaving Dallas, it was New Orleans and not K.C. that held Hunt's attention. Indeed, Lamar was just one step away from a commitment which would have meant no Arrowhead, no Worlds of Fun and, probably, no Jack Steadman as a general manager in pro football.

One stumbling block to the deal was that Hunt's New Orleans contact suggested local partners, which would have violated an old Hunt family maxim that the fewer the partners, the less the trouble. Another was that both Hunt and Steadman felt they might be relying too much on an outsider, the same sort of situation which thrust Jack into the GM's job in the first place.

It was the middle of the 1962 season when Hunt tabled the matter until after the AFL championship game, which was won by Hunt's Texans, 20 to 17, over its intrastate rival the Houston Oilers. That victory led to a phone call from Kansas City Mayor H. Roe Bartle. (Maybe this is where Nixon picked up the idea.) The mayor told Hunt that he, like everyone else, was aware of the Texans' attendance woes and that the newly crowned champions would be treated like champions if they came to Kansas City. (It's Steadman's opinion that the mayor was hot for a champion and that the call might just as easily not have come if Houston had won.)

Hunt and Steadman stopped off in K.C. on their way to a postseason meeting in Los Angeles and were whisked to the city hall in the mayor's private limousine. Everything had to be hush-hush because word had not yet leaked out that Hunt was contemplating a strategic withdrawal from the Dallas fan drought plaguing both the Texans and the Cowboys. Bartle introduced the two as "Mr. Lamar" and "Jack X," which sounds a bit corny but nevertheless had a number of people in town thinking that the visitors were IRS agents flown in specially "to get" certain local big shots.

Hunt took a look at Municipal Stadium and, despite being shooed off the playing field by the groundskeeper, George Toma, liked what he saw. Jack, too, liked Kansas City, but already was on record with Lamar that he didn't want to move his family out of Dallas. "Really I was planning to go back into the oil company operations," he says today.

And if New Orleans had been the choice, Jack probably would have gotten his wish. But unlike New Orleans, Kansas City had no front man for Hunt to rely on. Both men knew that if the press found them out before they had determined that K.C. was a feasible alternative, "we'd be dead in Dallas," as Steadman puts it.

So Jack agreed to stay in a Kansas City hotel room for several weeks putting together the many details of the transfer. Not even his secretary (he had only one back in those days) knew how to get in touch with him. Although basic agreements had been made with the city, it was Jack's job to get it all down in writing. He soon discovered that just getting the city council to pass a resolution for stadium improvements, an office and practice facilities could be a "major exercise" requiring more than a bit of jawboning.

Just before Hunt let his cat out of the bag, he asked Jack to reconsider his decision to stay behind in Dallas. In effect, Hunt sweet-talked Jack, telling him he didn't know how the move could be finalized now without him. When Hunt agreed to pay all moving expenses and threw in a raise, Steadman agreed. (Actually, it would have taken a lot less than that to convince him.) The two men shook on a three-year contract.

"And that's the last time we discussed it," Steadman says twelve years later.

Lou Spadia, President of the San Francisco 49ers, says Jack knew how to use his needles even back during the NFL-AFL player-signing wars of the early 1960s. Spadia remembers one time when Steadman showed up in the San Francisco area ready to hand over the keys to a new car to one college senior that both the Chiefs and the 49ers had drafted. Spadia says he signed the kid by convincing him that he'd rather play in the "big time." But so that it shouldn't be a wasted trip, Steadman proceeded to drive a few miles south and hand over the keys of this slightly used new car to another Chiefs' draft choice, one more impressed with Jack's set of wheels.

On at least one occasion, the previously mentioned Finks's factor—also known as luck—played a significant role in the wartime success of the Chiefs. In 1966, K.C. drafted a running back out of the University of Southern California on the twentieth and last round of the draft. His name was Mike Garrett and he was still available because everyone thought he was just a step away from signing a contract with the Rams of the NFL.

"It was 3 A.M.," Steadman remembers, "and we were still drafting because in those days we didn't have enough money to hold the draft over for two days. By the time we got to the twentieth round, things were really slim. Our people were going through all the scouting books when one of the girls called out kiddingly, 'I got one.' Nobody had drafted Mike earlier because we all thought the Rams had him locked up. But it turned out he had a lawyer who had talked him into taking the highest bid. And we," says Steadman, smiling widely, "made the highest bid." (Garrett scored two touchdowns his rookie year in the AFL championship game won by the Chiefs, 31 to 7, over Buffalo. He was named to the all-league first team that same season.)

Today, a pro-football general manager like Steadman has one natural antagonist seldom penetrated by any needle. The antagonist, strangely enough, is the NFL league office in New York. Jack characterizes his discussions with league officials as "one-way communication." Put another way: they tell you, you don't tell them. Nobody gets too upset about this state of affairs because most realize that without a strong league office the old wounds probably would surface, making any sort of united front difficult to achieve. And Pete Rozelle can't just walk into a House subcommittee meeting in Washington demanding reinstatement of the home-TV blackout rule if in Kansas City, San Diego or somewhere else a club is issuing a statement contrary to that position.

Even so, there are many minor irritations. One standard trouble spot is the season schedule, fashioned by league officials around weather factors, stadium conflicts with baseball and TV executives' desires for showcase attractions. No club is is ever really satisfied. In 1973 Jack complained by phone to Val Pinchbeck, Assistant to the President of the American Football Conference, both about having to play four straight away games in October and about having to start one home game at 3 P.M. just to accommodate television.

"Did you get my letter requesting the time change for our game?" Steadman asks Pinchbeck.

"Ahhhhhh . . ." The league man fumbles as Jack turns to someone in his office and whispers, "I bet he hasn't even read it."

Pinchbeck still hasn't responded when Jack complains

that "this idea of four straight away games in October is really too much. Why, that's when we have our beautiful weather around here."

Again a long pause, then Pinchbeck answers, "Well, maybe that's the price you have to pay for having six games on national TV this year."

"I'll gladly give up one of those TV games for a home game in October," Steadman needles him. "Our fans aren't going to like this schedule one bit."

"I really don't know what I can do," responds Pinchbeck without any emotion. "That's just the way things go."

Before hanging up, Jack also complains about having to finish the season in Oakland against the Chiefs' archrival, the Raiders. "We're never at home when it counts," he charges.

"Sorry," is the only response, followed by the standard I-gotta-go-now line.

After hanging up, Jack calls one of his secretaries into his office and asks her to make a copy of the schedule for Head Coach Stram. "Tell Hank to call Pinchbeck, not me," he shouts only half kiddingly as she leaves the room.

The call from the league office was just one of a steady stream of phone calls Steadman took this particular day. He says he has to come in Saturday because "that's the only day I can get my work done around here without being constantly interrupted."

The next call after the Pinchbeck tête-à-tête is from Jack's construction boss at Worlds of Fun, still under construction at the time. He thinks management should demand physicals as a condition of employment for all workers. "It'll probably cost us about $1,200," he figures, "but, hell, one hernia will eat that up."

Steadman agrees. "Let's make sure we protect our backside," he tells his lieutenant.

244

The construction man also wants better security for all the liquor that's being delivered to Arrowhead Inn in anticipation of opening day. "As it is now," he complains, "the construction crews can get good and drunk if they have a mind to."

Again Steadman concurs.

The next call is from the park's publicity man. He reads to Steadman a suggested press release, but Jack stops him short when $20.5 million is mentioned as the cost of the park. "Let's not throw that figure around too much," Jack tells him. "That could cause us some bad reactions."

Another caller actually wants Jack to go feed some ducks next week at a local park. And he agrees, seeing as it is part of another civic function that the executive vice president of the Kansas City Chiefs would be expected to attend.

Finally, it is Jack's turn to call, though it's only to get two seats to the Royals' baseball game that night for his son.

Jack's weekly schedule finds him answering mail Monday morning and "trying to grab think-time" Monday afternoon often about the regular Tuesday morning session of the Stadium Authority, on which Jack sits. On Tuesday afternoon a meeting of all department heads is held in Jack's office, while all day Wednesday may be spent troubleshooting over at Worlds of Fun. (He has an office there, "though I may never get the time to move in," he says.) Thursday and Friday see a "variety of meetings and things," while on Saturday during the season Jack is either checking final preparations for a home game with assistant GM Jim Schaaf, or traveling to an away game. On Sunday, Jack has no official duties other than to be available for the usual distress calls from his staff. "Make sure you say we've got the best staff in all of professional sports," he emphasized to this writer.

Steadman attends many league meetings, but unlike Finks

of Minnesota manages to find time to take a skiing vacation around February and a swimming and water skiing vacation at the traditional lakefront cabin around the Fourth of July.

More than phone calls, what bugs Jack Steadman most is the mountain of mail he has to answer every day. As he launches into a summation of all the different letters in his box this day, his secretary—the one who also organizes the cheerleaders, not the one who's also in charge of half-time entertainment—gently pats him on the head, indicating that this front office is anything but stodgy.

One letter is from the city approving the use of gas logs for the fireplace in Arrowhead Inn. Another is from Standard Oil Company requesting to be the sponsor of certain park rides in exchange for a prominent display of the corporate shield. There's a copy of a letter from Ed Garvey, Executive Director of the Players Association, to the NFL management council, the league's negotiating committee, which Jack says he still has to read. Also still to be read are the minutes from the last league meeting.

One letter comes from the Church of Latter-Day Saints asking for dates when Arrowhead might be available for a conclave a few years down the road. Another is a purchase order for a special stadium water meter and still another is a purchase order for a chandelier he says he knows absolutely nothing about, but will find out about in short order. A picture of Joe Robbie, owner of the Miami Dolphins, is on the cover of the Dolphins' new press guide, and Jack smiles when he sees it, commenting, "Looks like a Cheshire cat, doesn't he?"

Steadman pays particular attention to a progress report on, of all things, how to paint the multicolored balloon symbol of Worlds of Fun on the water tower adjacent to the park. "We've been trying to figure that one out for weeks," Jack says. "A balloon is round, right? And a water tower isn't quite, right? Now how the heck can you paint that thing on there?" (He found a way.)

When the boss comes to town, which he does on the average of thirty-five times a year, his sessions with Jack may run well into the night—leaving that day's mail to be answered who knows when. (Hunt, Steadman and all other Chiefs' executives fly tourist wherever they go, even if it's a trip coast-to-coast for the Chiefs' 6-foot-5-inch general manager.)

On one recent daylong Hunt trip to Kansas City, the talk centered around that same really essentially dull, nitty-gritty detail work that can, as witness Jack Steadman, all but inundate a pro football general manager. Most owners don't like to roll up their sleeves that far, but Hunt does, which is why the day began with a walking tour of the park and a close examination of every aspect of the construction by a man conservatively worth several million dollars.

This was right after Worlds of Fun opened, and Hunt was worried about the park's low attendance. He and Jack decided to intensify promotional efforts. They would mail park flyers to the 18,000 or so Chiefs' season-ticket holders. They would also offer group rates for company outings, borrowing another idea from Chiefs' history.

The afternoon session was back at Arrowhead and dealt a great deal with stadium problems (for one thing, water leaks, especially over all those expensive corporate boxes) and personnel problems (one department was doing a job something less than satisfactory and personnel changes seemed in order). In addition, Hunt took a look at the bids for the new parking lot at Arrowhead, gasped a little, and told Jack to reduce the outlay somehow or other.

This session went straight into dinner and evolved into a general discussion on "how on earth can we keep costs from spiraling?" Player salaries, as might be expected, were

247

deemed the worst culprit, having gone up an average of 15 percent to 20 percent a year over the past few years, according to Hunt.

"At some point," Hunt said in a voice reminiscent of Jim Finks, "we're going to have to say no and just let the unrealistic players play out their options. It's either that or we'll be out of business."

Hunt says that he and Jack think very much alike, and when Hunt's not in town, Steadman gives the appearance that he wants things done the Hunt-Steadman way or no way at all. Indeed, though quite capable of enjoying a lighter moment with his secretary, Jack will chew out an employee—even fire him—if the cause seems sufficient to him.

A case in point: in 1972 a writer in Kansas City complained to Steadman that the Chiefs were forcing their season-ticket holders to buy seats for all preseason games as a package rather than just those that they really wanted to see. Jack told the writer he was a liar, but had to apologize when he discovered that the charge was correct. He called on the carpet those responsible and they defended themselves by saying that there was no other way to program the computer, except to purchase all or none. But Jack, in effect, asked who's running this show, men or a computer? He asked why the staff couldn't simply stuff the envelopes by hand. "We used to handle our whole ticket sales that way," he said.

For most front-office executives, winning the Super Bowl is the ultimate accomplishment. For Steadman the accountant, what's almost as important is that hunk of concrete called Arrowhead. For sure, there's nothing vicarious about Jack's football thrills. "The great pro franchises," he says very seriously, "are those with the big-capacity stadiums. The others," he adds, sounding more like IBM than K.C., "are going to ultimately fall behind."

248

Though Steadman is shy about opening the Kansas City books, simple arithmetic tells you he has a point. If my stadium seats upward of 80,000 and yours can only hold something around 60,000, then I'm going to make a barrelful of money more than you. One NFL club with a stadium seating in the 60,000 range says that in 1972 it grossed between $5 million and $6 million and netted after taxes somewhere in the neighborhood of $750,000. That same team paid its players (a club's biggest expense) something in excess of $2 million, a figure owner Hunt says sounds a little high for his ball club. To be sure, the Chiefs are carrying significant financing charges on the bonds and operating costs for the new stadium. But the rental fee the other club is paying for its city-owned facility certainly isn't small. When you also consider all the extra beer and hot dogs consumed by an additional 20,000 or so per game, the Chiefs come out smelling like financial roses compared to this other club, which is fairly representative of NFL franchises.

"Others can be critical all they want," says Jack, "but when they see what we're doing here they all want to do it too. Pro football in the 1940s and 1950s was a $400,000 gross business at best. We still have operations today that have not progressed far beyond the $400,000 stage."

Says Hunt: "I don't think the public really cares about the financial situation of pro football. By and large, I bet the public's attitude is what the hell difference does it make to Hunt whether the Chiefs make money or not. He's got plenty himself anyway."

But nothing could be farther from the truth.

"Either get on board," Steadman says, smiling, "or watch our dust."

9

A Man for All Seasons

Art Rooney
Owner
The Pittsburgh Steelers

THOUGH HE HADN'T WORN THE UNIFORM in thirty-four years, John Karcis was still rooting for the Pittsburgh Steelers in the summer of 1972. A running back for the club in the 1930s, John now was one of its quarterbacks, armchair variety, still waiting for his team's first championship.

In 1972 the Steelers won that championship. In 1973 they buried John Karcis.

Among the mourners his wife greeted were the Rooney boys, Art, Jim and Dan, a priest known as Father Silas. The Rooney boys are all in their seventies now. Father Silas does the driving and brings along the Mass cards whenever the friend who has passed away was a Catholic. So many have, these last few years. Players from Art's Steeler teams of the '30s and '40s. Neighbors from the old First Ward. A city which was once so many Old World communities. A sport which was once run by a bookie, a horse player and a slightly sneaky lawyer who chaired all the meetings because he was the only one who knew the rules of order.

The drive to the funeral home where John Karcis has been taken takes Art Rooney through the neighborhood that isn't there any more.

250

"That used to be where Guilfoyle's saloon stood," Art says from the back seat of Father Silas's car as it passes a dirty-faced tavern on a ghetto street. "Guilfoyle was a great politician. He was an even greater Notre Dame football fan."

The car climbs a hill and passes a park void of people. "That's where Mike Griffin's football team used to play. All of us used to play on neighborhood teams. That's what you did on a Sunday afternoon. And then on Thanksgiving morning you played the best guys from another ward. Those could get to be pretty physical games."

First Ward wakes often ended in a saloon where the mourners would tip a few in memory of their pal. Times change, but Art still pays his respects by telling a story or two his pal John also would have enjoyed. On the ride back to Three Rivers Stadium, the Steelers' new multimillion-dollar home, Art stops chewing on his cigar long enough to say, "You know, none of my five boys thinks I was a great athlete. They just think of me as an old man. But," he adds with the look of a man who'd love to go five more rounds with the champ, "I was a heck of an athlete in my day."

Of course if your father had been a saloonkeeper who made damn sure you went to parochial school every weekday and Sunday school every Sabbath, you too probably would have had the two prerequisites of a top-notch athlete: toughness and discipline. Art never worried about the yardstick his teacher would whack kids with on Monday morning if they had been AWOL on Sunday morning. What Dad would have done would have been worse.

Art doesn't say that his father was the toughest man in town. He just says that the beer he made was so strong that when you drank it you needed a whiskey chaser.

The younger Rooney's forte was probably baseball. "I remember playing for Indiana State Normal against Duquesne University [in the early 1920s]. The score was nothing-nothing. It was the last inning and I got on first, then stole second and third. They had a big guy pitching by the name of Bevil Boone, who is a doctor around here now. The Duquesne coach was Father McWiggin, whom I'd known for years. The Father told Bevil not to wind up because I might steal home. But Bevil wound up anyway and I stole home and we won the game. The Father"—Art pauses to laugh—"was most unsaintly in his reaction."

Another time, "I had a kids' team from the neighborhood and I took them over to play Duquesne High School. Duquesne had one priest who was a kind of mild-mannered fellow and he coached the high-school team. Then they had Father McWiggin, who coached the college team; he had been a heck of an athlete in his day. We came to the top of the ninth and I decided to pinch-hit myself because we had three runners on base and we were behind. Well, the one priest looked at me and told the umpire that I shouldn't be allowed to hit. But Father McWiggin, he says, 'Let the big bum hit. He won't hit it anyway.' The first ball that pitcher threw I hit over the fence, which was pretty unusual for that field. They still talk about that hit today."

Art Rooney was also a welterweight boxer. Fought a lot of the toughs who toured the country with carnivals and circuses. Twice reached the quarterfinals of the National AAU boxing championships when they were fought in Faneuil Hall, Boston. Defeated the fighter who represented the United States in the welterweight division at the 1920 Olympics.

"I could have gone to the Olympics, but I turned pro instead. I fought a kid, I think his name was Joe Azevedo, on a Pinky Mitchell-Tommy O'Brien card in Milwaukee. My manager, Dick Guy, talked about matching me with Benny Leonard [the champion of that day]. I never quite made it, but I don't know, the style of fighter I was I might have wound up without all my buttons."

Art Rooney was also a football player. He played halfback on his high-school team and was good enough for Knute Rockne to send him two recruiting letters—which Art is always glad to show a visitor. Instead, Rooney chose the way of a "tramp athlete," as they were known in the '20s. He played football for a couple of different colleges in a fashion resembling more a paid professional than a collegiate amateur. (Played baseball for them too.) After a couple of years, Art dropped out altogether.

But even though Rooney never did earn a college diploma, that doesn't mean he was just another dumb jock. Next to long-distance swimming with his boots on, probably Art's best sport was politics. The swimming episode occurred when Art was seventeen. It had rained long and hard, and Exposition Park, today the site of Three Rivers Stadium, was covered with several feet of water. (Exposition Park was pretty much a big hole in the ground.)

"It was me and my brother Dan and a fellow named Squawker," Art recalls. "We were floating across Exposition Park in a canoe and Squawker just wouldn't sit down. I kept telling him that if he didn't sit down, he was going to tip the canoe. So Squawker sat down and that's when he tipped the canoe. The other fellows managed to get their coats and boots off, but I just couldn't get my boots off. It was a long swim to the nearest bleachers [the park's bleachers were only partially submerged] and for a while there I didn't think I was going to make it. I was almost right."

Art Rooney the politician was a ward leader, a member of the Republican machine in the city of Allegheny, now part of Pittsburgh. ("I got a secretary now who's a Democrat," Art says of his current gal Friday. "Sometimes it's hard keeping her in line.")

253

Back then Art kept them in line, and the Republicans in power, by doing what political machines were supposed to do: feed the hungry, bail out the jailbirds, go to all the baptisms and wakes. The Rooney saloon was a focal point of activity. "Sometimes the mourners would start drinking and get so happy that they didn't go home until the next day. I remember one time we just left the corpse at the door on the street."

The Rooney home was another focal point. "Everybody came to our house," he says. "We never called my mother on the telephone to tell her we were bringing someone to dinner. My mother didn't care. Our house was like a boarding house. We'd bring our friends home and they'd stay overnight, and sometimes they'd stay and stay. They never left."

(Unlike his mother, Rooney's wife, Kathleen, did mind after they were married. Art didn't marry until he was around thirty years old. Girls, he admits rather shyly, were not one of his better sports. Even now, Art says his wife can still surprise him. "Just the other day I heard this phone ring in our bedroom. The silly thing was under the bed, and it turns out my wife has kept a phone hidden from me for the last three years. I don't know why she did it, but at least now I know why she was always so anxious to get the mail whenever the phone bill was due.")

Rooney the politician ran only once for elective office. The party asked him to run for the position of Registrar of Wills, an office Art readily admitted he knew nothing about.

"But if I'm elected," Art told one crowd, "I promise to put someone in the job who knows what he's doing." That line went over big, even in front of a group Art later found out was outside his election district. Anyway, Rooney was cited in an editorial in *The New York Times* for his unusual candor and honesty, all of which was insufficient for him to overcome an F.D.R. Democratic landslide.

It was because of politics that Rooney got started promoting sporting events. It takes money to feed people, and he raised it by putting on boxing matches and football games featuring his own semipro teams. Pennsylvania had Blue Laws in those days, but it didn't seem to bother the 10,000 or so who showed up for games featuring the Rooney Reds or the Hope-Harveys, both teams managed by Rooney.

To say these contests were quite unlike a Harvard-Yale tussle is putting it mildly. One time in a Hope-Harvey–West View game, Rooney hired the Duquesne coach, Joe Bach, as a player for $75. "Early in the first quarter," Art remembers, "we blocked a punt and for some unknown reason that started a fight. Pretty soon the crowd was all over the field and instead of having a fight we had a riot. Joe Bach went home. He said he knew that game would never be finished, and it wasn't.

"Next day I sent a guy over to pay Joe his $75. He wouldn't take it, but the guy told him, 'Go ahead. The Hope-Harveys never finish any of their games!' "

Rooney proved so skilled as a promoter that Madison Square Garden sought him out. Instead, he bought a franchise in the carnival-like National Football League. As the story goes, Art bought into the NFL after winning a king's ransom betting on the horses one day at Saratoga Racetrack. He gave several thousand away to a priest he didn't know who came up to him asking for donations for a new roof for his church. He used another $2,500 to buy a franchise from Tim Mara, a New York bookie and owner of the New York Giants.

A good story, but it bugs Art, his sons and others in the

Steeler organization who know it's not true. All of them, Art included, have grown tired of sportswriters who use this and two or three other grossly exaggerated tales whenever writing about the Steelers' longtime owner.

The Saratoga mindbender was still four years off when Rooney bought a franchise for $2,500 in July, 1933, from his friend and NFL Commissioner Joe Carr. Not that Rooney hadn't already shown this "thing" for picking winners at the racetrack. Art's friend Gilbert L. (Gibby) Gilbert, an all-American football player at the University of Pittsburgh in 1927, says, "Art was an Irish kid who didn't have the money, who wanted the money and wanted it bad."

Adds Richard Easton, another friend and fellow devotee of the $100 window: "Art's got guts. A lot of people when they win figure they've only got so much luck in them. It's when he wins that Art becomes a player. He rides that luck and cleans up."

So Art had the money to get into football in 1933, and the fact that NFL franchises lasted about as long as Nixon's Cabinet officials do now didn't faze him. Among the failures that preceded Rooney's arrival in the NFL were Canton, Decatur, Pottsville, Racine and Hammond. Only George Halas's Chicago Bears (which started in Decatur), Tim Mara's Giants, George Preston Marshall's Washington Redskins (which started in Boston), and Curly Lambeau's Green Bay Packers had shown the ability to endure.

In his office, surrounded by pictures of Marshall, Carr and others, Rooney says: "I don't know why you're interviewing me. You should have picked Halas. He was on the running board when this league first got going."

Unlike Halas, who spent all his time either coaching, playing or managing his team, Rooney treated the Pittsburgh Pirates, as the Steelers were originally called, as

256

just another promotion. In the old days, Rooney ran all his sporting ventures out of a first-floor room in the Fort Pitt Hotel in downtown Pittsburgh. The room was the epitome of the musty, cluttered, smoke-filled office, complete with cronies just coming in to rest their feet and bums coming in to put the squeeze on a guy they knew was an easy mark.

"I guess at one time the Fort Pitt had been a high-class hotel," says Art. "My office had windows as high as the ceiling and as low as the floor so people left through the window because it was a lot easier than walking back through the lobby. We were the door next to the men's room, and I can remember guys rushing in pulling down their flies and me having to tell them that they had come to the wrong place."

(A story often told even though it's not true is that when Art moved his sideshow to the fourth floor of another hotel, one regular visitor in his haste one day forgot where he was and stepped out the window and down. This visitor then picked himself up and walked away, or so the story goes.)

The Pittsburgh Pirates lost money just like the clubs in Pottsville and Racine. But the losses didn't amount to that much for Rooney, the horse player. Indeed, in one afternoon at Saratoga, Art won enough to offset the losses from his football team for several years.

That day, Art picked seven winners and pocketed more than $200,000. Some $80,000 was won on an eight-to-one shot who stuck his nose in front at the very last second. The unfortunate bookie who handled that transaction brought Art his money in a men's room, where the winner was at that moment explaining to an attendant the difference between the single wing and the double wing.

Probably no one would have known of Rooney's big

day except that Art ran into a sportswriter who was also a friend of Marshall, the latter a reformed horse player who was out to tell the world about the evils of four-legged devils. The sportswriter wrote a story on Rooney's streak as a joke for Marshall, "and it's been growing ever since," Art says with a what-can-I-do-about-it look on his face. "Like I'm supposed to have given money to a priest I'd never met before. Well, I did give a priest money, but I had known him for years."

Maybe because Rooney used up all his luck at the track, but more likely because he spent all his time at the track, the Steelers were from the start a team with a natural affinity for last place. The club went forty years, until 1972, before it finally won some sort of championship, and then it was only the Central Division championship of the American Football Conference of the National Football League.

The Steelers, frankly, were always a mess under Rooney, Sr. The men Art picked to be head coach were especially comical. Probably the funniest was Johnny Blood, who coached in the 1930s and who didn't show up for one game because he had forgotten one was scheduled. Another strange one was Walter Kiesling who, in the 1940s, fancied himself one of the country's great handicappers and who, on occasion, might be found at the track when practice was supposed to begin.

"On most clubs," Art says, "the coach has to worry about the players showing up for practice. On our club the players always worried about the coach showing up."

Maybe it would have been better if the coaches hadn't shown at all. The Steelers had some great quarterbacks over the years. Unfortunately, the coaches traded nearly all of them away, including Johnny Unitas, Len Dawson, Sid Luckman and Earl Morrall.

258

And then there was the time in 1953 when Coach Kiesling had the chance to draft Joe Schmidt, a University of Pittsburgh product who was later to become a member of the Pro Football Hall of Fame after an outstanding career as middle linebacker for the Detroit Lions. Rooney's sons and his longtime publicity director, Ed Kiely, tried to impress upon Kiesling the abilities of this superstar in their own backyard. Art, on the other hand, simply told his sons not to interfere because the more they talked, the more they were talking Kiesling out of it.

When Kiesling passed up Schmidt for some offensive tackle by the name of Black Cat Barton and then cut Barton the first week of training camp, Art still kept silent. Dan, who has disagreed with his father on how to run the club on more than one occasion, says, "In those days the draft went thirty rounds and Kies [Kiesling] would draft twenty-nine offensive tackles."

The record shows that from 1933 until the arrival of Chuck Noll as head coach in 1969, the Steelers won 161 games and lost 254, with nineteen contests ending in a tie. Excluding ties, that's a won-lost percentage of only .388. Moreover, it took ten years before the club had a winning season. Under Noll, and also Dan Rooney and Art Rooney, Jr., the club has finally become a winner.

Though Art kept his vow never to interfere with his coaches' running of the club, today he regrets he didn't. Not that Art wishes he himself had been coach. It's just that some coaches who should have been removed weren't because Art liked them too much as friends.

One man Art still wishes had interfered more often was a certain Father Slee. In 1952 Father Slee walked into Rooney's office one day late in the season and asked for a job. "The Father came right to the point," Art recalls. " 'Mr. Rooney,' he said, 'I'm crazy about football and I'm a real fan of the Steelers. I wonder if you would consider me for the job of team chaplain, at least give me a tryout, and let me sit on the bench for the Giants' game next Sunday.'

"Somehow this Father Slee didn't have the kind of priestly manner I was accustomed to, so I asked him, 'You a Roman?' And he said, 'No, sir, I am an Episcopalian. Does that mean I can't sit on the bench?'

"I said it meant nothing of the kind. I told him I hoped I was as broadminded as the next man. I told him to come on Sunday, and he was so grateful that I kind of eased him toward the door before he started giving me an Episcopalian blessing.

"That Giant game"—Art laughs—"not only did Father Slee show up, but he brought us the biggest bundle of luck we ever had. We played in the snow at Forbes Field [in Pittsburgh] and we beat the Giants, 63 to 7, the worst licking in their history. I thought I was dreaming.

"Afterward Steve Owen, the Giants' coach, growled at me, 'What got into your guys today?' I said, 'We got a chaplain. You didn't have a chance.'"

The following game Father Slee divined the Steelers to a 24-to-7 win over San Francisco. But the next week, the last week of the season, the Father wasn't on the bench when the Steelers traveled to Los Angeles and lost, 28 to 14.

Says Rooney: "The Father got transferred the week before the game. Got transferred to L.A. and was on the bench for the Rams when they beat us."

Like Will Rogers, Art Rooney's never met a man he didn't like. The feeling is mutual.

His friend Gibby Gilbert remembers how in 1973, when Art and his sons were negotiating to buy Yonkers Raceway for more than $50 million, Art called him at home one night from Chicago to make sure he'd gotten the baseball tickets Art ordered for him. "Now that's a fantastic guy," Gibby says. "Humble though he's worth millions."

Ed Kiely, who has been with Rooney as the Steelers' head PR man for more than twenty-five years, says: "Art's always thought of the average fan first. We're the only team left with a $3 ticket. He may not be the most learned man, but he is a bright man. He operates on common sense and his handshake is as good as any written contract."

Richard Easton, Rooney's fellow handicapper, says: "When the Duquesne Brewery here closed down a few years back, Art tried to get jobs for all those workers. So many people came to his office that he said, 'Looks like I'm running an employment agency.' By the way, he got a lot of those people jobs."

Jim Finks, Rooney's quarterback in the early 1950s and today General Manager of the Minnesota Vikings, says: "I've never met a man who had more character. My top salary was $13,000 as a first-team NFL quarterback. This isn't much by today's standards, but I always got treated fairly."

"The world's greatest sportsman" is the way *Chicago Tribune* sportswriter David Condon referred to Rooney. In one column Condon told how the late Ben Lindheimer, who ran the horse casinos at Arlington and Washington parks, paid Rooney the "supreme compliment" when he said, "I'd rather have Arthur Rooney's hand than any other man's bond."

Prescott Sullivan, sportswriter for the San Francisco *Examiner*, remembers the time Rooney spotted him in a Pittsburgh bar and told the bartender, "Give this fine gentleman from San Francisco everything he wants and take none of his money." Says Sullivan, with a grin, "From that moment on I knew Art Rooney was my kind of guy."

Art Rooney's best friends are almost all dead now. These

were the nine or so old-time owners in the NFL, men like Marshall of Washington, Bert Bell of Philadelphia, Lambeau of Green Bay and Halas of Chicago. Halas is still very much around, but the rest aren't. And with them went much of what Rooney calls the "romance" of pro football. "Everything's all big business now," he laments at a table in the swank new eating club in Three Rivers Stadium which overlooks the field.

"You know, Marshall was really a sneak," Rooney says, while at the same time emphasizing that he loved him dearly. As the only lawyer in the group, "George just sort of assumed he should run the meetings. The rest of us didn't care. Charlie Bidwill [of the Cardinals] and I usually couldn't wait until those meetings were over so that we could go to the track.

"If George knew he was going to lose a vote, he would table the matter until the meeting was just about to break up. Then he would say, 'Hey, what about this thing?' And we'd say, 'Sure, George, whatever you want is fine with us.'

"One thing you never did with George," Rooney adds, "was go to the bathroom if there was any chance they might vote on something you cared about a lot. I can remember I wanted this fellow to be a referee in our league, but the moment I left the room they took a vote and turned him down. I came back and waited until the meeting was just about to break up and I asked what about this fellow. And they said with their big innocent looks, 'Sorry, Art, you must have missed that vote.'"

But Marshall didn't bulldoze Tim Mara, the bookie-owner from New York. "Charlie, Bert and I just used to sit back and watch the two of them get redder and redder as they yelled at each other. Maybe it was the schedule or a change in the rules. It didn't make no difference. They just naturally liked to fight."

Art adds: "Tim always carried this prayer in his pocket. It was a prayer on hate and he used to pull it out and read it every time he flew off the handle."

Nor did Marshall bulldoze Halas, who now is in his sixth decade as owner of the Bears. "Art and Bert and the other owners always acted in the best interests of the league," Halas recalls, "but George had a tendency to act in his own best interests. For example, he might try to schedule just those teams he knew would bring in big crowds. The Bears were one and the Giants another. The Steelers usually weren't too good a drawing card because of their record. But we never let him get away with it and one of the best things that ever happened to this league was when we decided to let the commissioner make up the schedule for all of us."

Halas remembers besting Marshall on one very famous occasion. It was 1939 and it was late in the season when the Bears played the 'Skins in Washington. Both teams had legendary quarterbacks—Sid Luckman for Chicago and Slingin' Sammy Baugh for Washington. The Bears trailed, 7 to 3, late in the game when Luckman started driving his team toward the Washington goal line. But a questionable last-second call by an official left the Bears losers, and Halas and his squad were still browbeating that referee when the final gun went off. Afterward, Marshall told the press that the Bears were just a big bunch of "crybabies. They're front runners. They're not a second-half team. The Bears are quitters."

Halas pasted the inflammatory remarks all over the Bears' locker room when the club started getting ready for its championship game that year against Washington. Marshall and the Redskins never knew what hit them. Final score: Chicago 73, Washington 0.

In the championship game two years earlier, Marshall

and Halas had almost come to blows. It started as a fistfight between two players and quickly grew into a free-for-all between both teams. Then Marshall leaped to the field from his front-row seat and went in swinging.

"Get back in that box," Halas ordered, according to Arthur Daley, sportswriter for *The New York Times* until his death in 1974, in his book *Pro Football's Hall of Fame* (Quadrangle/The New York Times Book Co.). "Too bad it isn't a cage, you [a few prime-cut curse words followed]."

"You shut that filthy mouth of yours," Marshall responded, "before I punch those gold teeth down that red throat of yours, you miserable . . . [more prime cuts]."

The two men were finally separated, while still in the shouting stage. But when a friend later told Marshall that she found Halas's language "positively revolting," George responded: "Don't you dare talk about Halas that way. He's my best friend."

Halas says that Rooney was mostly a listener at league meetings. "But Art had been a professional athlete himself, so you could always count on him doing the right thing at the right time," including voting to move the goal posts up from the end line to the goal line and spotting the ball in 15 yards from the sideline for greater maneuverability.

Halas says that one reason why the Steelers didn't win more often was because Art had other interests. "My whole life was football," says the man who guided Bear teams to seven world championships between 1920 and 1945. "I was the first person to hold daily practice sessions. We also had a lot better scouting system than Art had."

Another Steeler problem was money. In those early days there was no league draft. The best players went to the teams that could pay the most money. And while Rooney was never flat broke, he never got the tremendous crowds that would have enabled him to compete against Chicago, New York and Washington.

"Art couldn't afford to be aggressive in signing players," says Halas. Indeed, Art worked out one deal after the institution of the draft whereby the Steelers picked Luckman and passed him along to Chicago in exchange for a number of players, none of them a superstar like Luckman.

Halas agrees that Rooney's long suit was gentlemanliness. "We played an exhibition game in Chattanooga one year," he recalls, "and the crowd was so bad that Art suggested we both give the preacher who had sponsored the game $500 so that he could break even."

Rooney's nature differed sharply from that of Curly Lambeau of Green Bay. "If that buzzard ever died," said Cal Hubbard, one of Lambeau's best players in the early 1930s, according to Daley's book, "they'd have trouble finding six guys to volunteer as pallbearers."

Hubbard meant what he said. In 1930 Lambeau got so mad at his players one game that he put himself in as quarterback to show them how a team should be run. At Hubbard's suggestion, the Packer offensive line didn't block on the next play, leaving Lambeau at the mercy of clawing enemy tacklers. He limped to the sidelines, glaring at the traitors.

According to Daley, Lambeau's personality finally became his own downfall. In 1949 the Chicago Cardinals beat Green Bay in a game that left Curly again infuriated at his own charges. He fined every player one half of his game salary for indifferent play, which shot to hell any semblance of team morale. Though he returned the money after the season, Lambeau left town under public pressure in 1950.

To be sure, the early NFL had more than its share of hotheads. In addition to Lambeau and Marshall, there was Dick Richards, who owned the Detroit franchise for a time. "I've got a burial ground out at my place in Palm Springs," Richards reportedly said at one owners' meeting in the

265

1930s. "One tombstone is marked 'Tim Mara' and another is 'George Halas.'"

(In 1935 Richards tried to have Joe Carr fired as commissioner. When the other owners wouldn't go along, Richards tried to hire someone else who would be above Carr, another abortive effort.)

Rooney of course was Catholic and so was Tim Mara. When Bert Bell turned to Catholicism after years as an agnostic, Marshall asked cynically whether the next league meeting was going to be held in Rome.

Says Art: "I remember one time before Bert converted when he called me on the telephone to say he thought there might be something to all this religion stuff of mine. He said he had given a seat on the bench to a priest friend of his. That same day his Eagles won their first game of the season.

"Well, the next week Bert's got this same priest sitting on his bench. The Eagles beat us even though we're favored to win. After the game I go over to the priest and say, 'I know what you're trying to do, Father. You're pulling all these miracles to try to convert Bert, and I'm all for it. But for heaven's sake, you better convert him this week because next Sunday you ain't gonna pull any miracles. Next Sunday he plays the Chicago Bears and even you won't make any difference.'" (As usual, the end of the story brings on a smile turned downward at one corner by a cigar. The smile is followed by a rib-tickling, hoarse kind of laughter.)

After Art finishes lunch in the stadium club, he meets with his son Dan. While he's gone, Ed Kiely tells a visitor how Art once backed the late Dan Reeves in a fight for control of the Los Angeles Rams against a gentleman by the name of Edwin Pauley.

"Pauley came up to Art and said that Dan's got things all wrong. He asked Art if he would support him if he

266

could prove that Reeves was in the wrong. Art said, 'I don't care whether Danny's right or wrong. I'm supporting him.' Pauley was really shocked. He said he couldn't remember having met a man with that kind of loyalty to his friends."

The way things run now, Art meets with his son Dan at least once or twice a day so that the younger generation can keep the older generation abreast of trades in the wind and money in the bank. Dad says he usually just listens. Once a month Art's other three sons, Tim, who runs both Yonkers Raceway and the Palm Beach Kennel Club (a dog track) in Florida, and the twins, John and Pat, who run Liberty Bell Park in Philadelphia, come to Pittsburgh for a family summit. Again, Dad says, he usually just listens.

Counters Dan: "Maybe he listens more than he used to, but he's still the boss."

While Art gambled on horses, his sons gamble on the tracks where they race. Art says the family borrowed to the hilt to swing the purchase of Yonkers Raceway in 1972 for $45 million in cash plus assumption of $7 million in liabilities. "Sometimes I wonder whether we're stretching ourselves too thin," he says, shaking his head slowly.

If so, things will probably get thinner before too long. Dan says the family is looking into one or two other ventures that would complement nicely three horse tracks, a dog track and a thoroughbred breeding farm Art, Sr., has owned for many years in addition to the football club.

Art and his son Dan have differed several times on how to run a football team. Both generations have scored a few points. "My father," says Dan, "is a great baseball fan and when we've got a conflict with the baseball team here he may just as easily be on their side as ours. Like when we were planning to move into Three Rivers Stadium. I wanted the baseball team to play on an infield without a skin [or dirt] portion because of the problems a skin creates for football. Well, my father thought that was terrible. It took me two years to convince my father [and also the baseball team]."

One battle the son lost was when he threatened not to move the Steelers into Three Rivers Stadium in 1970 unless the club got a take from the concessions as most teams do in the NFL. "I was really determined," Dan says, "but my father didn't agree. Finally, I agreed that they [the Pirates] would get our concessions and that they would then pay for the maintenance of the stadium. But I agreed grudgingly. And I'll tell you one thing: they make a great deal of money off us. A fan spends an average of $1.25 a game on concessions and 40 percent of that is profit that goes to the Pittsburgh Pirates Baseball Club. Of that 50 cents per person per game profit, not a heck of a lot is spent on maintenance, believe me."

Another one the son lost was over whether the Steelers would switch into the American Football Conference along with two other old-line NFL teams in order to complete the NFL-AFL merger in 1969. Dan said no, vehemently. "My reason was strictly emotional," the son explains—a posture you would expect more from his father.

"I had geared myself for war, not peace, with the AFL. When an agreement was reached, I felt that we were one of the oldest teams in the National Football League and had been in there much longer than most so why did we have to be the ones to change?"

Says Dad: "We argued and argued about it. Even after we decided to switch, we went into the meeting and there was a temporary misunderstanding about something and Dan said that's it, it's off.

"The reason I decided to switch was that for a time there a stalemate seemed probable and that would have meant pulling names out of a hat to see what division you would be in. That scared me. I was afraid I'd wind up in a division without guys like Cleveland, Cincinnati, Philadelphia and New York, and wind up with guys like Miami and San Diego.

"I decided I wouldn't do anything without Modell [Cleveland Browns' owner Art Modell whose team has always played Army to Rooney's Navy]. Now Modell was in a hospital when all this was going on, so me and Danny and Wellington Mara [Tim's son] went up to see him. We talked for an hour and decided that if Cleveland, Pittsburgh and Cincinnati were in the same division, then we would consider it.

"Another thing I thought I got but didn't get was a guarantee that we'd play five exhibition games with five of the old clubs who had been our rivals for so long: the Giants, the Eagles, the Bears, the Redskins and the Packers. I thought I got it but it wasn't in writing. I don't think anyone ran out on me; I just think I didn't present my case strongly enough."

Adds the father: "I don't think the fact that we were each going to get $3 million for switching made any difference to either Modell or me."

Adds the son: "He [Dad] wanted to go because of where it would have put us financially had we stayed. You see, we would have had to pay the other clubs that switched, and that would have made our financial position difficult."

Such major policy decisions are of course few and far between. Funerals are a time consumer, as are family meetings and trips to the farm in Maryland. But around the office, Art, Sr., doesn't have much to occupy his time anymore.

"The last thing Dad used to do was handle any investments or use of money," says Dan. "But I'm pretty much involved in that now," and the Steelers are now involved in owning apartment units—a good way to generate some income and a great way to cut the club's overall tax rate. Dan is also seeking to diversify through acquisition of a communications or similar company.

"I can't retire," says the Steelers' owner of forty years. "What would I do? Stare at four walls?"

Instead, Art spends a great deal of time writing postcards (a trait he's been known for since time immemorial), arranging for tickets for all the nuns and priests he knows (Wellington Mara used to look at the crowd in Pittsburgh and say to Art, "I didn't know there were that many nuns in Pittsburgh"), and also taking visitors on tours of the new stadium.

As the tour begins, the "guide" dresses down city officials for supposedly dragging their heels on building Three Rivers Stadium, so named because of its location on the north bank of the Allegheny River at the juncture of the Allegheny, Ohio and Monongahela rivers. "When the bids for this place were first submitted in 1967, the lowest bid was $12 million above what the city wanted to spend. But when they got around to getting new bids, they all wound up higher than the first ones. So to save money the city cut our seating capacity from 60,000 to 50,000. But we still paid more and got less than we would have originally.

"And look at that thing," Rooney says disgustedly as he points out the Allegheny Club, the ritzy and privately owned eating club overlooking the playing field. "I should never have given in on that one. Look at all the seats that thing cost us. We've been negotiating with the city for more seats for several months now, but they just keep saying that if you want more seats, go build them yourself."

Unlike Super Boxes in other stadiums such as Dallas and Philadelphia, the decor of the Rooney Super Box at Three Rivers resembles a $6-a-night motel room. Dan wanted to jazz things up, but this was another battle he lost. What the heck? Certainly all the nuns and priests who sit there every week don't need fancy furniture. And Art usually just deposits his wife and walks around to the other side to sit in the press box with his boys.

(With all the publicity Art's been getting the last couple of years because of the Steelers' new-found success, it was decided at one point that security guards should be posted outside his box to protect him. But the first time they showed up he shooed them away. "Who? Me? Need protection? You must be crazy!")

The tour is interrupted while the guide has his daily conversation with Steve Dinardo, the head of the stadium grounds crew. This day Art wants to make sure Steve waters down the dirt around home plate before tonight's game (it's still baseball season at this point) because last night when that player for the St. Louis Cardinals slid home on a close play, he stirred up such a dust storm "I felt I was seeing my first Pittsburgh tornado," Art says.

"I like to bother them so that they can't get their work done," he adds upon returning to the group.

Next the tour goes underground through the Steelers' locker room. Practice has just ended (it's the exhibition season) and as Art passes, he kids kicker Roy Gerella about seeing him the other night with "another filly" on his arm.

"Yeah, and he never shares them," chimes in Rocky Bleier, a running back. (Gerella smiles as if he's heard it all before.)

Art then passes John Dockery, a defensive back, who is studying his play book. "You can show me how to make book, right, Mr. Rooney?" Dockery asks.

"You better believe it," the old man replies without turning his head.

Back inside his office, Art suddenly remembers he wants a get-well card sent to a Philadelphia sportswriter who, he was told last night by Pirates' announcer Bob Prince, is laid up in the hospital. Also, he wants a ticket for the Steelers' preseason game this weekend sent to a doctor friend of his whom he saw this morning. "I got up early thinking I had this appointment, but it's not till tomorrow."

Though the Rooney boys are different businessmen than their father, they still show respect for the old man's iron-fist authority. In fact, it was only a few years ago that they dared dress in public in something other than a white shirt and dark suit.

The three sons who don't live in Pittsburgh talk to their father by telephone nearly every night. Dad should consider himself lucky because if he was raising five sons today and wielding that same iron fist, chances are that by now at least one son would have told Dad exactly what he could do with all that authoritarian crap.

One story often told about Art and his offspring concerns the day Father went to watch three of his boys play baseball. Tim singled to the outfield and when he reached first base he turned to his right rather than left toward second base.

"You're supposed to turn toward second," Dad scolded after the game.

"That's the way you old guys did it," challenged little leaguer Tim.

"Give me those balls and bats," Art demanded. "I don't want people to know you're a Rooney."

In 1973 Roy Blount, Jr., wrote in *Sports Illustrated* that "the Rooneys seem to have resolved their hostilities toward one another in furniture-smashing fights when they were boys. As adults they . . . slip away from convention sessions to drink milk shakes together. . . ."

But Art, who is grandfather to thirty-two, may be planting the seeds for a new generation of furniture smashers.

272

The whole clan gathers at Grandpa's house on Thanksgiving day, and just like he did back in the First Ward, Art kids around, calling his grandchildren wops, heinies or Polacks depending upon who their mother is. "They all go running to Mommy asking what Grandpa means," Art laughs.

The sons wish their father would move out of the old neighborhood. Forty years ago they were all fine homes. But today those houses that still stand are, with the exception of the Rooney home, falling apart. The streets are filthy; racial tension is evident. In short, Art Rooney lives in a ghetto.

But home is only a few minutes walk from Three Rivers Stadium. And even when Pittsburgh had its racial disturbance back in 1968, Art Rooney was able to move about without apprehension. Still, his car was broken into in 1973, and for a while now Dan and Art, Jr., have made a point of driving their father home as often as they can and never pulling away until he's safely inside.

Halas said you could always count on Art Rooney's doing the right thing at the right time. Rooney says probably the most important thing he has done right in terms of the league was backing Pete Rozelle for commissioner upon the death of Bert Bell in 1959. Most people know that Rozelle was a compromise candidate. Not many know what all the hassle was about that led to Rozelle's nomination after twenty-two fruitless ballots.

Explains Rooney: "The fighting on a commissioner went on for five or six days. Leahy was the front runner [Marshall Leahy, San Francisco attorney and then counsel for the league]. Gunsel was right behind him [Austin H. Gunsel, Treasurer of the NFL and interim president upon Bell's death].

"The reason Leahy didn't become commissioner was that

he wouldn't move his office to this side of the Mississippi River. Pittsburgh, Baltimore, Philadelphia and Washington were for Gunsel. Dallas was neutral and they passed. The rest [seven teams] were for Leahy.

"Finally Wellington Mara presented Rozelle's name to me and I talked to Philadelphia and Washington and Baltimore and we all agreed on Rozelle. Mara then made a strong presentation that convinced all the others right off.

"It was like fate," Rooney adds. "I don't know any commissioner in sports who could have done a better job with television and the league as a whole. He has a way about him so that even if he fines you, he makes you like him while he's fining you.

"We had a ward leader one time who was very close to me, and he was tremendous on doing everything he could for anybody. Like people would come to him for, say, $20, and he would give it to them. But he would do it only after calling you names and everything else. I used to argue with him that if he was going to give it to them, give it to them with a smile."

Probably the dumbest thing Rooney has ever done in football was leaving his seat seconds before Steeler fullback Franco Harris caught a deflected pass and ran for a last-second touchdown to give Pittsburgh a 13-to-7 win over Oakland in the 1972 division play-offs.

"I wanted to make sure I was outside the locker room when the game ended so I could thank every one of them for such a tremendous season. I heard all the shouting and I asked an attendant what had happened and that's how I found out.

"Here we finally win something after all these years and everyone writes about the Steelers' dumb owner missing the big play. I wish they would have left me out and just written about Franco and all the other fine boys."

274

Says Dan: "I think what Dad wants most is to be known as a humanistic man. He tries to think of everything in its relation to people. Money doesn't really mean that much to him. He tries to be good to people rather than a good businessman or a successful club owner."

Adds Ed Kiely: "Not long ago one of our banks held a directors' meeting and asked Art to speak at their luncheon. They asked him to talk about the finances of football and you could tell he was delighted that people would ask him to speak on something other than the good old days, if you know what I mean."

But legends are made of baggy pants and cigars, not of money. They're made of carnival fighting and wakes in a saloon. They're made of a lifestyle, not a job, which is why Pete Rozelle will never be a legend but why Joe Namath may. Outside of Rooney and Halas, there are no living legends today in the front offices of professional football. Nor are any likely to appear very soon for the simple reason that there's too much money in the game now.

"I honestly feel we would be better off if TV hadn't given us so much money," Rooney says. "TV is a hot and cold business which drops guys all the time. Then we have to rip out the whole system and start over again."

"He [Art, Sr.] is a brilliant man," says Ed Dougherty, President of the Harness Tracks of America. "But he's a man of the handshake. He finds the transition to tax lawyers and comptrollers uncomfortable."

In the good old days, not even a con artist like Winnie the Weeper made Art Rooney feel uncomfortable. He once told a reporter:

"I was at the races at Narragansett one day and happened to have a winner. I was coming away from the cashier's window when I noticed a little old lady dressed all in black. She was standing against a wall, crying bitter tears. I walked over and said, 'Ma'am, are you ill? Can I do anything for you?'

"She turned to me, the tears streaming. 'No, sir,' she said. 'Nobody can help me now. I've lost my rent money for my little grandson who's lying there in our furnished room getting weaker by the minute with the whooping cough. I came out to the track, praying that I would have a winner to buy medicine for the little tyke. But my horse lost by a lip, and now I don't know what to do. But it's all right, sir. Don't you mind. You're a fine gentleman and you just go ahead and enjoy your winnings with a champagne-and-lobster dinner somewheres. I'll get by somehow.'

"Well, I reached into my pocket and pulled out a $100 bill. 'Take this, dear lady,' I said. 'Pay your rent and get the medicine for your little boy. Say a prayer, and I'm sure something good will turn up for you.'

"Well, on the way to my hotel, I was riding with a well-known tout and I told him the story. I thought he would laugh himself sick. 'You've been taken by Winnie the Weeper,' he said. 'That old doll has been hanging around the $50 cashier's window and working that act with strangers for years.'

"I still think The Weeper deserved the money. She gave a great performance."

Carroll Rosenbloom, Los Angeles Rams' owner. *Owning a championship team is good; doing it all over again is better.*

Carroll Rosenbloom. *The future kingpin as a young halfback at th
University of Pennsylvania.*

Jim Finks. *A pirouette as the Steelers' quarterback.*

Jim Finks, Minnesota Vikings' General Manager. *Building a winning club is not a sometime thing.*

John Free, New York Jets' Business Manager and Traveling Secretary. *Next crisis please.*

John Free and friend in the pause before battle.

Jack Horrigan (left) and one of his first "boys," Cookie Gilchrist (second from right). Ralph Wilson, owner, is far right.

Jack Horrigan, Buffalo Bills' Public Relations Vice President. *Finally at ease watching the team play.*

The Morabitos. *In an earlier more innocent time.* (Left to right, Mrs. Morabito, Sr., Vic, Jane, Tony, Josephine and Mr. Morabito, Sr.—1941.)

The Morabito ladies, San Francisco 49ers owners. *In an age taken with feminism, they certainly rate a special citation.* (Josephine left. Jane right.)

Rommie Loudd, former New England Patriots' Director of Pro Personnel. *Black will be beautiful when black is an owner.*

Jack Steadman, Kansas City Chiefs' Executive Vice President. *Management also scores points.*

Art Rooney (first row, far right). *Early proof that football, Rooney and Pittsburgh are three words with the same meaning.* (Brother Dan Rooney, first row third from right, is now Father Silas Rooney, a Franciscan priest.)

Art Rooney, Pittsburgh Steelers' owner. *From back-lot pioneer to modern mogul, he's seen it all.*